Restorative Just Culture
in Practice

A restorative just culture has become a core aspiration for many organizations in healthcare and elsewhere. Whereas 'just culture' is the topic of some residual conceptual debate (e.g. retributive policies organized around rules, violations and consequences are 'sold' as just culture), the evidence base on, and business case for, restorative practice has been growing and is generating increasing, global interest. In the wake of an incident, restorative practices ask who are impacted, what their needs are and whose obligation it is to meet those needs. Restorative practices aim to involve participants from the entire community in the resolution and repair of harms. This book offers organization leaders and stakeholders a practical guide to the experiences of implementing and evaluating restorative practices and creating a sustainable just, restorative culture. It contains the perspectives from leaders, theoreticians, regulators, employees and patient representatives. To the best of our knowledge, there is no book on the market today that can function as a guide for the implementation and evaluation of a just and learning culture and restorative practices. This book is intended to fill this gap. This book will provide, among other topics, an overview of restorative just culture principles and practices; a balanced treatment of the various implementations and evaluations of just culture and restorative processes; a guide for leaders about what to stop, start, increase and decrease in their own organizations; and an attentive to philosophical and historical traditions and assumptions that underlie just culture and restorative approaches. The interest in 'just culture', not just in healthcare but also in other fields of safety-critical practice, has been steadily growing over the past decade. It is a trending area. In this, it has become clear that 20-year-old retributive models not only hinder the acceleration of performance and organizational improvement but have also in some cases become a blunt HR instrument, an expression of power over justice and a way to stifle honesty, reporting and learning. What is new in this, then, is the restorative angle on just culture, as it has been developed over the last few years and now is practised and applied to HR, suicide prevention, healthcare improvement, regulatory innovations and other areas.

Restorative Just Culture in Practice

Implementation and Evaluation

Edited by
Sidney Dekker
Joseph Rafferty
Amanda Oates

Routledge
Taylor & Francis Group

A PRODUCTIVITY PRESS BOOK

First published 2022
by Routledge
605 Third Avenue, New York, NY 10158

and by Routledge
4 Park Square, Milton Park, Abingdon, Oxon, OX14 4RN

Routledge is an imprint of the Taylor & Francis Group, an Informa business

Library of Congress Cataloging-in-Publication Data
A catalog record for this title has been requested

ISBN: 9780367755294 (hbk)
ISBN: 9780367754617 (pbk)
ISBN: 9781003162582 (ebk)

DOI: 10.4324/9781003162582

Typeset in Garamond
by Deanta Global Publishing Services, Chennai, India

Contents

About the Editors

Sidney Dekker
A Professor at Griffith University Brisbane, Australia, Sidney founded the Safety Science Innovation Lab as part of his groundbreaking work on human factors and safety. He was also Professor of these disciplines in Sweden and flew 737s as First Officer in Denmark and he remains an avid pilot. He has been Professor (Hon) of psychology at the University of Queensland and Professor (Hon) of human factors and patient safety at Brisbane Royal Children's Hospital. Sidney is the author of a series of books on Just Culture and 'human error', a term he firmly puts in inverted commas. He is recognised internationally as a leading scholar and is an expert on human factors and safety.

Prof Joseph Rafferty CBE
Dr Rafferty has been consistently named in the top 100 most influential people in healthcare by the *Health Service Journal* and as Chief Executive of Mersey Care. Joe is currently number 9 in their list of top 50 Chief Executives. Joe joined the NHS in 1999 as a National Trainee on the NHS General Management Training Scheme. He previously worked at a post-doctoral level as a team leader in molecular genetics at the Paterson Institute for Cancer Research in Manchester and before that in Cambridge. Previous high-level NHS roles include national leadership as Director of Commissioning Support at the NHS Commissioning Board. Joe has been CEO and Director at other NHS Trusts and was part of the team that set up the Greater Manchester Strategic Health Authority. Now heading Mersey Care, Joe has led the Trust through massive expansion as it acquired new services. He is co-founder of the Zero Suicide Alliance and has spoken at Westminster, around the UK and beyond about suicide awareness and restorative just culture.

Amanda Oates

Amanda is the Executive Director of Workforce on the Board of Mersey Care NHS Foundation Trust. She was previously the HR Director at two other trusts and after joining Mersey Care she led the team to win most improved HR team of the year. Amanda spearheaded a regional Health and Wellbeing initiative through the development of the NHS Games. She was recognised with the Health and Wellbeing Leader Award at the NHS Leadership Academy Awards in 2012 and as HR Director of the Year 2018 as well as at the National Social Partnership Forum for partnership working for the trust's Just Culture work at the Healthcare People Management Association Awards. Amanda is the lead for Mersey Care's award-winning Restorative Just Culture agenda, bringing in academics and industry experts, and she is now a sough-after speaker on the topic. This work was highlighted in the 'We are the NHS: People Plan 2020/21'.

About the Contributors

Ted Baker
Professor Baker became the Chief Inspector of Hospitals in August 2017. He joined CQC in 2014 as Deputy Chief Inspector of Hospitals. Before joining CQC, he worked in clinical practice for 35 years. He was Medical Director and Deputy Chief Executive of Oxford University Hospitals NHS Trust from 2010 to 2014 and Medical Director at Guy's and St Thomas' NHS Foundation Trust from 2003 to 2010.

Kristina Brown
Dr Brown is Senior Lecturer in Leadership and Management and Restorative Just Culture working at the Newcastle Business School of Northumbria University. She is also a doctoral student at Durham University Business School and has an extensive background in public health research including at the Department of Health.

Peter Cheese
Peter is Chief Executive of the Chartered Institute of Personnel and Development. He is a Fellow of the CIPD, a Fellow of AHRI (the Australian HR Institute) and the Academy of Social Sciences. He's also a Companion of the Institute of Leadership and Management, the Chartered Management Institute, and the British Academy of Management. He is a Visiting professor at the University of Lancaster and sits on the Advisory Board for the University of Bath Management School. He holds honorary doctorates from Bath University, Kingston University and Birmingham City University. Prior to joining the CIPD in July 2012, he was Chairman of the Institute of Leadership and Management and a member of the Council of City & Guilds.

Joanne Davidson

An award-winning organisational development practitioner, Jo has more than 25 years of experience in the private and public sector, including working in leadership roles in health and social care in both the NHS and the local government. Jo is Mersey Care's Associate Director of Workforce, Organisational Effectiveness and Learning.

Robert J. de Boer

Trained as an aerospace engineer, Professor de Boer is Director of the Amsterdam Campus at Northumbria University. His most recent work is called 'Safety Leadership – a different, doable and directed approach to operational improvements'.

Amy Edmondson

Professor Edmondson is the Novartis Professor of Leadership at Harvard Business School. She graduated in three years with a double major from Harvard University. As one of the world leaders in studies into psychological safety in the workplace, Amy is the author of 7 books and more than 75 articles and case studies. Amy has been ranked by the biannual Thinkers50 global list of top management thinkers since 2011 (most recently number 13) and selected in 2019 as the number 1 most influential thinker in Human Resources by *HR Magazine*.

Joe Farmer

Joe is a psychiatry CT1 doctor in the West Midlands. He graduated from Warwick Medical School in 2015, completing a Foundation Training in the West Midlands and is working closely with Dr Chris Turner on a shared interest in civility and medical education which started over a cup of coffee and became the Civility Saves Lives campaign.

Jeremy Hunt

The Rt Hon Jeremy Hunt MP was the UK's longest-serving Health Secretary, holding the post between 2012 and 2018. He went on to be Foreign Secretary and a candidate to be Leader of the Conservative Party when Theresa May stepped down from office. In his time in office his principal focus was patient safety. He introduced Ofsted-rankings for hospitals, care homes and GP surgeries; set up the Healthcare Safety Investigation Branch; and introduced the Statutory Duty of Candour and Freedom to Speak Up Guardians amongst many reforms designed to create a just culture when it came to issues of patient safety. As Foreign Secretary, he persuaded the WHO's World Health Assembly to vote for the creation of an annual Patient Safety Day, which now happens on September 17 every year. Last year's World Patient Safety Day was marked in 87 countries with 130 monuments worldwide lit up in orange to mark the theme of Health Worker Safety. Jeremy's work in mental health has particularly focused on the insight that safer patients also mean safer staff. He strongly supports the Zero Suicide Alliance as he was the first Secretary of State to offer it national funding.

Penny Hurst
An ST2 doctor in Obstetrics and Gynaecology working in a large teaching hospital, Dr Hurst graduated from Warwick Medical School in 2015. Penny completed her foundation year training in the West Midlands and is a founder member of the healthcare professionals' campaign group Civility Saves Lives.

Nico A. Kaptein
Nico is Associate at COT Institute for Safety, Security and Crisis Management in The Hague, The Netherlands, and has published widely on safety and design issues. He teaches at Northumbria University and was COT Head of Research and Consultancy from 2012 to 2018.

Steve Mallen
A co-founder of the Zero Suicide Alliance, Steve is also a member of the National Suicide Prevention Group within the Department of Health and Social Care with oversight of the National Confidential Inquiry into Suicide and Safety in Mental Health (NCISH). Following a long corporate career in international chartered surveying and fund management, Steve is now a committed mental health campaigner and reformer. He is also a Governor at Cambridgeshire and Peterborough NHS Foundation Trust (under whose care his son had died), and he works closely with several mental health and suicide prevention charities. A member of The National Children's Bureau, Steve is also the Chairman of The MindEd Trust, a charity focused on mental health in children and young people.

Jill Mason
Jill is a Healthcare Law Partner in the national law firm Mills & Reeve. Jill's work, and that of her 25 strong immediate team, has involved advising health and care providers in both the public and the private sector and

commissioners on all manner of patient-related issues for over 25 years. This includes advice and support in respect of serious incident investigations, inquests and risk management work, all under the umbrella of key pieces of legislation such as the Mental Health Act 1983, Mental Capacity Act 2005 and Human Rights Act 1998. Jill is a client relationship partner for many clients including large mental health trusts in England and also leads the whole health and care sector at Mills & Reeve. Jill appreciates the importance of governance too as she sits on the firm's Audit, Governance and Oversight Panel.

John Rowbotham

As communications manager in Mersey Care, John leads on promoting the restorative just culture agenda and has designed training materials. He has an MA (Hons) in English Literature, Language, Politics and Sociology. John is also involved in education leadership as a Chair of School Governors and previously worked in communications in local government.

Kick Sterkman

Kick is an expert in safety operations in high-risk environments. He holds a BSc in maintenance engineering, an MSc in management and an MSc in Human Factors and System Safety. He is the group HSEQ Director for Neptune Energy, leading health, safety, environment, quality and security teams.

James Titcombe OBE

James is a patient safety specialist at Datix Ltd and before that the UK Care Quality Commission's national advisor on patient safety, culture and quality. He was also a project manager in the nuclear industry. The story of the death of his son led to a number of investigations of 18 other babies where findings revealed cover-ups, claims of records being destroyed and ultimately the closure of a maternity ward.

Chris Turner

A founder of the widely respected healthcare professionals' campaign Civility Saves Lives, Dr Turner is a consultant in emergency medicine at University Hospitals in Coventry and Warwickshire NHS Trust, working in a tertiary trauma centre. He has delivered a TED talk on civility and regularly lectures and publishes, including making contributions to Mersey Care's online training packages.

Chapter 1

Introduction to Restorative Just Culture

Sidney Dekker

Contents

A just culture is a culture of trust, learning and accountability. The primary purpose of a just culture, to most people, is to respond appropriately to incidents. Their idea is that a just culture should not only enable you and your organization to learn from failure but also hold your people 'accountable' for undesirable performance. This chapter and this book show that a just and learning culture, or a restorative just culture, is actually so much more than that. Restorative practices that build toward a just and learning culture enable people in an organization to become more involved, to speak up and

DOI: 10.4324/9781003162582-1

to become part of the solution – independent of untoward things happening or not.

The Retributive Dead End

Most of the guidance available on just culture today – and the typical model adopted by many organizations – considers justice in retributive terms (see Dekker, 2016). It asks questions such as:

- What rule was broken?
- Who is responsible?
- How bad is the violation (honest mistake, at-risk or reckless behavior) and so what should the consequences be?

Such a 'just culture' is organized around shades of retribution. It focuses on the supposed 'offender' and asks what they have done and what they deserve. But many managers have found that simplistic guidance about pigeonholing human acts does not take them very far: how do you fairly judge, for instance, how 'bad' a supposed violation was? There will almost always be a lack of clarity, agreement or perceived fairness about who draws the line between the acceptable and the unacceptable behavior. Does this person who draws the line actually know the nuances and messy details of the practitioner's work? If not, how can they really know what constitutes risk or risk-taking in that world? And of course, hindsight and outcome biases have been shown to have a considerable influence on how people judge the actions leading up to an outcome (LaBine & LaBine, 1996).

   Knowledge, power and justice get easily muddled in this. Research shows that the more powerful people in an organizational hierarchy typically consider their organization's culture to be more 'just' (von Thaden, Hoppes, Yongjuan, Johnson, & Schriver, 2006). Also, there is not always a well-developed process for appealing a decision that is made on the basis of a 'just culture' policy. Being 'just cultured' is known by some employees as a good way to get yourself fired, demoted or suspended. It is probably not surprising that there is actually no convincing evidence that organizations with a retributive just culture have higher reporting rates or that they learn more of value after an incident. They may in fact create cultures of 'risk secrecy', of hiding evidence of wrongs and harms, of pushing blame around.

Restorative Just Culture as a Strong Alternative

A restorative just culture presents a strong and viable alternative. The principles of restorative justice are these:

■ An event causes harm, and the response to that event should aim to repair that harm. This includes taking responsibility for the harm and making amends for it.
■ The people most involved in, and affected by, the harm should all be able to participate in designing and deciding the restoration needed.
■ The result often includes restoration of trust and a transformation of relationships between stakeholders and reintegrates participants into the community of practice.

What this means in practice is that a restorative response is organized around three very different questions (as compared to a retributive response):

■ Who is impacted?
■ What do they need?
■ Whose obligation is it to meet those needs?

Identifying and meeting obligations is ultimately about putting right what went wrong. It is about making amends. In restorative practices, this means promoting reparation and healing for all affected by the incident. This notion of reparation, of restitution or 'paying back', is central to retributive justice too, of course. In restorative practices, however, everything possible is done to reintegrate the practitioner into the community, and the 'payment' typically gets made in a different currency. Restorative practices ask you to:

■ Address the harm done to first and second victims of the incident, as well as the surrounding community.
■ Address the systemic issues that helped produce the incident by asking *what* was responsible for it, so that other practitioners and first victims are less likely to end up in a similar situation.

For restorative practices to be meaningful and seen as just by all involved, you have to be collaborative and inclusive. Effective restoration relies on this engagement. An incident can affect many people, and its aftermath typically has many stakeholders. These might be given access to, and information about, each other. All can then be involved in deciding what justice requires in their case. This may mean an actual dialogue between parties (e.g. first and second victim) to share their accounts and arrive at an agreement on what should be done. How might the creation of restorative justice look in your organization? It will likely involve the following steps and people:

- Encounters between stakeholders. The first one is likely to be between your organization and the practitioner(s) involved in the incident. Remember your organization's obligations above!
- An encounter between the first and the second victim, appropriately guided, may follow. Surrogates or representatives may need to be used in some situations.
- Encouraging all stakeholders to give their accounts, ask questions, express feelings and work toward a mutually acceptable solution.
- Acknowledge the harm, restore the balance and address your future intentions.

Restorative justice has the possibility to deal effectively with both the consequences *and* the causes of an event. Rather than just pursuing the narrow and limited 'legal' facts that would be necessary to secure, for example, dismissal, restorative justice facilitates a dialogue that helps identify many sides of the event. It seeks to lay out, for and with help of all participants, the complexity and diversity of an incident. This begins to display the complex causal web beneath it and can let participants in on a diversity of leverage points to make changes. It does this by:

- Getting people from the *community of practice* involved. These are most likely the people who understand intimately the messy details of how work is done and how success and failure are created locally. Without a deeper understanding of how success is normally assured, and how a negative event could come about, there is neither a good chance of a fair response to it nor a good chance of finding entry points for change and improvement.
- Engaging in *forward-looking accountability*. Forward-looking accountability deals with causes and consequences because it directs accountabilities toward prevention. It holds people accountable not by fixing

blame for something past. Rather, people collaboratively fix future responsibilities for things they need to accomplish in and for the community.

And, as said in the introductory paragraph, there is more to a restorative just culture than how you respond to incidents. The best post-event processes in the world, after all, cannot do much if there is no prior relationship of confidence and trust between the people in an organization who need to figure out what to do next. Restorative practices, and how they touch everything from people's interactions to human resources to processes and procedures, are made to help an organization build that confidence and that trust.

A restorative just culture doesn't mean that it is a culture without rules. But because a restorative just culture so consciously invests in the engagement and enabling of people, it generates a number of advantages that can bring *work-as-imagined* (as it is in all the rules) and *work-as-done* (as it is in actual practice) much closer together (Hollnagel, 2012):

■ Involvement of those who will have to do the work enhances the legitimacy of the rules that apply to people's work.
■ Taking part in the process of developing the rules increases the sense of ownership the workers feel toward the rules. The rules derive from their own insights, arguments and experiences.
■ Developing the rules in connection with the workers ensures that the rules are connected with reality. The standards are not designed for an ideal environment, imagined without time pressures, complicating factors and conflicting information. Instead, the written rules (and practices taught by educators) align with and support normal practice in the field.

The two forms of just culture (retributive versus restorative) also approach trust differently. Retribution builds trust by reinforcing rules and the authority of certain parties or persons to patrol and enforce them. It says that where people work to get things done, there are lines that should not be crossed. And if they are, there are consequences. Think about it like this: if you find that people 'get away' with breaking rules or doing sloppy work, you don't have much trust in the system or in your community's ability to demand accountability. Your trust can be restored if you see an appropriate and assertive response to such behavior. You can once again rest assured that the system, or your community, does not accept such behavior and responds in ways that make that clear – to everyone.

Restoration, on the other hand, builds trust by repairing fiduciary relationships. Fiduciary relationships are relationships of trust between people who depend on each other to make something work. Consider the work done in your own organization. People in your organization depend on each other. Every day, perhaps every minute, they have to trust each other that certain things get done, and get done timely, appropriately, safely. They might not do these things themselves because they are not in the right place, or because they lack the expertise or authority to do them. So they depend on others. This creates a fiduciary relationship: a relationship of trust. It is this relationship that is hurt or broken when things go wrong. And it is this relationship that needs restoring (Table 1.1).

Table 1.1 Different Ways in Which Retributive and Restorative Processes Try to Create Justice

Retributive	Restorative
Wrongdoing creates guilt and demands punishment that compensates it	Wrongdoing creates needs and obligations to meet those needs
Account is something the offender *pays* or *settles*	Account is something the offender *tells* and listens to
Asks *who* is responsible for the incident	Asks *what* is responsible for the incident
Learns and prevents by setting an example	Learns and prevents by asking why it made sense for people to do what they did
Focuses on what people involved in the incident deserve	Focuses on what people involved in, and affected by, the incident need
Creates justice by imposing proportional and deserved punishment	Creates justice by deciding who meets the needs arising from the incident
Meets hurt with inflicting proportionate hurt	Meets hurt with healing
Looks back on harm done and assigns consequences	Looks ahead at trust to repair and invests in relationships
Builds trust by reinforcing rules and the authority to impose and police them	Builds trust by repairing relationships between people whose work depends on each other

From Dekker, 2016

A History of Restorative Justice

Perhaps one might think that restorative justice is a morally superior practice; that it is inherently a better, fairer or more natural way for people to resolve differences and right wrongs. That, though, would be both ahistorical and morally problematic. The history of restorative justice, such as it is, is best seen as a constant push–pull between – or co-existence of – different modes of responding to hurts and infractions. Restoration and restitution often co-existed with other, more retributive approaches. Cultures where we can historically find the outlines of restorative justice practices also typically applied retribution (Braithwaite, 1989).

Restorative practices have existed for as long as people have lived in communities. Anthropologists have found evidence for them in so-called acephalous societies (meaning societies or communities without a head and without a state), such as hunter-gatherer clans. Inter-clan transgressions were often the object of restitutive practices. Negotiations between elders followed a transgression (say, a theft of something from another clan) and were concluded with some form of compensation to the victim and his or her clan. Restorative practices understood a transgression mainly as an offense against the victim but also against the community as a whole (Mulligan, 2009). This meant that victims, and their communities, needed to be meaningfully involved or represented in the negotiations. Pursuing restitution could have been pragmatic rather than moral: restorative practices kept clans from being drawn into cycles of blood revenge (Weitekamp, 1999).

Early written codes also contain restorative procedures. The Babylonian Code of Hammurabi (circa 1700 BCE) prescribed restitution for property offenses, for example, and others demanded restitution for violent crimes (e.g. the Codes of Ur-Nammu and Eshnunna). Ancient Hebrew law uses the word 'shillum' for restitution and a return to healing and wholeness, which is etymologically close to 'shalom', the word for peace. This is how it aimed to establish fairness in the wake of harm – interestingly with the shadow of capital retribution (or what we would today call 'mob justice' or 'vigilantism') hovering in the background:

> The case of two men involved in a fight that resulted in non-fatal injuries to one of the men. The one who inflicted the injury was required to pay for the employment time the other man lost due to the healing process. Similarly, if an ox was known to be dangerous but the owner did not take proper precautions and the ox gored

a person to death, both the ox and its owner were to be killed unless the victim's family was willing to accept reparations instead.

(Weitekamp, 1999, p. 84 *supra* note 12)

Early Germanic tribal laws similarly encouraged restorative justice for a wide range of infractions, including homicide (Mulligan, 2009). A seventh-century collection of English Laws of Ethelbert, named after the late 6th century English king, contained detailed compensation schedules proportionate to the harm caused to the victim(s). Anglo-Saxon laws, too, were based on restorative principles. As with Babylonian codes, restorative practices weren't limited to acephalous or small communities. The early empire of Rome had its Law of Twelve Tablets (449 BCE) which required thieves to pay restitution for the property they had stolen and suggested restitution as an explicit alternative to certain physical offenses. Acephalous communities that exist today continue to apply restorative practices. These include Australian Aboriginals, Egyptian Bedouin, Native American and Canadian First Nation societies and the vast number of small, geographically or topographically isolated communities for whom the idea of a state is a mere whisper, a rumor from across the hills – from hamlets in the forests of Eastern Ukraine to the mountains of Afghanistan to the vast tundras of Siberia.

This doesn't mean that the sort of restorative justice practiced in these places – and indeed historically – necessarily coincides with what we now know as universal human rights. Discrimination and intense prejudices on gender, sexual orientation, age, religion or ethnicity were and are often deeply laced through the negotiations and resolutions. Some won, some had the power to decide – and some lost. These arrangements can create jarring injustices for a few, even if a sense of order and apparent harmony is maintained at the community level. This is a known problem of utilitarian forms of ethics: what is best for the whole can sacrifice justice for a few unlucky ones. What is seen as right (for the community) and what is just (for the individual) can diverge widely. The monstrous consequences that these forms of justice could have for some individuals, as well as their co-existence with threats of retribution (a threat, or lever, that was typically held by victims), mean that we should not mythologize restorative justice.

Nor should we see restoration as the dominant form of pre-modern justice. Indeed, the very term didn't show up to denote a specific kind of justice until quite late in the modern age. Retribution as a response to offenses had existed for a long time alongside other practices, even in acephalous societies. But of course, states, from Babylonian to Roman to early European, were particularly well-equipped to develop and apply systems of retributive justice, because they could develop an apparatus to administer justice *on behalf* of victims and their communities. In 1066, with the Norman invasion of England, William the Conqueror and his successors brought into existence a legal system that gradually replaced the church and local systems of conflict resolution. For the nascent state, the legal system turned out to be useful for exerting influence and extracting money. Crimes were seen not (just) as violations of a community's mores, or the victim's rights. They were seen as infractions against the state, and against the ruler, the king, as a disruption of the 'King's peace'. Fines benefited the ruler economically and often politically. The state and the offender were the primary actors around whom the justice was organized, and the victim played a lesser role.

The Goals of Restoration

From how restorative justice has been dealt with both historically and currently, we can derive four goals it should strive to achieve inside your organization:

■ Moral engagement
■ Emotional healing
■ Practitioner reintegration
■ Organizational learning

Moral Engagement

The Many Sides of an Incident

For those in your organization, an incident with an adverse outcome is seldom firstly acknowledged as a moral issue. It's not that it *isn't* a moral issue (more about that soon), but the event is first and foremost so much else. There is an immediate demand for damage control, for instance, for mitigation and for preventing even worse harm from occurring. Then an event with a bad outcome is very likely an economic issue. There are the immediate consequences of the disruption or delay in operations. If the incident is bad enough, work grinds to a halt on that site, or in that operating theater, or with that aircraft or truck. A job might not get finished in time, and in case of serious injuries or fatalities, people who could do the job are no longer around. A regulator could even step in and stop operations. Then there is the loss of an asset, for instance (this could be anything from a broken vessel in which concrete was being poured to a ship or an airliner lost in an accident).

The event is also, probably early on, a legal issue, generating questions about liability and responsibility. People will try to trace out what the legal consequences of the event could be, and how it might affect them personally or their roles or departments. Then the event is an insurance issue. It may result in various claims, either by external parties or by the organization itself. The claims could be associated with harm or loss caused to others, or with the loss of an asset, for instance. The event is a reputational issue too. Depending on the visibility of the incident, an organization's brand or reputation could be hurt significantly, which has financial knock-on effects (e.g. stock price if listed or loss of prospective customers). This can make the event a media relations issue too. In that case, moral questions often get put on the backburner, in favor of generic expressions of compassion ('our thoughts are with …'), hedging about causes ('we will fully investigate …') and stalling on responsibility ('we will fully cooperate …').

All these different guises of the same event can easily divert organizations from seeing that event as a pressing moral issue. It's just not the most immediate thing to be concerned about, as there is too much other damage control to be done. But what exactly does moral mean? Something is a moral issue if it invokes questions of right and wrong. Moral questions are typically without obvious answers as to which is which or have grave limits imposed on doing the right thing when you *do* know what that is. In some countries or hospital systems, for example, it is still a legally really bad idea to disclose the role one has had in harming a patient. This despite the fact that the impulse of some caregivers would be to rush out to the family immediately after the harm has occurred or been discovered. Lawyers and managers advise against it and might even endeavor to keep involved caregivers away from the family. From an emotional and moral point of view, however, sitting down with the family and disclosing one's role and expressing remorse for what has happened could be exactly the right thing to do. (This has actually been shown to often be the right thing legally too, as honest, open and timely disclosure can reduce liability costs down the line (Dauer, 2004).)

Restoration has the goal of moral engagement. Moral engagement means a couple of things at the same time (see Bandura, 1990):

■ *Accepting appropriate responsibility* for what has happened. This doesn't mean that a practitioner should shoulder the blame – quite the opposite. In many cases, accepting appropriate responsibility means that many others in the organization need to engage with *their* roles and responsibilities. They and their decisions (about equipment, procurement, deadlines and production pressures) may well have helped set the practitioner up for failure. Moral engagement is about embracing the consequences of decisions made in those roles across the organization and finding a balance of who carried what in steering things toward a bad outcome.

■ *Recognizing and acknowledging the seriousness* of the harmful effects on others. It is possible to work in an organization, even for a lifetime, and not understand the effects that incidents and their consequences have for those who were affected by them. I have seen a safety manager summarily dismiss a worker for breach of a safety rule and then turn his back. The manager did not realize, for example, that the worker had a family to support and came from a small town in which getting another job was virtually impossible. And even if he had, he surrendered to the role and its orders: the organization's life-saving rules were to be strictly adhered to and workers knew they would be fired if they violated even one of them. To be fair, the safety manager expressed deep remorse years later, wishing he could go back and undo his actions, or meet the dismissed worker and say sorry. Restoration avoids such dissociation by bringing relevant people together to discuss the impact the incident has had on them and others and by together finding appropriate responses to it.

■ *Humanizing the people involved* in the incident, thereby becoming able to recognize their hurts and needs. In some cases, I have seen the opposite, where nurses blamed the doctor (or vice versa), but where the other was depicted as a cut-out, as a one-dimensional stereotype – not as an individual with a story to tell and feelings to share. Doing this is, of course, one type of psychological protection. Dehumanizing makes it easier to blame others and deflect responsibility for moral engagement (with the event and with other people involved in it) away from oneself.

In a few cases, doctors have been noted to dehumanize patients who suffer harm by blaming them (e.g. a 'nonconforming patient') (Morreim, 2004).

If that is what moral engagement consists of, then how do you achieve it? And who should actually become morally engaged? There is, theoretically, no limit to the circle of people who might be negatively affected by the incident. It depends on the circumstances. It probably also depends on the resources the organization can make available for engaging the affected community of people. More will be said about inclusion later in the book. But this much is clear: to achieve moral engagement, there is no substitute for actually meeting the 'other' and being able to engage in conversation with them (indeed, just 'meeting' the other from across a court room doesn't really do that). Accepting appropriate responsibility can depend on learning from others what they see as *their* responsibilities. Recognizing and acknowledging the seriousness of harm is really possible only by hearing its consequences from the stories of others, by seeing the etches of suffering on their faces. And humanizing is critically dependent on getting to know the person – the human – behind the role or stereotype (Klein & Klein, 2007; Macaskill, 2012).

Emotional Healing

Since the 1980s, we know a lot about the common patterns of a reaction to a crisis – an incident in which the practitioner is involved. People typically experience a combination of any or all of the following (Mitchell, 1983):

- Helplessness
- Mental confusion or disorganization
- Difficulties in decision making and problem solving
- Anxiety, shock, denial or disbelief
- Anger, agitation or rage
- Lowered self-esteem
- Fear
- Withdrawal from others
- Emotionally subdued, depressed
- Grief
- Apathy

- Physical reactions such as nausea, shakes, intestinal or muscular issues, hyperventilation and more.

In cases where the practitioner was involved in the incident and feels personally responsible, it is very likely that the experiences also include guilt, shame, remorse, humiliation, worthlessness and empathy or intense concern for (other) victims of the incident (Dekker, 2013; Wu, 2000). The first steps of any restorative response have to address the needs that arise from these experiences. They have to mitigate the impact of the incident and facilitate normal recovery processes (Case, 2004). The provision of psychological first aid is a good step to start with. Cut access to stimuli from the workplace and provide some privacy, if possible. Acknowledge that a bad event has happened and that this likely affects the practitioner in ways that are both obvious and not yet visible. Tell what has been done to meet the needs of other victims of the incident, so that those concerns can be put to rest. Explore the options and plans available and make the practitioner aware of any rights and duties in the wake of the incident. Don't debrief yet; don't worry about the substance of the incident. That comes later. At this point, any steps taken have to help restore the practitioner to a normal level of functioning and create the basis for ultimately reintegrating them into work.

Emotional healing is a vital characteristic of restorative justice, too. Recovering from an incident represents a kind of symbolic reparation; a reparation of trust and confidence, of worthiness. The practitioner involved may, for instance, feel that the organization has long been indifferent to a particular issue or constraint (e.g. staffing, workload, equipment design, provision of tools) that played a role in the incident. Emotional healing in this case depends on engagement by the organization to show that it cares about the practitioner and the causes behind the incident. Ideally, of course, the organization engages in a conversation about the systemic issues that contributed to the incident and shows a commitment to actual repair. Emotional healing for the practitioner here means moving from indignation and resentment and anger to acceptance and empathy. It could even mean mustering the energy to help change things in the organization or industry. The processes of emotional healing between organization, practitioner and (other) victims of the incident tend to be intertwined. An employer can hardly expect a practitioner to show genuine remorse if its own role in contributing to the incident is left entirely untouched and unexamined. A victim of the incident cannot be expected to become willing to forgive (and this expectation should never exist anyway) if there is no confession and repentance on part of the organization, the practitioner or their representatives (Berlinger, 2005).

Reintegrating the Practitioner

A third major goal of restorative justice is to reintegrate the practitioner into the world of their work. The reasons for this are not just humanitarian. Doctors, pilots, train drivers, air traffic controllers, nurses, firefighters and other practitioners can be hard to find and expensive to train. Some countries are in fact facing acute shortages of suitably skilled and qualified people in some of these fields. Losing one to an incident whose aftermath wasn't handled constructively can be a huge waste. The driver for getting a practitioner 'back in the saddle' can thus be an economic one, and this is often a reason for organizations to support critical incident response teams and stress management programs (Leonhardt & Vogt, 2006).

An incident can seriously dent the confidence a practitioner has in his or her own skills. Reintegrating them into practice is then foremost an exercise in building that confidence back up. The way in which this is typically done is to ease the practitioner back into work through simulation or mentored practice where someone else helps them along. Some may need referral or additional support, of course. When I learned to fly in my teens, the folk or intuitive way that incidents were managed was by getting the student pilot right back in the airplane. The thought was that staying away from the cockpit after a near miss or incident would be a sure way to lose them altogether. Student pilots were thought to become fearful and averse to flying, or flying particular maneuvers or aircraft, if they weren't shown immediately after the incident that things would mostly go right if they just tried again. I never did check up on the theoretical or empirical basis for the practice (and I was too young and focused on mastering the various aircraft). But it would seem to make intuitive sense, if sometimes a bit rushed and harsh. An adequate defusing and debriefing (such as explained above) might have been good in some of the cases I witnessed, and I do recall some spontaneous attempts at versions of defusing and debriefing in some instructors. Unfortunately, many instructor pilots at the time had neither the inclination nor knowledge or skills to do so.

There is another reason for wanting to keep the practitioner who has been involved in a close call or an actual negative outcome. They have a unique perspective. What does the world look like, and how does it feel, when that which you are trained to prevent actually happens? An area of practice, which others might merely have experienced as brushing up against a margin, was wholly crossed by the practitioner involved in the incident. Knowing about the view from the other side of that experience, and learning from it, can be valuable for colleagues and leaders alike. The insights gained by the practitioner can be highly useful not only in safety training, in resource management and emergency training but also in the moral engagement of the organization's leadership. It allows them to learn more intimately what their organization is actually working with at the sharp end and what failures can do to people both inside and outside their organization.

I haven't actually met many leaders who truly embrace practitioners who have been involved in an incident. Leaders rather shun them, because the practitioner has made the organization look bad and made them look bad. And the practitioner perhaps reminds them of a vexing goal conflict in which the leaders themselves played a part, for example, the conflict to provide adequate resources under significant budget pressure or personnel shortage. It sometimes seems easier for leaders to leave the care of the practitioner in the hands of unions, colleagues, peers or professionals. But even if that is done, it is perhaps not entirely smart to avoid further involvement. Showing that you personally care as a leader, and that you take time to learn about the incident from the source the closest to it, is a critical signal not just to the practitioner involved but also to colleagues. Support, in whatever form and whether from colleagues, peers, managers or family and friends, has been shown to be critical to the eventual reintegration of the practitioner (Dekker, 2013; Eurocontrol, 1997; Scott et al., 2009; Ullstrom, Sachs, Hansson, Ovretveit, & Brommels, 2013).

Finally, some organizations may feel that some form of retributive accountability is appropriate and necessary for a reintegration to be possible. Even peers and colleagues may sometimes feel that way. Some years ago, one of my students, a European captain who flew for an airline based in Asia, told me of precisely such an instance. He learned of an incident that had happened to an Asian colleague captain. Bad visibility and hard winds had caused the aircraft to drift off the centerline of the runway after landing, pushing it partially into the soft ground next to it. The captain eventually initiated a go-around and pulled the aircraft away from the rough, troubling ground run. After circling back to the runway, the next landing was uneventful. As part of its response, the airline demoted the captain temporarily to First Officer (or second-in-command). He had to wear a

First Officer's uniform, got paid less and of course lost face and reputation. During the immediate aftermath of the incident and the hearings and investigation around it, colleagues had shunned him, probably because of the uncertainty of what was going to happen with him. Yet when he got back into the crew room for his first flight (again) as a First Officer, however, he was greeted heartily and gregariously by his colleagues. Laughing and backslapping, he clearly was part of the 'gang' again. He was seen to have paid his dues (or seen to still be paying them as a demoted pilot). That was, in the eyes of many, a just accounting. He also had to show that he could be trusted with an aircraft again. The reintegrative 'shame' he had to go through was part of his ability to come back to his profession. This didn't say anything about him as a person or a practitioner, but everything about the event he'd been involved in (see Braithwaite, 1989).

Organizational Learning

The fourth goal of restorative justice is organizational learning. Restorative justice is better geared toward addressing causes of harm than retributive justice is. The reason for this is simple: restorative processes go beyond the practitioner and their actions, whereas retribution often doesn't. A fine, a demotion, standing someone down, firing them – all of these responses merely focus on the practitioner and would seem to suggest that the unwanted actions will no longer occur simply because the actor is now removed or suitably punished. This supposedly also deters others from doing the same thing. None of that, however, addresses the broader causal picture in a way that restorative discussions can. A major ingredient of restorative processes (focusing on hurts, needs and obligations) almost necessarily directs part of the attention to what needs to be done to prevent a recurrence. Restoration not only involves reparation for hurts and harms but also includes the obligation to seek prevention. With the involvement of many stakeholders, restorative processes are likely to identify all kinds of system issues behind the incident – from goal conflicts, resource constraints, production pressures to procedural double binds and equipment issues (see Woods, Dekker, Cook, Johannesen, & Sarter, 2010). Considering the contributions of these factors, and seeing what can be done about them, is of course consistent with forward-looking accountability (Sharpe, 2003). It involves investigating and deciding what needs to be done now and in the future so that recurrence, or the occurrence of similar incidents, becomes less likely. Again, it is almost inevitable that this involves discussions about the many contributing factors and system issues behind the creation of both success and failure. For restorative justice, putting things right doesn't mean paying off what went wrong. It means addressing and repairing the harms that have been done, but also addressing and changing the causes of those harms (Zehr & Gohar, 2002).

Into Practice

This book is the work of many contributors, bringing academic and leadership experience, and in many cases, powerful and moving testimony, to draw out the theory and the processes described in its chapters. They culminate in what we believe is a practical statement, if not a definitive guide. We are clear that there is no off-the-shelf solution but a series of choices to be made.

While they may be read as stand-alone documents, each chapter progresses a loose but developing narrative. The frame we put on it is that of one organization, Mersey Care NHS Foundation Trust. All the learning in these pages has been seen and, in some form, used by Mersey Care, although the contributors relate their own accounts independently. We have brought in their respective viewpoints to offer perceptions of just culture from academia, from the voices of a patient, regulator, inspector, parliamentarian and from a provider organization. Mersey Care, a large trust based in Liverpool, has taken steps along the route we call restorative justice and has led much in the way of culture change, training and advocacy of just culture within the UK healthcare system. You will hear much from them as well as strong voices from these wider spheres. I have worked with them and spent time with staff in their services across their footprint.

It is a medium-sized National Health Service (NHS) trust, providing local mental health, learning disability and community health services to a population of around 1.2 million people in the North West of England and specialist high-secure and learning disability services to a population of around 11 million people. It is the largest provider of forensic learning disability services and is one of the major providers of high-secure services in England. The trust currently employs around 11,500 staff from more than 170 locations and it has an annual turnover of more than £600 million. The trust was established on 1 April 2001 and granted NHS Foundation Trust status in May 2016.

Since 2016, the trust has acquired three other NHS trusts and additional services, giving it a footprint across wider areas than its earlier Liverpool core. It has built and opened new hospitals in the same period, including a regional secure site for people with complex mental ill-health needs. Throughout this period, the Board of Directors has been headed by design engineer Beatrice Fraenkel as Chair and former cancer chemist Joe Rafferty as Chief Executive. The trust's work on suicide prevention, and their founding of an alliance of high-level national and international partners to promote education and reduce stigma, is of strong relevance to their whole approach to this topic.

The trust's services have been delivered through clinical divisions which are supported by corporate services such as patient safety, finance, workforce, communications and facilities. During the trust's journey with restorative just culture the four clinical divisions have been:

- The secure and specialist learning disability division comprising care prescribed by the Ministry of Justice as going from high, medium and low secure for people presenting a significant risk to themselves or others, plus services in two prisons as well as community and individualized packages of learning disability care.
- A local division comprising further mental health, learning disability and some social care services for the adult population of Liverpool, Sefton or Kirkby.
- Community health division comprising community (physical) health services provided to the population of Liverpool and South Sefton.
- From 2021, a Mid Mersey division comprising similar services from a newly acquired Trust which operate in particular geographic areas.

From April 2022 Mersey Care started a redesign of its operating model which will see a structure of three clinical divisions.

The cliché of the journey is often ill-used. Here we see described how, as Mersey Care came to see that there needed to be a step change in culture, the reality of their regeneration operated in a system bound by regulation and process. One which had to accommodate many modifications: incremental increases in staffing levels, the intricacies of real-life politics and indeed the expectation to operate complex services through a global pandemic. It also recognizes that their development is just that: a work in progress. This book is about much more than one organization, my work with them and my film about them, the circumstances of which are outlined later.

It does, however, provide evidence of a complex organization asking itself what, in daily practice, does the theory mean to people – both staff and ultimately patient care.

References

Bandura, A. (1990). Mechanisms of moral disengagement. In W. Reich (Ed.), *Origins of terrorism* (pp. 161–191). Cambridge, UK: Cambridge University Press.

Berlinger, N. (2005). *After harm: Medical error and the ethics of forgiveness.* Baltimore, MD: Johns Hopkins University Press.

Braithwaite, J. (1989). *Crime, shame and reintegration.* Cambridge, UK: Cambridge University Press.

Case, P. (2004). Secondary iatrogenic harm: Claims for psychiatric damage following a death caused by medical error. *Modern Law Review, 67*(4), 561–587.

Dauer, E. A. (2004). Ethical misfits: Mediation and medical malpractice litigation. In V. A. Sharpe (Ed.), *Accountability: Patient safety and policy reform* (pp. 185–202). Washington, DC: Georgetown University Press.

Dekker, S. W. A. (2013). *Second victim: Error, guilt, trauma and resilience.* Boca Raton, FL: CRC Press/Taylor & Francis.

Dekker, S. W. A. (2016). *Just culture: Restoring trust and accountability in your organization.* Boca Raton, FL: CRC Press.

Eurocontrol. (1997). *Critical incident stress management: Human factors module.* Retrieved from Brussels: https://skybrary.aero/sites/default/files/bookshelf/4578.pdf

Hollnagel, E. (22.02.2012–24.02.2012). *Resilience engineering and the systemic view of safety work: Why work-as-done is not the same as work-as-imagined.* Paper presented at the 58. Arbeitswissenschaftlichen Kongress GfA (Hrsg.) Gestaltung nachhaltiger Arbeitssysteme: Wege zur gesunden, effizienten und sicheren Arbeit, Kassel, Germany.

Klein, C. A., & Klein, A. B. (2007). Alternative dispute resolution: An overview. *Nurse Practioner, 32*(12), 15–16.

LaBine, S. J., & LaBine, G. (1996). Determinations of negligence and the Hindsight Bias. *Law and Human Behavior, 20*(5), 501–516.

Leonhardt, J., & Vogt, J. (2006). *Critical incident stress management in aviation.* Aldershot, UK: Ashgate Publishing Co.

Macaskill, A. (2012). Differentiating dispositional self-forgiveness from other-forgiveness: Associations with mental health and life satisfaction. *Journal Social and Clinical Psychology, 31*(1), 28–40.

Mitchell, J. (1983). When disaster strikes... The critical incident stress debriefing process. *Journal of Emergency Medical Services, 8*, 36–39.

Morreim, E. H. (2004). Medical errors: Pinning the blame versus blaming the system. In V. A. Sharpe (Ed.), *Accountability: Patient safety and policy reform* (pp. 213–232). Washington, DC: Georgetown University Press.

Mulligan, S. (2009). From retribution to repair: Juvenile justice and the history of restorative justice. *University of La Verne Law Review, 31*(1), 139–149.

Scott, S. D., Hirschinger, L. E., Cox, K. R., McCoig, M., Brandt, J., & Hall, L. W. (2009). The natural history of recovery for the healthcare provider 'second victim' after adverse patient events. *Quality Safety Health Care, 18*, 325–330.

Sharpe, V. A. (2003). Promoting patient safety: An ethical basis for policy deliberation. *Hastings Center Report, 33*(5), S2–19.

Ullstrom, S., Sachs, M. A., Hansson, J., Ovretveit, J., & Brommels, M. (2013). Suffering in silence: A qualitative study of second victims of adverse events. *BMJ Quality and Safety, 23*(4), 325–31. Nov 15. doi:10.1136/bmjqs-2013-002035.

von Thaden, T., Hoppes, M., Yongjuan, L., Johnson, N., & Schriver, A. (2006). *The perception of just culture across disciplines in healthcare.* Paper presented at the Human Factors and Ergonomics Society 50th Annual meeting, San Francisco.

Weitekamp, E. (1999). The history of restorative justice. In G. Bazemore & L. Walgrave (Eds.), *Restorative Juvenile justice: Repairing the harm of youth crime* (pp. 75–102). Monsey, NY: Criminal Justice Press.

Woods, D. D., Dekker, S. W. A., Cook, R. I., Johannesen, L. J., & Sarter, N. B. (2010). *Behind human error.* Aldershot, UK: Ashgate Publishing Co.

Wu, A. W. (2000). Medical error: The second victim. *British Medical Journal, 320*(7237), 726–728.

Zehr, H., & Gohar, A. (2002). *The little book of restorative justice.* Intercourse, PA: Good Books.

Chapter 2

Creating a Restorative Just Culture in a Large Public Organisation: A Personal Reflection from Mersey Care's Chief Executive

Joseph Rafferty

Contents

For much of my career in healthcare management and leadership, I have found myself focusing on organisational performance or being examined for it as a CEO. My more recent experiences have shown me that *organisational health* conducted in a psychologically safe workplace should

DOI: 10.4324/9781003162582-2

be the lens through which we seek to see organisational performance enabled and driven. In this chapter, I set out my experience of focusing on organisational health through developing *Just Culture* in a large National Health Service (NHS) mental and community physical health trust. I've led Mersey Care NHS Foundation Trust as CEO since 2012, and this is what happened.

The lessons are fuelled by conversations with patients, relatives and staff about their experiences with Mersey Care in the event of something having gone wrong in the delivery of healthcare.

Like many people, I have also been on the receiving end of healthcare; as a son, husband, father and friend. More than once, I have experienced sitting on my sofa at home talking about the loss of a loved one, knowing and experiencing the first-hand devastation of that loss.

As CEO of Mersey Care, there was a moment when I found myself sitting on another sofa – this time with a distraught mother, talking to her and apologising for the family devastation caused by the death by suicide of one of her children while they were in our care. That parent made the most reasonable of requests: '*surely* there must be something to learn from all of this'.

I want to be clear that in this chapter I describe not only an organisational journey but also a personal one. That one question from a bereaved mother triggered inside of me a desire to understand how to answer it as the Accountable Officer for Mersey Care; this in turn resulted in a leadership tipping point for all of the trust's Board of Directors.

Like many stories of significant change that resulted in deep organisational and personal transformation, both in healthcare and in other industries, ours was accelerated by a compounding series of tragic and troubling events.

Between the period of 2014 and 2015, there were a number of patient suicides and related serious incidents. These provoked fundamental questions about the effectiveness of the incident review processes used in Mersey Care. Specifically, there were three patients under our care, who over a short period of time died by suicide on a group of three wards on one of our hospital sites. Contextually it is important to appreciate that suicide is a rare event, and inpatient suicide in a mental health setting is even more uncommon. For example, for those in contact with mental health services in England in 2017, the suicide rate per 100,000 service users was 67.1 between 2007 and 2017; the rate of suicide for mental health inpatients in England, as reported by The National Confidential Inquiry into Suicide and Safety in Mental Health, was 9.6–6.0 per 10,000 admissions.

In response to these particular deaths, we could have spent many hours working out if what happened was in fact a 'statistically significant cluster'. However, it felt much more pressing to assess whether our safety processes were actually and fundamentally fit for purpose. Given that the purpose of these processes is to learn and iteratively reduce the risk of recurrence, I could still hear that question posed by our bereaved mother. I felt that I needed to be able to, more accurately, provide a response to her that assured her of our learning as the result of her child's death.

So, for us, this grouping of deaths in a relatively close window of time became a sentinel series (see the Joint Commission website) that signalled our need to clinically, corporately and philosophically reset our approach to service safety.

Processing the Lessons from a Shock Wave

The three deaths in Mersey Care acted as a shock wave to us that set actual and metaphorical alarm bells ringing. When the actual alarms stopped sounding, the more persistent signal – the one indicating a systematic problem – was impossible to silence. Patients who died whilst in our care, admitted because of their acute needs and who presented a risk to themselves, had been failed by our organisation if we accept that keeping at-risk people from fatal self-harm is at the apex of our safety priorities. The questions of accountability that emerged triggered a chain of traumatic events. They devastated relatives managing that awful cocktail of bereavement, anger and disbelief as well as their hunger to understand more; meanwhile, staff found themselves facing investigation and coronial examination. At the same time, the organisation itself behaved, in the words of some bereaved people, like it had 'blood on its hands'.

Some of our early actions, each punctuated by the next death, involved becoming increasingly 'grippy' and assurance driven. The logic at the time assumed 'operator error' and that signalling 'consequences' to all our staff would in itself result in improvements to safety processes and would also serve as a message to the wider stakeholder community that the Board of Directors were 'holding people to account'. Eventually we reached the point where several staff were suspended, pending detailed investigations into each specific incident as well as looking at the three incidents as a group. This produced a whole spate of processes and defensive investigations, which on reflection caused a great deal of unnecessary hurt. The industry of investigations and bureaucracy that followed, staff would tell us afterwards, felt like there was a barely disguised focus on finding the person who made a mistake or who overlooked a protocol and was, therefore, negligent.

We were told several years later that the trust's approach felt like 'culprit seeking' rather than a lesson learned. Although this chapter recounts the organisational story for Mersey Care, since being open about our experiences it is surprising to hear many senior leaders have said they don't recognise it as an issue in their organisation. However, it is interesting to note that several years later when the NHS Patient Safety Strategy (July 2019) was published, it highlighted that a patient safety culture and patient safety system cannot be ignored and that in NHS settings learning is too often thwarted by fear and blame. A pivotal point for Mersey Care was recognising that while much of our clinical risk is complex and adaptive (Woodward, 2019) we recognise that no safety process could ever eliminate all potential opportunities for error or mishap. We equally have to accept our processes that could have done so much more.

Later in this book, Mersey Care's Executive Director of Workforce looks in greater detail at the biases which exist when we review an error or incident. As leaders, we have to do more to avoid the potential pitfall of bias when incidents are reviewed; otherwise, patients, family members and staff themselves can be blamed inappropriately or disproportionality. So, while staff suspensions were labelled as 'neutral acts' or in HR language as 'a non-prejudicial action', staff told us that they were in fact symbolic of our blame culture. Our *processes* in Mersey Care caused us to reflect on the detrimental but largely invisible impact this had on our people and also the potential consequences for disclosure and learning in terms of patient safety. And for our bereaved families it did not allow us to fully reflect on the events and enabled only weak reflections on learning and prevention. These biases meant that full reflection and transparency inhibited true learning. They did not assist in preventing similar future occurrences, neither do they support individual team nor organisational reflections which we now know lead to really valuable learning from incidents and the means by which prevention can be enabled. As articulated by West and Lyubovnikova (2013), good team working is associated with benefits for staff and patients alike and is associated with lower levels of error, stress and injury. For staff who were suspended from duties, it resulted in accusations – firstly from the trust and then from the media – that the staff involved had somehow been solely to blame. In reality, our processes and actions, which were intended to create a virtuous cycle of learning, actually represented a vicious cycle that generated suspicion and defensiveness. They meant that harm was being met by harm.

I recall becoming increasingly irritated by what seemed to be a consistent, if subconscious, 'explaining away' of suicide events across the system. It was not just true of Mersey Care as an individual part of the NHS. Frequently, it seemed we arrived at a conclusion that there appeared to be no root causes, that those who took their lives had been 'determined' and that circumstances on the wards had been 'particularly complex'. We reassured ourselves that these are rare events and that actually, Mersey Care benchmarked in the lower quintile of all NHS mental health trusts for death by suicide – the implication being that because we get it right *most* of the time, we would not attract the attention of quality and other regulators. While each of these statements is more or less factually correct in isolation, they at best provided an uncomfortable and even unfeeling solace.

Corporately we were being less curious about understanding and learning than we needed to be. In particular, it felt like we were looking at the many relevant issues in silos rather than as a set of potentially inter-related factors. Almost certainly we had a reliance on a set of post-incident actions that produced repetitive confirmation that resulted in overconfidence in our systems, processes and their outputs. We did not consider or understand enough the impact this had on our patients' loved ones, friends or indeed on the wider community of caregivers, nor on our own staff and their personal networks either.

It is probably important to say here that what we were experiencing significantly reflected the more nascent state of safety thinking in mental healthcare in the NHS more generally. While there are some notable exceptions (ref NCHIS, RCPsyc/Joint Commission), safety thinking has lagged behind physical, acute healthcare specialities in having a more robust analysis of safety events and proactive management of human factors. Quite reasonably this reflects that not all aspects of safety in healthcare are uniform: risk in mental healthcare can often only be managed moment to moment and sits in the space of an ultra-adaptive system (Vincent and Amalberti, 2016). This description recognises that in services like mental health, especially those aspects with a high level of community activity generally feature a higher level of operator autonomy than in other disciplines. Continuously improving on safety is as much about helping people adapt and respond to the complexity they experience in other areas of their lives. It is also about recognising that ultra-adaptive environments dictate, by their very nature, a need for a different tolerance of risk and some level of acceptance that they can never be harm-free. But similarly, they are areas, given the right learning circumstances, that fast failures can be rapidly innovated into fast successes. It is true too for mental health that disease aetiology and research understanding of therapeutic efficacy have also not been in the same place as for acute physical presentation. However, as the chapter by James Titcombe in this volume will attest, knowledge of events from more reliable, process-intense care systems such as maternity does not always convert to the level and type of learning that one would anticipate.

This differential in approach across different clinical specialisms is a point well made by Suzette Woodward in her book *Implementing Patient Safety* (Woodward, 2020). There she describes a set of safety myths or misunderstandings that seem commonplace.

While published after these events, many of the myths on Woodward's list resonate strongly with the circumstances we encountered as a senior team as we started to explore how we approached systematic learning for safety improvement. Similarly, the NHS Patient Safety Strategy (2019), which emerged as Woodward was writing, highlighted the critical importance of having a safety framework that addresses culture and behaviours. At the time of the events being described, we did not have this. We were without either *adequate* patient safety processes or people processes. Hindsight is inevitable here. Indeed, Dekker (2014) explored the folly of looking back with a different viewpoint or from within a 'tunnel'. However, as with Woodward, the 2020 patient safety incident response framework now addresses the impact of culture and behaviours. It talks of openness with patients and their families and references just culture as potentially removing the potential for inappropriate blame, which is known to be very damaging to parties as well as discussing organisational safety culture. We are seeing, at least, the culture changes that Mersey Care embarked upon becoming normalised in our healthcare processes.

Organisationally, we could almost check off each of the areas that Woodward noted as potential drivers of blind spots in safety systems. Corporately, we:

■ Held a strong belief that our incident reporting systems captured, accurately and comprehensively, all of the things that needed reporting.
■ Relied strongly on the notion that the information in incident reports and, where appropriate, the ensuing root cause analysis were unbiased and unambiguous indicators of how to prioritise ongoing actions that will *directly and effectively* address the causes of harm.

- Believed that, provided we followed a mechanistic framework, learning would automatically ensue.
- *Rapidly* shifted to questioning capability and competency of staff when improvements did not follow as anticipated, often resorting to describing these as failures and enacting accountability mechanisms.
- Relied too heavily on existing and unchallenged benchmarking – in relation to suicide in care.

In short, it felt like our safety culture was heavily centred on an approach that focused more on compliance with what was expected by regulators, rather than on the extraction of real learning that could be actionable on the frontline. While that statement may implicitly suggest criticism of the people running our safety processes, we have been careful to describe it as a mindset driven by corporate and regulatory expectation rather than by any individual operator preferences. What this meant in reality was that we operated with a strong belief that good systems deliver good outcomes. In other words, if our policies (intent) and our actions in delivering those policies (behaviours) are aligned, then the organisation, service, team or individual will, by default, modify existing processes to the optimal, safer configurations. In the case of Mersey Care, there is no doubt that 'good process leads to good outcomes' dominated our narrative.

We were missing consideration of the need for real, deep and meaningful relational work required to explore the multiple perspectives and systemic issues surrounding such complex issues as deaths by suicide.

Developing a Focus on Quality and Safety Management

With this firmly in mind, we began in 2015 to explore safety and healthcare literature for clues as to how to structure our safety thinking in a way that would fundamentally reshape our (individual to organisation) ability to learn. Central to our thinking was the need to find mechanisms that not only altered our policies and behaviours but also shifted our mindsets in a way that challenged the safety myths already described.

This research journey was wide-reaching. Ultimately, we decided to adopt and adapt from two different and diverse approaches.

Firstly, we used the concept of Perfect Care championed by Don Berwick in IHI's Pursuing Perfection programme (as reported in a series of publications such as the *Joint Commission Journal on Quality Improvement*, June

2002) to follow an approach of progressive learning set against an ambitious backdrop of relentlessly seeking to close known gaps in care. This, along with the adoption of the six components of safety described, again by IHI, in *Crossing the Quality Chasm* helped us to focus more clearly on quality improvement conversations.

Our second influence was the work of Jim Collins and Jerry Porras described in *Built to Last: Successful Habits of Visionary Companies* (Collins and Porras, 1994) in which the idea of the big, hairy, audacious goals (BHAG) is socialised and developed. This notion is centred on releasing curiosity, creativity, cooperation, debate and dialogue and focus on goals, not just processes. We very much saw the BHAG approach as a means to draw us to a common purpose and act as a catalyst to focus our attention on the need to be relentlessly focused on safer services. In some respects, it represented our attempt to operate at the level of cognition by helping connect staff with their vocational instincts rather than purely reinforce their contractual obligations. Right from the start, we were also clear that the trust's Perfect Care approach and the zero-based delivery framework were not just about establishing some interesting but inert principles. We were determined to develop and codify a set of practices that supported the delivery of meaningful and practical operational systems that would work for frontline staff because they resonated with them.

The Plan and the Solution

The trust's executive leadership team made the decision to start to make this approach come to life. I was clear and we all understood that this was not a task-and-finish quick win. There was a considered vision and ambition regarding continual improvement, embedding a quality culture and compassionate care. The further development of the strategy and plans needed to be the result of our collective action. We recognised that our staff were experts in their field and had valuable contributions and ideas which were central to shaping the future of co-production. As a part of this commitment to real change, rather than a change in principle, our trust established a Centre for Perfect Care (leanly resourced!). This was a flexible association of senior clinical colleagues with a mind and skillset able to be more than an internal 'think tank'. The Centre for Perfect Care had a focus on addressing fundamental issues of awareness and the training needed to improve practice. They were asked to raise general capability across the

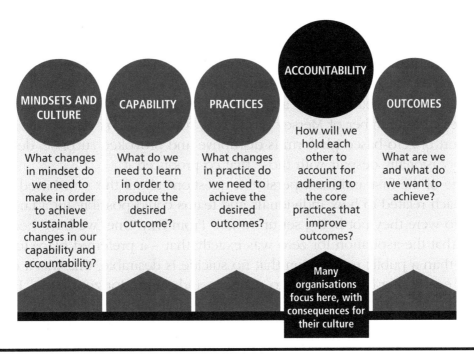

Figure 2.1   Mindset and culture.

organisation as indicated in Figure 2.1. Alongside the creation of the Centre for Perfect Care, we considered what impact resourcing an organisational development team within the organisation could have on our organisational health overall.

There was a comprehensive programme of engagement events to hear the perspective and reality of the workforce. At the very first 'Perfect Care Senate' in 2013 we asked clinicians of all professions to tell us what the barriers to delivering Perfect Care would be. Surprisingly, people did not say more money, staff or expertise. Instead there was unanimous agreement that the real barriers to achieving Perfect Care were values, mindsets and behaviours, the calibre and style of leadership and how teams work together and the organisational culture. We built on this through numerous ways to engage our workforce which are discussed in the chapter on organisation development.

We started by using our regular large group engagement events involving staff from all corners of the organisation. We engaged in a process of taking the idea of Perfect Care – and crafted our versions of BHAGs. The organisation was in a good place to discuss and even be bold in challenging what should be the priority, and we had solid links and connections, such as Dr Ed Coffey, whose work on Perfect Depression Care (*Journal of*

Clinical Outcomes Management, March 2015) was an inspiration and a challenge for us. Even the very acronym BHAG provoked debate as it sets itself out daringly to deliver something really substantive. Over time these have emerged into a small number of inter-connected zero goals as shown in Figure 2.2. Each goal presents a critical challenge in a way that gets right to the heart of a number of Mersey Care's core functions. It is easy to see how this sort of zero-based platform is disruptive and provoked surprise, delight and occasionally despair with those that co-produced it.

One of the first and most persistent questions about the zero-based approach related to how individuals and teams could possibly hit a target of zero were they not being set up to fail? From Day One, we have been clear that the aspiration for zero was exactly that – a preferred place to be. More than a public recognition that no suicide is desirable, this was a call to do everything in our power to redesign and reform for zero harm. But at no point have we set a target for zero and established the usual time-based trajectories. At the time, I was convinced that this was a very significant and assuring step, which along with establishing a very clinically relevant set of BHAGs would generate a real change in mindset for staff. It would stimulate the learning culture that was the objective of the entire framework. This is an important point and is well exemplified by the zero suicide BHAG, which really provoked the mindset issue of whether staff consider

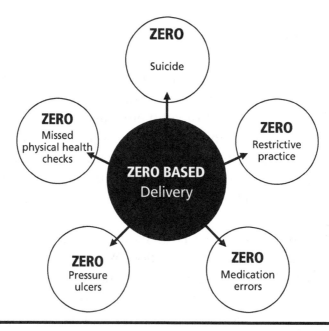

Figure 2.2 Zero-based delivery.

all suicides as preventable. Some, with proper experienced judgement, certainly considered it as an often-inevitable part of someone's life course, raising questions as to how this sort of thinking impacted learning about prevention. If something is inevitable, how can it be prevented, so what is there to learn?

Understandably, we wanted to make sure that we had the requisite skills to manage towards our audacious goals. Fundamentally we had begun to move from a safety and learning approach that started and finished with accountability to one that assured us that a learning-driven safety culture was 'front and centre' across all parts of the organisation. We focused on establishing good quality improvement skills, developed excellent monitoring and learning processes and focused on supporting leaders and staff to develop a clear mindset which really asked the relevant safety questions and collaborated with staff and service users to explore the improvements needed.

With the BHAG approach, the ambiguity associated with more traditional and cautious mission identification and objective setting is removed. The effect of this on staff was in some instances like a powerful release to try to exceed what had been conventional expectations. Over the period of a couple of years, it was certainly possible to see improvements as a result of the Perfect Care/BHAG approach. We observed advances in suicide prevention work and large shifts in our approach to removing restrictive practice from our clinical practice, both of which have far-reaching gains for improving clinical delivery, patient safety and staff safety. We saw reductions in staff assaults and workforce satisfaction improvements logged in the NHS staff survey. In benchmarking terms, progress was distinctly notable, yet it was clear that organisationally we had not shifted into top gear. It was a tenuous beginning that we could detect the 'seeds of the future'.

For too many others, it seemed that aspirations for Perfect Care and our BHAGs at that time were adverse, with the approach posing a threat to their working parameters and the safe space in which they operated. As a result, many staff considered that these goals were unachievable and served as another unrealistic NHS target and would 'set us up to fail'. Although staff struggled with the concept of continually striving to improve against standards which were aspirational, it began to emerge that there were very deep mindset issues relating to being able to engage safely in improvement and learning. We were beginning to surface a set of tensions that would, surprisingly rapidly, give rise to our restorative just and learning culture work.

Psychological Safety

We now recognise that as obvious as it seems, we had not sufficiently considered that a mindset shift could be undermined by a lack of psychological safety for some of our staff. Or perhaps better put, that the mindset shift is needed to one of psychological safety. Whatever the semantics, at a senior level, we clearly had not engaged deeply enough to hear and understand the real issues. We were in fact a good working example of a team of leaders who considered that 'work as imagined is how work is actually done'. As a senior team, we had not considered that changing established practice, never mind introducing novel methodologies, without the ability to safely raise concerns in a way that assured the protection rather than the exasperation of the organisation, would be so rate limiting.

Once we knew the need to focus on organisational health, which would support improvement in performance, the trust began to invest in organisational effectiveness through the appointment of Organisational Development (OD) practitioners. The trust's Director of Workforce articulated the need for an OD approach to our structures, design and processes to support learning and drive changes in organisational behaviour. Her view at the time and currently is an OD approach to facilitate continuous improvement and supporting teams to make a meaningful change would deliver that change in a much more focused manner than through the more regular HR processes.

Unlike more conventional views, the approach to our trust's employer relations started with an evidence-based organisational development approach to reviewing HR practices. The profound impact of holding the mirror up to ourselves in this reflective way is discussed by Mersey Care colleagues in more detail later in this book.

The review process highlighted some significant systemic issues across the organisation which impacted team relationships and performance. These issues of course in turn clearly had implications on service delivery and ultimately patient safety. At this point, relationships within and between some teams could be described as ranging from strained to dysfunctional. Lack of role clarity between professions and teams across the care pathway affected the quality and continuity of care. Moreover, as staff talked more openly, it became evident that we had silo-based defensive cultures that were embedded in traditional clinical training approaches. Given the scale of the organisation and its wide geography, this perhaps should not have been a surprise.

The level of transformation required to address this was significant within the trust and more so against a backdrop of continual service change and cost-improvement programmes in the NHS. Traditional tools for change management used in the sector at that time majored on project management and or top–down quality improvement which invariably failed to effectively involve and engage the people closest to the point of care or the people receiving it. The impact of this approach to delivering change was compounded by a 'command and control' style of management. The implications were that safety concerns and risks were often identified and proscribed to the level of individuals, whether that be the people in services or staff, to maintain the *status quo*. It was *not* about the adoption of a critical analysis of the governance systems and the hard-wiring of the associated formal and informal processes.

The absolute impact of this was brought home when we asked a small team, independent of Mersey Care, to try to understand these issues better. What they would find would give us another wake-up call.

A Second Shock Wave

During a review period with a large group of senior leaders, we were challenged by colleagues representing our unions to consider another BHAG – one that focused on zero blame. The simple fact that such a challenge could be made by the staff side at all gave us some level of affirmation: we were pleased to have an openness where such critical reflections were permissible. Their question ensured we were sighted on this significant omission in our quest for 'perfection' – the fact that we might be missing 'crucial voices'. The realisation became clear to us all that the trust's patient safety and HR systems were completely focused on supporting vulnerable patients and their families to improve care and prevent reoccurrences of harm. We had not sufficiently considered carefully enough the vulnerability of our own staff during what we organisationally considered to be learning events but which were actually considered by those involved to be the manifestation of a corporately condoned blame culture.

As a leader, already immersed, practically and emotionally, in a significant change programme, it is tempting to listen in order to respond or react, rather than to understand. As a result, it is relatively easy to become defensive and be persuaded that 'the solution' is to:

■ Restate the mission again because it must not have been clear enough to everyone;

- ■ Assume that counter or alternate views are anomalous and largely rooted in perception thereby widening the gap between work as imagined versus work as done;
- ■ Conclude that dissent and challenge is noise from those not on board and proceed to generate micro-aggressions towards all those who want to express a different or alternate view;
- ■ Switch into performance mode or reach for the accountability button.

It is fair to say that at times we strayed into some combinations of these behaviours. But the stark reality about how it feels following an incident in Mersey Care emerged when we asked an independent and external team to ask approximately 400 of our senior clinicians these relatively simple questions:

- ■ What does it feel like when an incident is being investigated?
- ■ What were the barriers to transparency – and subsequent onwards learning?

What followed was a harsh but compelling confirmation for senior management that could not be rationalised away nor ignored by the Board of Directors. The significant response was not about the issues that we naively assumed might get predominantly aired such as processes, time consumption or training. These did feature but paled in comparison to a group of concerns that were overwhelmingly and unambiguously about relationships and an utter lack of trust.

The overarching response – virtually half of all replies – cited the fear of the consequences, of blame and even dismissal as the predominant staff response to an incident where harm had occurred (see Figure 2.3). Astonishingly and tellingly, not a single responder saw the immediate response to an incident as being about the opportunity to learn and reduce the likelihood of recurrence. Yet these were senior and highly experienced clinicians, all valued people working in some of the most complex areas of care in the NHS. Instead of feeling supported to carry out their duties in very complex adaptive situations, these colleagues were worried about what would happen next if they got it wrong.

It is not hard to imagine how such an environment would result in little or no learning and therefore little or no subsequent prevention. In short, the intended virtuous circle of learning envisaged was actually a vicious cycle of fear. This significant disconnect between those at the top level of the organisation and people on the 'shop floor', on the wards and in our services,

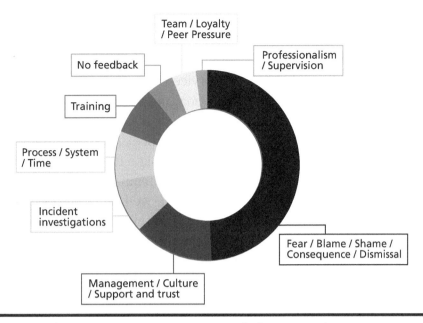

Figure 2.3 Barriers to transparency – terms and phrases used.

has since occupied a great deal of leadership reflection and is now a litmus test question for progress. This incongruence, if left unaddressed, risked our organisation's ability to move forward with any sense of sustainable improvement, with potentially cataclysmic consequences for some patients and staff.

For the Board of Directors, the dissonance disclosure from the frontline of our organisation produced shocked us to the core. It was a lesson that brought to life the old adage that culture eats strategy for breakfast. But it also energised us. We worked to understand the steps needed to support the creation of psychological safety as a route to delivering the sustainable learning and improvement system that we originally envisaged. As a leadership team, we considered the information we had as needing immediate actions that would re-establish trust with all staff and begin a genuine psychological contract with them to truly focus on impacts that would allow each person to do their best work. Our teams in human resources and organisational development were enthusiastic to support this process. However, we knew that authentic cultural and behavioural change is the result of a much wider redesign of the service delivery and organisational operating model, not a stand-alone piece of work in any one team. To progress the required collective ownership and leadership to foster commitment and accountability, we were very clear that the first steps had to be modelled by the Board of

Directors. We had to recognise the organisation as a complex and dynamic human system. Between 70% and 80% of the organisation's capital is people. It is therefore a feeling, thinking entity subject to bias and strong cultural norms. Generally staff and people in service have the knowledge, skills and insight that can lead to transformational improvements. To release this potential, we needed to shift and encourage positive leadership capability, behaviours and levels of emotional intelligence. The cultural change is needed to develop leaders' competence to translate the vision into practice and engage and develop safe, high-performing teams.

This effective team working is critical to the well-being and safety of both patients and staff. It comes about by facilitating relationships and culture at the team level to improve communication, collaboration, safe challenge and decision-making. Making it happen in practice requires engaging and involving people closest to the work and to the decisions which sit around it to take an inclusive approach to quality improvement. There must be both identification and then the removal of the barriers which interfere with psychological safety, well-being and support. Only once this is achieved will staff be able to reach their full potential and provide excellent safe-care.

The challenge to the executive team was to translate these ideas into something more substantial than the rhetorical phrase about 'valuing and investing in our workforce'. For a real cultural change to come about and become embedded as business as usual for the trust, we had to develop the infrastructure, capacity, capability and resilience of everyone and to recognise the skills, ability and talent we have within our teams and the positive impact it has on people's lives. Striving for perfect care is not achievable without continuous learning, education, training and development. Moreover, just talking about it – as can happen in any political or cultural sphere – without it being seen to be led or driven, without it being backed up and actually leading to a set of practices and changes – is itself harmful. Empty promises, as colleagues attest in chapters of this book, are especially distressing in the healthcare system. We had to do more than rally around the slogan: Perfect Care had to live as a true aspiration for every member of staff.

Responding to the Complex Cultural Challenge of Building Trust

The reader, observing from 'the outside in', may consider the phenomenon that we uncovered as fairly self-evident. After all, many volumes have been written on the cultural iceberg and the inevitable focus that leadership brings to the part above the waterline, while expertly ignoring the much greater mass of submerged issues. Why, when we had identified mindset as a critical transformational component, did we not go on to fully evaluate and understand its impact? One reason is that from the 'inside out' the perspective of the iceberg can be a challenge. What amounts of cultural issues are submerged? How deep are they below the surface and how do you know? How profound is the hegemony that permits the punitive way of doing things to persist, despite the best intentions of leaders? These are the questions that we continue to ask. And the first and most difficult question was: What do we do now?

The one thing we did quickly and well was to acknowledge that the information provided by those 400 respondents needed to be believed and understood. Accepting their individual and collective testimonies was a crucial step forward for us all. It recognised the courage it had required for staff to be so candid. In return, it was essential that the members of our trust's Board of Directors took a strong role in being the stewards of establishing a new direction and a new deal with staff. They were willing to do this and that championing cannot be understated or underestimated in all that followed.

This willingness to not only acknowledge the gap between the work as imagined and the work as delivered but also respond by holding the mirror up to ourselves for new insights, rather than pushing blame back, developed a maturity that helped us work through the next steps.

In reality, our people and patient safety processes had been too focused on the actual process and what the policy said. They would always, if unintentionally, focus on 'who was involved' and 'what rule did they break'. It was a system which was directed at what they did 'wrong', rather than asking the much wider and useful question about what had happened, the context in which incidents occurred and the contributory factors. It was in fact a system loaded with confirmation bias that favoured the institution's narrative rather than those who could give a first-hand account of working in complex, adaptive environments.

Worse still, we sometimes merely defended or justified our action and position ahead (or instead) of seeking to extract full understanding and honest learning. In a very real sense, we were structurally designed to be defensive, which suppressed the institutional and personal curiosity necessary to learn objectively.

In every human system, errors will happen. Mersey Care's services are often delivered in very complex, adaptive and fast-changing environments and the consequences of a small sub-set of mistakes can be life changing for some patients and families. As an organisation, we were slow to realise that how mistakes and incidents are handled can be devastating for the staff involved too.

How we had historically responded to those mistakes meant some people did not feel able to raise concerns or give their true account of what actually occurred. In hindsight, it seems likely that at the time, even if our people gave their true account, we were not truly ready to listen to understand and make sense of it. We listened with a different intent. Specifically, we listened to react by instigating proceedings, creating terms of references for investigations or root cause analysis and by developing action plans. It was what might be described as a classic corporate response; perhaps it was more important to be seen to be holding people to account as opposed to being meaningful in our endeavour. Or maybe it was, as so often in public services, that there was an overwhelming naive belief that a good process will deliver a good outcome. Either way our response was mounted from the perspective of a defensive and misguided attempt at being proactive. By taking responsibility for learning out of the hands of those who knew best what had happened, there is an implicit charge of some level of guilt and the immediate creation of suspicion of the corporate intent. The need for objectivity, specialist review and conversations about accountability became blurred and part of the blame game.

At its very best, our approach surfaced some level of individual learning and outcomes because it was, implicitly or otherwise, rooted in the 'who' question. The opportunity to understand the context and system in which an incident occurred largely passed us by. This was because the unintentional impact of our approach was to impair the psychological safety of all involved, including the wider team and communities.

The aftermath of these incidents triggered both patient safety and people processes (HR) investigations, which had profound consequences for our people. As I've set out in this chapter, Mersey Care recognises and acknowledges that the old ways of identifying the causes of harm in patient care were often inhibited by a fear of our people being blamed by the very procedures in place to protect them, a classic *Catch 22* scenario. Simply speaking, we put our policies and processes before our people and by doing so prevented transparency and learning. The question, of course, was what to do next?

About this time, the Executive Director of Workforce, Amanda Oates and I were further studying the literature on just culture. We had been intrigued by the idea of developing a restorative just culture as outlined by Sidney Dekker in his book *Just Culture: Balancing Safety and Accountability* (Dekker, 2007). In a subsequent series of collaborations we have explored how to move the logic and notion of restorative just culture into a set of meaningful and repeatable practices to underpin our safety and improvement programme. Several chapters in this book explore this work.

We have a very simple (disarmingly so) definition of just culture, taken from Dekker's *Just Culture: Balancing Safety and Accountability.*

> A just culture accepts nobody's account as 'true' or 'right' and others wrong … Instead it accepts the value of multiple perspectives, and uses them to encourage both accountability and learning.

In this model, as we took it at that time, the working assumption is that learning, candour and transparency, in both organisational and personal contexts, can only flourish if the culture is built upon non-punitive practices and when the responses to incidents are first and foremost compassionate. In such a system, accountability is forward-looking and prospective. It is centred on candour and learning, rather than retrospective biases. As the Professor states in this volume, it is not 'an anything goes (blame-free)' culture but instead one which balances responsibility, professional accountability and organisational learning.

By establishing a routine, repeatable and meaningful restorative just practices, we established our own null hypothesis that we would create a psychologically safe environment for our staff to learn and improve because:

■ Of the absence of threat or arbitrary penalty;
■ We bring information about improvement opportunities to those most able to action improvements;
■ We ask what, when and how, rather than who as the starting point of any learning exercise.

Since we focused on accountability driven by learning, we have taken that critical step to creating a virtuous cycle in which we can continue to invest in safety benefits for patients as we are now diverting fewer resources to legal defence and liability protection. We are realising safety dividends as discussed by Dekker. In subsequent chapters, we show evaluation findings that support the benefits we have realised through establishing restorative just culture approaches across Mersey Care.

Summary

A focus on the organisation's perception of human error simply results in corporately doing almost all of the wrong things and responding in a way that sent a signal that our culture was vindictive and punitive. In the process we will almost certainly have lost opportunities to close safety gaps and to improve outcomes for those using our services because of the pernicious nature of a lack of trust in the governance mechanisms of the organisation. Dekker (2014) describes this as a classic safety risk, in which organisations attribute error existentially to human presence and see it separate to the organisational systemic design and complexities of real circumstances. This is not uncommon in many healthcare organisations and may contribute to the variable patterns of outcome in many health systems. Certainly, it seems that many types of incidents continue to persist in health systems, despite many reviews, sets of recommendations and the passing of years. The experiences of both James Titcombe and Steve Mallen, which this book vividly set out, highlighted that stories had been changed and simply speaking showed where the system had worked against a duty of candour. They are stark reminders of why all this matters. Sadly we know these examples are not unique. I hope that we can now begin to understand and ask why 'does this happen' – what makes institutions and individuals within behave in this way.

In this chapter, I have asked questions which I know to be critical to improving quality and safety across organisations. I have described the impetus and context of the start of Mersey Care's at times painful journey to making change through adjusting mindset and culture. The focus on Perfect Care ensured the organisation was able to ambitiously raise the standards. It was the audacious nature of our strategy that in the end focused on just culture as the cornerstone of creating a system of governance at the board level that constantly tests the gap between our view of work and that experienced by all on the frontline. I have thrown light on the very real and disabling impact of an over-reliance on transactions in safety management and investigation. I have described the pivotal importance of having an approach to quality and safety improvement, which while underpinned by good standards of governance around its processes, nevertheless guards against judgements about people as the problem and instead sees them as the solutions. There is indeed 'no trade-off between high standards and psychological safety' (Horizons, June 2021).

I have explored the importance of moving from a retributive model of accountability, which by default seeks to identify the person or persons at fault, to a restorative model focused on getting a calibrated approach to learning and professional responsibility. The COVID-19 pandemic further exposed the fragility of the care system and reinforced the need for strong relationships with local partners. Technical solutions alone are not transformative, nor do they satisfactorily mitigate risk. Now more than ever, solutions must be socially constructed, collectively owned and collaboratively delivered. Mersey Care's strategy to deliver Perfect Care places people at its core, recognising the sector as a human system, creating congruence between culture, structure and process in order to achieve the organisational health required to deliver organisational performance. The two are intrinsically linked and support the ability to manage complexity whilst sustaining quality.

Much of the rest of the book is devoted to understanding how to take the concepts of restorative just culture into reliable, measurable, evidence-based practices.

My Personal Reflection – Amanda Oates, Executive Director of Workforce

For this book, I wanted to look back on the HR practitioner and HR Director that I was to the one I have become.

My immediate reflections are guilt and sorrow for the hurt I have caused. I have acted and led many workforce practices and functions within the organisations I have worked for which I know have had profound impacts on our people. Many of them will have been positive and I have witnessed many excellent outcomes in my career. However, despite good intentions, some actions have had consequences that were divisive and hurtful, for which I now feel a huge sense of remorse.

I also feel an immense frustration that at the beginning of my professional training and career it was never highlighted to me that there was a very different way to understanding and handling employee relations issues. Hindsight can be very upsetting, but we must use it to inform our learning.

When I read Dekker's book *Just Culture* in 2015, the words 'Second victim' hit me like a ton of bricks. Whilst I wish that I had read it years ago, I also know I might not have been ready at that time to act on the lessons within it. Why? Because it is easy to be defensive and justify your positioning and actions, as others are doing the same and you have had a lot of success. Reading it at that time resonated, it felt it was describing what it felt like to work in Mersey Care. It struck me that there had to be another way, but at that moment I didn't have any idea how we could put it into action or practice.

From reading the book and in conversations with the staff side and our staff, I heard one too many stories and experiences of the hurt we had caused our people. It was the worst feeling; putting staff through unnecessary formal proceedings, suspensions, sanctions, hearings, processes we can only now describe as punitive and an unnecessary legalistic approach. All these had taken the trust to the point that too many staff didn't have enough faith in our systems or in our leadership to tell us what had happened and what was really going on for them.

There was some cause for optimism. I was also amazed how many of our people were prepared to talk to me and use their experiences to help shape a new way. As an HR lead in the NHS I know the compassion needed every day in challenging complex workplaces but I will forever be in awe of so many people's personal sacrifices and their ability to put former conflicts aside and walk this journey with me as an ally.

Looking back without bias I accept at the time there were significant challenges that HR had to address which I did not see. I had been blinded by the old institutionalised way of approaching employee relations. I knew if we wanted to drive a cultural shift we had to work significantly in partnership with our unions to forge a new way ahead. This new teamwork means I will be forever in debt to my own HR team and to union colleagues. I single out our former staff side chair Mandi Gregory who trusted me and took the leap of faith that despite the organisation's history, she believed the trust genuinely wanted something different for our people. If we were going to see a real change of culture we had to work with HR, staff side and managers – truly together – and absolutely not a tick-box approach to partnership working. It required honesty, reflection and for us all to hold the mirror up to what we had been doing. It also required taking the risk of doing something different without fear of blame.

My key reflection is that we often gloss over the impact of incidents on our people, the caregivers. Our patients and family members of course are fundamental. Yet we cannot forget our staff. We have a responsibility for all our people: patients and staff alike. As a consequence, our former way of reviewing incidents did not fully consider the importance of staff's psychological safety in capturing learning, improvement and prevention of risk.

From my 25 years of working in HR, across both private and public sectors, I have seen the best and worst of HR in practice. When I look back, I constantly question if I was blinded by the way we had always done things so that I never significantly questioned my approach or that of others. My new understanding highlights how having a robust methodology and framework that embodies a restorative approach has helped to redesign the way my trust operationalises HR.

It has been a full-on professional and personal challenge. Along the way it has itself has caused conflict, new policies, new training, new processes and new understanding. We even use a new language to speak of these issues. My trust has been at the centre of this change in the NHS; we've driven the change, developed the change and witnessed the change first hand for the better. At times I have felt overwhelmed and vulnerable by the challenge this has prompted within me and supporting that prompt in others. Throughout I have questioned if I/we have done the right thing. It is important to be reminded how many more people we have got this right for. Yes, I admit we have a long way to go. I am driving a bus without a road map. We are continuously writing and rewriting that road map on route and that's tough. Yet what drives me and drives my colleagues is that we are doing this for our people. My aspiration is simple: I want all HR professionals to see the opportunity for this change. I want to enable them to move away from policies and practices that have the potential to punish to policies that reflect practice and offer restorative, compassionate HR. Simply put, I want to put the human back into human resources.

I have said sorry more times than I wish was needed. I am conscious for some that will not be enough, and I understand that. I was brought up in an era where I was told my actions speak louder than my words, I hope I will be remembered not by our former way, or by the incidents and outcomes which still today still do not always go to plan, but that I was brave enough to try a new way. I know we are still on that journey, but I also know that we have had a positive impact for many in my trust and beyond.

There is a further dimension to this. One that traces its roots in Mersey Care all the way back to the changes we made in areas such as restraint reduction, where positive risk taking allowed us to move away from physical interventions and to initiatives like 'No Force First'. The huge level of professionalism and the desire to deliver a different answer to something really difficult was inspiring and powerful – and we delivered great results, in particular for our most vulnerable service users. That idea of positive risk-taking flows through what has to happen as we embraced the new culture of restorative justice.

As I moved away from the HR Director I was to the one I have become – or hope I am becoming – I felt safe to experiment and innovate into the unknown. I was not just in a position of power, but as a member of a collective and accountable board, I still felt trusted to share my vulnerability. I still had to account for myself and this new direction to my peers, my Chief Executive Joe Rafferty and across a system of regulation that still to some degree thought in traditional ways. I felt safe to do this with Joe. I had psychological safety. It would have been very easy for Joe to take a different approach. And those investments of faith, trust and shared goals began to spread through my team and the whole of Mersey Care. We had to understand how power and authority can be shared in an organisation and how positive risk taking, delivered with proven experience, delivers.

To close, I am sharing one paragraph of a reflective poem I drafted following the release of the joint collaborative *Just Culture* movie we made with Professor Sidney Dekker. That first screening of his film was a pivotal moment and the atmosphere of the room was astonishing:

> Our staff shared their stories of hurt some recent and some of many years ago,
> To hear them was emotional, more than many of you would ever know.
> Yes, I am a leader, but I still feel your pain. I cried tears with you, I'm so sorry they may have been too late.
> Today is a new chapter, help me take new strides, I can't promise it will be easy and we will get everything right,
> So I look forward with hope optimism and pride, I genuinely feel together it's the only way we can learn and get things right.

References

Coffey, E. (2015). Perfect depression care spread: The traction of zero suicides. *Journal of Clinical Outcomes Management*. 2015 March, 22(3).

Collins, J., & Porras, J. (1994). *Built to Last: Successful Habits of Visionary Companies*, Harper Business Essentials.

Dekker, S.W.A (2007). *Just Culture: Balancing Safety and Accountability*, CRC Press.

Dekker, S.W.A. (2014). *The Field Guide to Understanding Human Error*, Routledge.

Horizons (June 2021). A practical guide to the art of psychological safety in the real world of health and care. *Horizonsnhs.com*.

Institute of Medicine (2001). Crossing the Quality Chasm: A New Health System for the 21st Century. http://www.ihi.org/resources/Pages/ImprovementStories/HealthCareMustBeSafe.aspx#:~:text=The%20Institute%20of%20Medicine's%20 2001,%2C%22%20number%20one%20is%20safety.

The National Confidential Inquiry into Suicide and Safety in Mental Health (2019). Annual Report: England, Northern Ireland, Scotland and Wales, University of Manchester.

NHS Patient Safety Strategy (July 2019). www.england.nhs.uk/wp-content/uploads /2020/08/190708_Patient_Safety_Strategy_for_website_v4.pdf, page 7.

Sentinel Event Policy and Procedures: The Joint Commission, One Renaissance Blvd, Oakbrook Terrace, IL 60181. www.jointcommission.org

Vincent, C., & Amalberti, R. (2016). *Safer Healthcare: Strategies for the Real World*, Springer Open, pp. 27–38.

Woodward, S. (2019). Moving towards a safety II approach. *Journal of Patient Safety and Risk Management*, Sage, June 2019. https://journals.sagepub.com/doi/full /10.1177/2516043519855264

Woodward, S. (2020). *Implementing Patient Safety*, Routledge.

West, M.A., & Lyubovnikova, J. (2013). Illusions of team working in health care. *Journal of Health Organization and Management*, 27(1), 134–142.

Chapter 3

A Just Culture for Mental Health

Steve Mallen

Contents

> Welcome to the world my son, I don't know if you are going to have a mother.

These were the first words I said to Edward, our eldest child, minutes after he was born at noon on a cold and crisp Sunday in December 1996 in the Rosie Maternity wing of Addenbrooke's Hospital in Cambridge. Following protracted labour, there had been an unforeseen and incredibly rare complication with the afterbirth. My wife had suffered an enormous haemorrhage. With a panic alarm sounding in the background, I gazed trembling out of the hospital window and prayed for the first time in my life.

Following emergency surgery and a very large blood transfusion, Edward's mother was saved. The following nine days prior to discharge on Christmas Eve were traumatic and difficult, fraught with anxiety and exhaustion. The hospital staff, from auxiliary personnel through to senior consultants, were, however, extraordinary. Their professionalism and empathy were exceptional. When we left hospital that day, our faith in the National Health Service (NHS) was both affirmed and unshakeable. They were marvellous.

DOI: 10.4324/9781003162582-3

And so family life began. Post-natal services were also exceptional, supporting our young and nervous family through the rest of that long winter. In the following six years, we were blessed with two other fine and happy children: a daughter and another son. Both born at the same hospital, our trust in the NHS strengthened still further.

Time passed.

Eighteen years and three weeks to be precise. On a cold, wet Tuesday afternoon in January 2015, dear Edward walked into Fulbourn Hospital on the outskirts of Cambridge, not two miles from where he had been born. Unbeknown to his doting parents, he was suffering from the sudden, inexplicable and cataclysmic onset of clinical depression. With a recent history of serious but concealed self-harm and pronounced suicide ideation, he had been referred, in extreme crisis, by his GP – who had known him all his life – on an acute emergency, 24-hour basis.

Edward left that facility with nothing more than a scrap of paper ripped from a notebook on which a couple of barely legible website addresses had been scribbled. Downgraded to 'routine' status, a social worker had told him to expect a letter which would offer a first consultation for cognitive behavioural therapy (CBT)-based treatment in six to nine months' time.

Let me repeat that: six to nine months, for an initial consultation.

A little under a month later, at seven minutes past three on a cold, bright sunny Monday afternoon in February, our son was destroyed by an express train travelling at 82 miles an hour on a railway line not 500 yards from the front door of the family home where he had spent his entire childhood. The railway line is arrow-straight at that point. It was a clear day with perfect visibility. The train driver reported that Edward had his headphones in and, with eyes open, was looking up to the sky.

The NHS experiences surrounding Edward's birth and his death could not be more different, or more troubling. As outlined in this chapter, the NHS experiences were exemplary on his arrival into the world. They were disgraceful both before and in the aftermath of his death.

Reference should be made here to the principle of Parity of Esteem, which placed physical and mental health on equal footing in law, as enshrined in the Health and Social Care Act 2012. For the most part, the narrative surrounding parity remains little more than empty rhetoric and a hollow vision. The principle of Just Culture in mental health is severely compromised in consequence.

Towards the very end of 2014, it was clear that all was not well with Edward. He had suddenly, for no ostensible reason, become withdrawn and

remote. A loss of appetite and insomnia were shrouded in general mal-
aise. He had stopped playing the piano, a life-long daily passion. Perhaps
now, social change, amplified by the COVID pandemic, has sensitised us to
well-being, resilience and the vital importance of maintaining good mental health. Back then, despite our obvious devotion as parents, we knew
nothing about mental illness. It was not something we had ever knowingly
encountered, let alone been educated in.

Following a difficult Christmas cloaked in worry, Edward was persuaded
to visit our family GP shortly after New Year's 2015. The diagnosis was
immediate and life-threatening: severe depression with serious self-harm and
clear suicide ideation. With Edward present, an immediate call was made to
secondary care. A prescription for fluoxetine (Prozac) had been prepared but
was thrown away there and then in favour of one for citalopram (Celexa)
on the advice of the mental health nurse on the other end of the phone.
Recognising that prescribing authority is vested in the GP, the nurse at
Edward's Inquest flatly denied recommending citalopram. This was a lie. It
was verified as such at the Inquest, and this was one of the primary factors
which led the Coroner to issue a Regulation 28 Prevention of Future Death
notice when the Inquest was concluded.

I'm aware that there are many parents who are convinced that selective
serotonin reuptake inhibitor (SSRI) medication is responsible for the death of
their child or that it may have been a contributory factor. I will never know
the role that citalopram may or may not have played in Edward's demise.
Suffice it to say that his condition deteriorated rapidly and markedly within
two weeks of the rewritten GP prescription. The risks were never explained,
no follow-up or monitoring protocols were put in place, no literature or
signposting was offered and there was no consultation with Edward's family – all in direct contravention of the National Institute for Health and Care
Excellence (NICE) Guidelines.

The fact that the clinician, NHS Trust and their lawyers subsequently lied
about this in an attempt to position the GP as a scapegoat only compounds
the tragedy. 'The truth will out', and this formed the basis of the Regulation
28 Prevention of Future Death Report (under the Coroners and Justice Act
2009) issued by Edward's Coroner at the conclusion of his Inquest, censuring
the Trust's conduct and issuing a system-wide warning.

What role do NICE Guidelines play in mental health? Based on my very
extensive research, the answer seems to be very little. The vast majority of
frontline mental health personnel are not familiar with NICE Guidelines, let
alone conform to their inherent standards and protocols. How is it possible

to aspire to excellence if one does not know what excellence looks like? How can one follow the rules when they have never been explained? Meticulously prepared via extensive consultation and a deep dive into the evidence base, NICE Guidelines are often viewed internationally as being akin to a Gold Standard for clinical care. In the harsh world of mental illness though, their application and impact are negligible. It is a plain and uncomfortable truth that, had NICE Guidelines on Depression been adhered to, it is highly likely that my son would still be alive today.

Mental health services in the UK might well be transformed at a stroke if every patient-facing clinician and manager took a crash course in the relevant NICE Guidelines. From a restorative justice perspective, the NICE framework is for guidance only, leaving little room for redress or restitution when it is routinely ignored or abandoned.

In the absence of enforcement or adherence methods, NICE Guidelines in mental health start to look like being superfluous and a waste of time and resources. Whilst a Just Culture should be based on a shared empathy and common values, its realisation would be accelerated by a clear, defined and deployed framework of evidence-based excellence. Surely NICE Guidelines should be a statutory element in the training and continuing professional development (CPD) protocols of all frontline clinicians?

As it stands, diagnosis and risk assessment in mental health and suicide are frequently based on the unconscious bias of the clinician rather than their alignment with best practice and clinical excellence. Notwithstanding the fact that mental illness is often directly linked to impaired lifepaths, there is a near-blinding infatuation with how and where people, especially young people, grew up. Not every patient needs a social worker.

At the time of his death, Edward had been offered a place at Cambridge University and been voted by his classmates as being most likely to go on and be Prime Minister one day. From an affluent, professional and stable family with no history of trauma, his clinicians were incapable of seeing beyond the superficial presentation of 'a polite young man wearing a clean shirt' sitting in front of them.

Following referral, Edward was initially assessed via telephone by the same mental health nurse with whom the GP had spoken. We later learnt that the nurse was in only his second week of unsupervised working – which might explain his clear and subsequently flatly refuted contravention of the rules on the prescription of medication. I believed that he had a limited command of the English language and had a career entirely restricted to the care of highly violent, maximum-security adult criminals, and it is quite possible that the nurse had simply never met anyone like my son.

The misalignment between the clinician and the patient could not have been more pronounced. There was no connectivity here. Whilst many in psychological trauma are prone to fantasy and delusion, my lad was neither delusional nor a liar. The dismissive tone of the nurse's notes and the comment that he 'claims he has a place at Cambridge University!' left me in bewildered sorrow when I read them many weeks later. Crucially, Edward gave his consent for his family to be consulted in his care during this first interview.

Despite the emergency, 24-hour referral, Edward was downgraded to 'routine' status and a consultation with a nurse and a social worker was arranged for a week later – on that wet Tuesday afternoon in January. Following this second assessment and with complete disregard for basic medical procedure, Edward's medical notes were never properly written up, and there was no letter back to his GP which might have formed the basis of a 'triangle of care'.

Edward was assessed as being at 'low risk' solely on the basis of his persona and outward presentation. His repeated and clear suicide ideation was ignored, as was his serious self-harm. When asked again whether his parents could be consulted in his care, he reaffirmed his consent. He felt 'embarrassed' by his condition and asked that somebody 'please tell my Mum'.

By this point, Edward had twice given his consent for his family to be consulted in his care. On the second occasion, consent was forthcoming in the form of a direct request. He had also told four different medical professionals that he intended to take his own life on the railway, voicing a clear plan and access to means – he travelled to and from college every day on the rail line which runs through our village. The very line he was to die on.

It is against this backdrop that the scrap of paper, with a couple of websites scrawled on it, and the promise of a possible first consultation for talking therapy in several months' time came to represent the sum total of the NHS care extended to my son. The gulf between the NHS experience at Edward's birth and his death was enormous and far greater than the mile or two which separate the two hospitals in the same locality. The disparity between physical and mental health services in this country is thus thrown into sharp and painful relief.

With incomplete notes, no correspondence and no attempt whatsoever to act upon the consent for his family to be involved we, as parents, were left in near-complete ignorance with regard to the nature and severity of our son's condition. Having referred the matter, the GP was also left uninformed and any potential care structure and pathway evaporated.

Despite a diagnosis of deep depression, with a how-do-you-feel-today-out-of-ten score of two, the nurse and the social worker could not even make the effort to give Edward the 36-page self-help *Coping with Depression* booklet sitting in boxes in the corner and bedecking the shelves in Reception. The manifest apathy, failure to adhere to even basic medical procedure and total neglect in the face of blatant and repeated risk – unfortunately so common in mental health services – are nothing short of an indictment on our health system.

There are other relevant details. The clinicians who saw Edward had been substituted in from another team owing to staff shortages and workload pressures in the normal triage team. Edward never saw a psychiatrist or a psychologist despite his extreme risk presentation. The administration systems were so weak that the wrong address was entered into the patient database.

A single letter was issued regarding the consultation for therapy six to nine months hence. This was issued two days after he had died. Coincidence? I think not. In any case, with the wrong address, the letter never reached us. With no contact from his GP or secondary care and with having had to explain his trauma multiple times in the most dire and draining of circumstances, Edward was left alone and devastated. His loving parents had no idea of his condition or his intention to take his own life. Edward said to his mother shortly afterwards one evening: 'I don't think anyone cares Mum'.

It is with bone-crushing hindsight that I now know Edward proceeded with his plans to take his own life two weeks later with this intent fully known to four different medical professionals. One telephone call, for which consent had been given – twice – would have saved my son. His condition was evident, his plans were clear, the method was established, access to means had been recorded on several occasions and yet the nurse and social worker did nothing. Nothing at all. They did not even write up his notes. Pathetic, shameful, unprofessional, negligent … pick a word: How would you describe it?

Aware that the crisis with Edward was deepening and in a complete vacuum of communication and information from health services, we hurriedly organised very expensive private therapy for Edward. He attended a first appointment on a Friday afternoon which seemed to have gone well and offered a glimmer of hope. Unfortunately, it was too little too late. He was dead the other side of that fateful weekend. Ever diligent, Edward had actually made the journey into college to hand in an assignment on the morning of his death. I had waved to him on the driveway to the house as he left to catch the train, little knowing that that would be the last time I was to see my boy alive.

Time stopped.

The issue of consent and confidentiality is one of the most complex and controversial themes in modern medicine, especially in the field of mental health. The basic tenets of the current law emphasise the privacy of the individual and their absolute personal sovereignty over their body and being above all else. This can present extreme challenges and difficulties to the Just Culture paradigm and also frequently conflicts with the current drive towards patient safety led by former Health Secretary, Jeremy Hunt and others. Even when there is clear risk to an individual, the right to privacy is sacrosanct, provided the individual is adjudged to have 'capacity' – itself a complex and ultimately subjective notion.

If someone is clearly at a very severe risk of harming themselves and potentially others, with clear intent and access to means, should not their 'capacity' *de facto* be called into question? Should they not at the very least be assessed by an experienced psychiatrist? As matters stand, a request not to share information overrides all other considerations and the most junior and ill-equipped personnel are often left to make life-changing decisions. This results in many people dying or coming to serious harm, events which could so easily be prevented. Information sharing is thus central to the Just Culture paradigm.

In Edward's case, he had capacity (under current definitions), was clearly at severe risk and had given his consent for family liaison (requested it in fact). The clinicians' appalling failure to act in these circumstances underpins his terrible demise. However, matters become more complex when consent is withheld, as is frequently the case in mental illness situations. Virtually every investigation involving inpatient and outpatient suicide references a lack of consultation and a failure to share information, whether that be between the agencies involved in someone's care or with their families and frequently both. This was one of the key findings of the NHS Resolution (NHSR) report *Learning from Suicide-Related Claims* published in 2018. The forlorn and plaintive phrase 'if only we had known' echoes hauntingly around nearly every NHS suicide investigation.

Families are commonly plunged into deep anguish when it becomes clear that others were in full possession of knowledge and information which might have saved their loved one had it been shared. Similarly, clinicians and other professionals frequently experience a crisis of conscience and emotional distress when it emerges that they could have potentially averted a tragedy if only they were not excessively fearful of outdated, draconian and insensitive legislation. It is to be hoped that the current reforms to The Mental Health Act (1983) will address some of these concerns.

At any point in time, there are tens of thousands of people in society, typically sitting on unacceptably long waiting lists awaiting therapy, whose nearest and dearest have no knowledge of their condition, the supportive interventions they might make and how they might create a nurturing environment which offers the prospect of improvement rather than a lonely and steady descent into deeper crisis. Consent protocols negate the ability to create a triangle of care, impede the sharing of potentially valuable information and prevent families becoming fully invested in the care of their loved ones. How can you look after someone if you do not know what is wrong with them, have not received guidance and have not been signposted to appropriate resources?

A reversal of the current position – whereby information would automatically be shared with relatives – is also clearly not appropriate. There are situations where sharing information, in cases of domestic abuse for instance, could be very dangerous and profoundly irresponsible. It is also very important that service users are not deterred from accessing services by the prospect of sometimes extremely sensitive and personal information potentially being shared more widely, most especially with those they love.

However, Edward's GP, our family doctor and a 20+ year friend of mine, did not even ask Edward whether he was happy for his family to be consulted and it never occurred to him to entrust confidences, in the face of a clear and imminent risk to life, to a long-standing acquaintance and a responsible father. Such is the effect of the excessively stringent current regulations, framed in a fear of professional misconduct and liability.

Fear is the antithesis of Just Culture. The vast majority of clinicians are naturally and demonstrably dedicated to the well-being of their patients and to acting in their best interests, together with that of those close to them. Fearful that even minor errors or misjudgements could lead to censure, recrimination and worse, is it any wonder that many clinicians in mental health hide behind confidentiality as an excuse for inaction?

More pragmatically, well-intentioned clinicians are commonly so overstretched, under-resourced and low in morale that it is difficult for them to find the time and energy to engage with families and friends in the creation of positive and triangulated care pathways, underscored by healthy exchanges of information. Whilst it is so much easier to do nothing and whilst the law is predicated against acting in the patient's best interests even in the face of severe and blatant risk, preventable tragedies will continue to occur.

The current law and supporting regulations require reform. Until we dispel the post-tragedy mantra of 'if only we knew', constructive learning and restorative justice can never be fully realised. It is extremely difficult for stakeholders and families to come together following a serious incident or a death in an atmosphere of mistrust, poor communication, withheld information, prospective liability and a culture based on the apportionment of blame. System learning and improvement are severely compromised in consequence. I have never met the social worker who knew Edward was suicidal and who had been asked to tell his parents about his condition. It is probably best that I never do. The foundations of restorative justice thus crumble at a stroke.

It is difficult to convey the severity and agony of the prolonged torment and chaos that society and the health system inflicts on families impacted by suicide. Following extensive research and representation from myself and a handful of other similarly bereaved and committed individuals, the current NHS Long Term Plan contains policy provision and funding for the creation of support after suicide services in every locality in England. When Edward died, there was no such support. The great big policemen left the house and nothing. There was no signposting, no offer of support, no follow-up, no information and not even a verbal outline of what we could expect to happen next. Just a bottomless abyss of shock and sorrow.

There are more than 6,000 suicides every year in the UK, as the Office for National Statistics reports. Even conservative estimates suggest that five to ten people will, on average, be very seriously impacted by each suicide. They will be impacted to the point of it being life altering and potentially seriously damaging to their health and well-being. Academic research has established that someone close to a suicide loss is 60–70% more likely to take their own life than someone who has experienced a loss through physical illness. By inference, this means that there are approximately 50,000 people a year in the UK plunged into misery and possible crisis. The societal impact is very considerable. Each suicide costs £1.67 million in direct costs and lost productivity, suggesting an annual economic impairment of around £10 billion+ each year and over £100 billion every decade.

Restorative justice is now well established in a criminal context. Victims of even minor crimes in the UK are routinely offered access to victim support services, counselling and well-established compensation and restitution systems. Police and legal liaison are ingrained throughout to guide victims through the stresses and complexities of the Criminal Justice System.

In 2018, I was the victim of a very serious, life-threatening and unprovoked grievous bodily harm attack which left me scarred – mentally and physically – for life. The signposting, guidance and support I received from the police and other agencies were exceptional and highly efficient. It was also activated within 24 hours of discharge from hospital. All was concluded satisfactorily, and opportunities for restitution and compensation were extended automatically and with ease. It was nearly a year before the matter came to trial and I was fully supported throughout.

When I lost my son and could barely function, myself and my family were left completely isolated in terrible grief and trauma with our only consolation being the torrent of condolence cards which started to arrive. Restorative justice must begin at the point of tragedy if it is to be effective. This is very rarely the case for inpatient and outpatient suicides, marking a severe system imbalance which impacts on national well-being and productivity. We look after violent criminals (and their victims) better than we do families impacted by terrible tragedy as a result of failings in the health system.

The inequity between physical and mental health is also repeated in the legal arena which sees families impacted by clinical negligence well served in acute settings, albeit by incredibly complex and long-winded processes, whilst those impacted by mental health tragedies are left largely floundering.

The Fatal Accidents Act (1976) makes provision for bereavement awards in situations of clinical neglect for families and dependents. Astonishingly, this excludes parents who are not financially dependent on children who may have died. Extremely difficult to prove in cases of mental illness and suicide, the statutory settlement under this legislation was revised to £15,120 in May 2020. In the vast majority of mental health cases, most lawyers are unable to justify representation given the enormous work involved, only a slim chance of success and the paltry sums involved. By comparison, the Criminal Injuries Compensation Scheme, administered by the Criminal Injuries Compensation Authority (CICA) is well established, efficient and based on a clear scale of restitution. There is no equivalent in mental healthcare.

In rare instances, action has been brought in cases of suicide under Article 2 (Right to Life) of the Human Rights Act (1998) following a mental health inpatient or outpatient death. Only the most capable and experienced lawyers, and those (very few) who are prepared to work on a *pro bono* basis, are, however, likely to even consider such projects. These cases can run for years with a typical settlement barely equivalent to standard funeral expenses.

This is clearly a very complex theme. In essence though, the disparity between acute-care tragedy and tragedies in mental health settings once again makes Parity of Esteem look like vacuous rhetoric. This in turn also highlights a glaring gulf between the health system overall and the criminal justice system. A Just Culture in mental health needs to be replicated in law and statutes. Restorative justice is very difficult to realise in mental health situations when the actual law of the land is so incredibly weak and biased against restitution. It is also brutal from a family perspective.

We only survived Edward's loss, thanks to a supportive family and a wonderfully kind community. Many others impacted by suicide are not so fortunate. There are many now lost who should still be with us. There are countless lives broken beyond repair. Better support, restitution, learning and guidance are desperately required at a system level.

The errors in entering Edward's address into the NHS Trust system meant that all the post-incident documentation relating to his death and the ensuing Serious Incident Report (SIR) went to the wrong address. This included notice of a visit by the Trust CEO, other directors and investigating personnel to our home. This incredibly private and sensitive documentation was returned to the sorting office where it resided for five days, being opened and passed around the postal workers who were trying to ascertain its correct destination. Eventually, a shame-faced postman approached the house with a ripped parcel of documents wrapped in a plastic bag offering his condolences and suggesting that he thought this material was for us. This was an hour before the proposed Trust visit and thence, totally unprepared, I was met on my doorstep shortly after by a group of Trust officials. I did not even know what a Serious Incident Report was, let alone how it is generated. Surely somebody could have quickly verified Edward's address before sending out his death papers!

Ill-fated from the start, the SIR process deteriorated from there. As it so often does, miring families in bureaucracy, obfuscation, concealment and conflict for months. Sometimes years. Why is it that we inflict such protracted torture on broken and bereft people in the wake of appalling tragedy when they are in many instances trying desperately to cling onto reality and their sanity? Injustice and torment are endemic in the system from the outset despite NHS protestations to the contrary. This resonates with the very essence of what a Just Culture has to offer as an alternative.

Although just an outpatient in the care of the Trust for less than a month, it took a year to complete the SIR process into Edward's death. A year! An all too oft-repeated litany of errors unfolded as the weeks and months passed.

The social worker who assessed Edward was mysteriously signed off sick a few days after his death and then, equally mysteriously, was no longer in the Trust's employment. They then refused to participate in the SIR process and the Inquest, having to be subpoenaed to the latter. The police lost material evidence from the death scene, resulting in a formal complaint six months later. The Trust did not respond to emails and phone calls from an anxious family seeking progress updates. It was blatantly obvious that draft SIR documents were almost entirely constructed of cut-and-paste extracts. The Chief Medical Officer attempted to assert that Edward could not have been saved and that his death was inevitable despite the medical notes, such as they were, clearly stating that he had every prospect of a full recovery with appropriate intervention. It took more than two months for me to obtain a copy of the (incomplete) medical records.

And so it goes on …. This roll-call of errors, mistakes and contradictions will be familiar to nearly everyone who has lost an NHS patient to suicide.

Whilst the SIR process is mandatory, it is vested in internal process; the Trust inspects itself. The principle of Duty of Candour was articulated in the Health and Social Care Act 2008 (Regulated Activities). This piece of the legislation, underneath all the legal-speak, essentially adds up to three themes: honesty, transparency and disclosure. Self-inspection, by predisposition, does not lend itself to the tenets of Duty of Candour and so it proved to be in Edward's case, together with a multitude of others my work has led me to encounter these past years. Absent personnel and falsified or manufactured documentation are common themes as is a failure to engage properly and empathetically with families.

I had to elicit the intervention of my MP, the Chair of the Trust, the local Director of Public Health, the Chair of the Clinical Commissioning Group (CCG) and two Directors from NHS England (NHSE) before Edward's Trust (Cambridgeshire and Peterborough) would even countenance an independent SIR, such were the inaccuracies and omissions in the internal SIR and the absence of faith I had in the process based on the behaviour of Trust officials and their lawyers.

I later discovered, at Edward's Inquest, friendship connections between seemingly independent parties and false testimony. There was nothing independent about this at all. Independent investigators are also paid by the Trust (sometimes handsomely) which only adds to the sense of suspicion and collusion.

Under Jeremy Hunt's tenure as the Secretary of State for Health, SIR protocols were revised in relation to infant mortality during childbirth in NHS settings. Independent SIR processes are now mandatory in these tragic instances. There are fewer than 100 inpatient deaths in mental health facilities in the UK each year. None are automatically subject to independent investigation. Outpatient numbers are much larger but the same principles apply, especially for those recently discharged from inpatient care.

The trauma of suicide is such that families would instantly be better assured with regard to Duty of Candour if suicide deaths were also subject to independent investigation as a matter of course. It is obviously clear that such an approach would also promote better learning in the wake of tragedy and enhanced restitution whilst mitigating against falsification, subterfuge and a fundamental lack of trust in the process.

The Royal Colleges could so easily create national panels of independent experts to work with Trusts and families through these deeply painful experiences. One suspects that Coroners would also welcome more independent evidence at Inquests as NHS professionals sit with litigation-averse lawyers on one side of the room whilst grieving and distraught relatives huddle together alone and unsupported on the other. This is clearly not conducive to honesty, learning and healing.

Edward's Inquest was concluded 16 months after he died. Sixteen months! With the media in dogged, voyeuristic pursuit, box files of documentation piling up and no support other than that offered by kindly neighbours, myself and my family were at the lowest possible ebb. Hope, vitality and well-being had all vanished and the prospect of destitution and permanent ill-health loomed large. It is not just the fact of suicide which destroys many families but also the over-bearing and unrelenting thunderclouds of confusing officialdom and bewildering due process which follow in the aftermath. There is nothing 'just' about this.

A brief history of the English coronial system is presented elsewhere in this book. To me, Coroners and the coronial system occupy a unique and peculiar position in the statutory landscape which has more in common with medieval assizes than it does with modern, integrated and consistent legal proceedings. Largely autonomous local officials, dispensing common law rulings, have created a system characterised by a well-documented lack of consistency and under-reporting with regard to suicide. It is also a system notoriously disengaged and lacking in empathy from a family perspective. We spent much of Edward's Inquest in a filthy, cobweb-ridden storeroom designated as 'private space'.

In cases of suicide, there are enormous variations in the quality, rigour and conclusions stemming from the coronial process. Despite suicide being decriminalised in 1961, it was only in November 2020 that the Supreme Court finally, in rejecting an Appeal, ratified lowering the Inquest standard of proof in relation to suicide from a criminal standard ('beyond all reasonable doubt') to a civil standard ('on the balance of probabilities').

It has taken 60 years for common law practice to catch up with legal reform, such is the stigma and shame which has persisted through the decades. Having spent very considerable time poring over suicide data and looking at bar graphs which now include my son, it is clear that official data are only one version of reality at best, such are the vagaries of the coronial system. Myself and others are now engaged with statutory authorities in a drive towards establishing real-time surveillance for suspected suicides in the hope of getting better data more rapidly and more consistently. This will have the contingent benefit of laying the foundations for the rapid and effective provision of postvention support to families affected by suicide – as now set out in the NHS Long Term Plan.

The first Coroner appointed to Edward's case began by cracking repeated and inappropriate jokes in front of a tearful mother at a pre-Inquest review. A subsequent total failure to communicate and admit evidence, amidst persistent and unacceptable delays, only compounded the situation. It is very difficult to recuse a Coroner from an Inquest once it has commenced – not unlike sacking a Judge halfway through a trial for misconduct. However, it is not advisable to cross a bereaved and capable father. The Coroner was duly replaced and advised into early retirement. He was replaced with a far more professional, empathetic and diligent individual.

In considering the postvention landscape, insufficient attention is directed to the coronial system. Here once again, restorative justice is firmly linked to external process. Many families find Inquest proceedings as difficult and trauma-inducing as SIR processes. Inexplicable delay, failures in communication and concealed evidence seem to be the standard operating procedure in many jurisdictions. Recrimination rises, anger mounts, learnings are lost and mistrust becomes pervasive. For restorative justice to be fully effective, all agencies and stakeholders, not just health services, need to unite under a common philosophy and clear operating model. This includes Coroners.

When it finally arrived, with TV crews waiting outside, Edward's Inquest actually ran rather well, despite the personal horror we inevitably endured. A very thorough and empathetic Coroner had ensured that all the evidence and relevant witnesses were properly collated and aligned. In contrast with many families, we were treated with respect and kindness. Notices were issued and followed through, apologies were secured and corrective actions implemented.

In retrospect, it is clear that I was only able to achieve this by securing excellent legal advice, having the initial Coroner removed, launching a civil action against the Trust and applying all of the education, skills, determination and experience gathered in a long and successful corporate career to the process over many long months. Most families are not able to build such a robust position and many are left broken and angry by the coronial process. Here again, restorative justice fades away.

A conclusion of suicide was reached and the Regulation 28 Notice confirmed, both with our approval. I shall never forget the surreal experience of watching myself on the national news that evening whilst numb with grief and exhaustion. Overall, it is clear to me now that accurate and constructive determinations in cases of tragedy are frequently only arrived at in circumstances of combative opposition. This has been confirmed by the hundreds of families who have subsequently shared their terrible stories with me. Without lawyers, threats of sanction, media attention and extremely strong personal determination, many SIR processes and Inquests end up in travesty and painful acrimony. In the interests of learning, restorative justice and common humanity, I continue to this day to help families struck down by young suicide as they try and navigate the torrid waters of a very cruel, complex and unfair system.

Epilogue

In June 2015, four months after Edward died, I was myself plunged into deep psychological trauma. Those initial months of gut-wrenching grief, funeral arrangements, media attention, battles with officialdom and a resolute determination to shield my remaining family from the onslaught had taken their toll. As I have said, those impacted by suicide are at greatly inflated risk of taking their own lives, and sadly, many either try or succeed.

I went to see my GP. Edward's GP. Himself deeply affected by Edward's loss and with a welcome and heightened desire to protect us, I was immediately referred to a neighbouring mental health trust in Hertfordshire. The fact that it was recommended that I should not visit my own trust, which had so disastrously served Edward and with whom I was by this time already deeply engaged in mutual and acrimonious confrontation, speaks volumes. Under the circumstances, I was more than content to place myself in the hands of another locality.

It took ten weeks for me to get an appointment with a psychiatrist within the Hertfordshire Trust. Ten weeks. A desperately bereaved father in extreme distress, exhibiting at least moderate and perhaps severe risk, I do not quite know how I survived that nightmare period.

Reaching out for care is one of the most difficult steps for someone with mental affliction to take, especially if you are male. However, I was still self-aware enough to know that I had to do this. My expectations for care and support from the neighbouring locality were therefore high. Some local notoriety might have garnered their focused attention and professionalism.

Unfortunately, I was deluded. Having met with the psychiatrist and a mental health nurse over two consultations, I received a lengthy letter to the effect that I was suffering from depression and post-traumatic stress disorder for which various interventions might be suitable. However, the letter concluded with:

> It has come to our attention that you are currently engaged in legal action with a neighbouring Trust. In our experience, the stress and anxiety associated with such action means that any treatment we are able to offer is unlikely to be effective. We are therefore unable to extend treatment to you at this time.

Sometimes the world is as bad as you are afraid it might be!

It is not melodramatic when I say that I nearly joined Edward after he died. I certainly thought about it. This inhumane and possibly illegal refusal of care affirmed my total and utter lack of faith in the mental health system at that time. The fact that I am able to write these words now is not because on the health service, but in spite of it. The mountain we have to climb in promulgating a Just Culture becomes all too clear.

My son was ill, he could have been cured, he should have been cured and he should still be with us. End of.

The appalling experiences of my family following his death represent just one drop in an ocean of misery and similar cases, repeated every day. There must be a better way, and this is precisely what restorative practice and a Just Culture are all about.

Following the death of his son, Steve Mallen has dedicated himself to improving the mental health system and reducing suicide. He is a Co-Founder of the Zero Suicide Alliance (ZSA) and a member of the National Suicide Prevention Advisory Group (NSPAG) within the Department of Health and Social Care (DHSC). He is also Chair of The MindEd Trust, a charity created in memory of Edward and focused on improving mental health in the education system. Still resident in Cambridgeshire and with a long career in the international chartered surveying, fund management and consulting sector, Steve has recently joined the Board of Governors at Cambridgeshire and Peterborough NHS Foundation Trust (CPFT) under whose care Edward died.

References and sources

Suicide Rate in England and Wales 2019: quoted as 5,691 and Scotland 833. www
.samaritans.org/about-samaritans/research-policy/suicide-facts-and-figures/
www.ons.gov.uk/peoplepopulationandcommunity/birthsdeathsandmarriages/deaths
/bulletins/suicidesintheunitedkingdom/2019registrations
An article in *The Lancet* (20 April 2021) Notes that though 'the coronial system in
England is not suitable for timely monitoring of suicide because of the delay of
several months before inquests are held', more recent data bare comparison to
pre-pandemic levels, with discussion of the wide professional concern of the
effects of COVID-19 on long-term mental health. www.thelancet.com/journals/
lanepe/article/PIIS2666-7762(21)00087-9/fulltext

Chapter 4

Joshua's Story

James Titcombe

Contents

In October 2008, our world was very different. Our daughter Emily was just three-and-a-half years old, and at the time, I was working as a project manager at a large nuclear facility on North West Coast of Cumbria. At 7.38 am on 27 October 2008, our second child Joshua was born at Furness General Hospital (FGH), part of the Morecambe Bay NHS Trust. I remember staring at him in his cot, thinking how perfect he was and how lucky I was – how lucky we all were. But just 24 hours later – that world ended.

An early morning phone call broke the news. I remember the words as if it was yesterday:

> Joshua is having problems breathing and your wife is very upset –
> can you come to the hospital.

I remember phoning my mum and hearing her voice break (mums have an instinct), getting to the hospital and seeing Joshua in the Special Care Baby Unit – initially breathing by himself but quickly put on a ventilator as I'm ushered out the room. Confusion, uncertainty, desperation, fear, hope and despair followed.

Joshua was transferred by ambulance to a specialist unit in Manchester and my wife and I followed him by car. At this point, we were uncertain as to what was wrong. We were told there might be a problem with his heart, but even then, this explanation did not seem to fit.

My wife had been feeling unwell in the days before Joshua was born and shortly after his birth, she collapsed with a high temperature and was given intravenous fluids and antibiotics. She recovered quickly, but we both raised worries with staff about Joshua – if my wife needed antibiotics, wasn't Joshua also at risk of infection? Despite raising these concerns with staff, we were repeatedly reassured that 'Joshua was fine'.

Surely his collapse 24 hours later could not be due to infection? Not after we had specifically raised concerns with staff about this and been reassured repeatedly that Joshua was ok?

The following day the team in Manchester confirmed our fears; Joshua had collapsed due to an overwhelming pneumococcal infection – the same strain that had now been identified as having caused my wife to collapse shortly after the birth. Questions about how this could have happened raced around my mind. Could I have done more to raise concerns and insist Joshua was seen by a paediatrician sooner? These feelings of regret and guilt have never left me.

But these questions had to be put on hold for now. Joshua was still fighting for his life and all that mattered was getting him the right care and treatment so we could bring him home.

At Manchester, we were told that Joshua's best option was to be flown to a specialist unit in Newcastle to be put on a heart and lung machine for babies. The treatment had risks, but the unanimous view of his clinical team was that this treatment would give Joshua the best chance of recovery.

Joshua was flown by helicopter to Newcastle. For what would be the final time, my wife and I followed him by car. When we arrived in Newcastle, Joshua had already been hooked up to the medical machinery that we hoped would save his life.

We were greeted by a kind consultant who told us that Joshua's prognosis was good. We were shown a wall of cards, letters and photos from the families of other children who had been cared for at the unit and had recovered and who were now doing well at home with their families.

We had seven hopeful days in Newcastle; Joshua was sedated but able to open his eyes and squeeze a finger.

We hoped that we would get to take our baby boy home too, but that was not to be. Those hopes were dashed when Joshua died at just nine days old as a consequence of internal bleeding caused by the damage the pneumococcal infection did to his lungs.

Although over a decade has passed since these moments, I remember them as vividly as if they had happened just yesterday. Seeing Joshua for the first time after his death with all the tubes and medical equipment removed – he looked like a perfect baby boy. How could he have died for want of a simple dose of antibiotics at the right time?

The loss of any child in whatever circumstances is a life-changing tragedy – but coming to terms with Joshua's death was made incalculably worse by the way that the trust and healthcare system responded.

Crucial medical records of Joshua's observations went 'missing'. Staff accounts of what happened at Furness General Hospital conflicted with the events as my wife and I remembered. The initial report from the hospital concluded that Joshua's observations in the 24 hours after his birth before he collapsed were all within 'normal' limits and that therefore no one was to blame for what happened.

As Joshua's father, I knew that no one intended the tragic outcome for Joshua, but I was not going to accept false narratives and dishonestly either. I had failed to keep Joshua safe during his short life, but I wasn't prepared to allow the truth about his death to be swept under the carpet.

I soon discovered that seemingly at almost every level the healthcare system was not open to looking for, let alone acknowledging the truth about what happened to Joshua and why.

The journey since has been long, hard and at times lonely. Eventually we did establish a truthful account of what went wrong and in doing so uncovered a far wider scandal at the maternity unit at Furness General Hospital. After meeting other families who had experience of tragic outcomes following poor care at the same unit, I started a campaign group and worked to try and secure a national inquiry into the safety of the unit. The campaign was successful, and the Morecambe Bay Investigation report, chaired by Dr Bill Kirkup, was published in March 2015.

The report concluded that between 2004 and 2012, a 'lethal mix of failures' had led to the avoidable death of 11 babies and one mother at Furness General Hospital – Joshua was just one of many preventable deaths. It described the maternity unit at FGH as characterised by 'denial and cover up'. The report made 26 recommendations for national change and triggered a programme of work in England with the aim of halving avoidable harm in maternity units across the country by 2025.

In the aftermath of Joshua's death, as well as struggling to deal with deep trauma and grief, I was also consumed with a burning sense of injustice and anger. The more I learned about the culture of the unit where Joshua was born, the more I realised that Joshua's death was far more than an unavoidable accident. The Kirkup report concluded that the first opportunity that the trust had to identify serious systemic issues was following the avoidable death of another baby in 2004 – more than four years before Joshua died. But the investigation that was carried out by the trust was superficial, 'protective of the staff involved' and failed to result in any meaningful action to learn from what happened and makes the service safer for others.

Why Is Transparency and Learning so Elusive in Healthcare?

Human beings are prone to error and mistakes – but where that normal variation in human performance can lead to serious or catastrophic outcomes, for example, in the nuclear industry or aviation, considerable effort is usually placed on designing and building systems and processes to prevent those mistakes leading to harm.

Joshua was born in a maternity unit characterised by dysfunction. Staff lacked basic competencies and skills, processes and guidelines were out of date, midwives and doctors perceived themselves to have different objectives and there was distrust and blame in place of teamwork and shared goals.

Overriding all of this was a leadership culture that was toxic to transparency, learning and improvement. The trust at the time was preoccupied with achieving 'Foundation' status, which would have given them greater control and financial freedom – but crucially this involved persuading various regulators that they met the appropriate standards of governance and quality. A seriously dysfunctional maternity unit with a history of avoidable harm was a problem that the senior leadership team sought to manage and they focused on doing everything possible to reassure the local community and regulatory system that their services were safe.

Unpicking all these behaviours is complex. The healthcare system at the time seemed to be influenced by perverse incentives; pursuing strategic objectives and meeting performance targets, seemingly put above the safety of mothers and babies.

But the barriers to transparency and learning in our healthcare system go much deeper. The truth is that existing systems, processes and regulatory incentives and levers often make it hard for healthcare professionals to do the right thing.

In the aftermath of harm, the relationship between the patient and the bereaved family can almost instantly become adversarial. In Joshua's case, there was initially no inquest – we were told to raise our concerns about Joshua's care via a formal complaint.

Rather than our family and the trust working together via a process to understand and learn, immediately the process became one of 'allegations' for the trust to respond to.

The vast majority of tragic outcomes like Joshua's death occur without any deliberate intent, but rather as a consequence of normal human performance/error and a combination of unsafe systems and processes. However, healthcare staff often have little faith that trust investigation processes will be candid about systemic problems and instead fear being singled out for blame or referral to a professional regulatory body. Fear and safety are conditions that cannot sit together side by side; healthcare systems must choose one or the other.

American patient safety campaigner Professor Lucian Leape states that 'the single greatest impediment to error prevention is that we punish people for making mistakes' (Leape, 2015), and he is right. Countering fear is crucial if we want to create the kind of learning culture in healthcare that has played such a decisive role in making other high-risk sectors safer. Furthermore, the focus on inappropriate blame detracts from where clear and meaningful accountability should lie.

How Could Things Be Different?

Although it took nearly ten years, eventually I did manage to reach a point of reconciliation, healing and to some extent forgiveness, following what happened to Joshua.

After the Morecambe Bay Investigation report was published in 2015, that trust agreed to some further work around Joshua's death. Although several years had passed, they carried out the kind of comprehensive investigation that should have happened if current best practice guidance was followed. The investigation highlighted serious failures that other external processes had already found but also issues with Joshua's care and treatment that we were not previously aware of. But the crucial difference with this investigation was that the trust themselves had carried it out. For the first time since Joshua's death, I felt confident that the trust themselves owned and understood Joshua's story and therefore could be trusted to take its learning forward.

The final aspect of the work the trust carried out was by far the most difficult but also the most healing. A midwife who had a direct role in failures relating to Joshua's care had been heavily criticised by the Nursing and Midwifery Council. The resulting hearing concluded that her role relating to Joshua's death was serious enough to warrant a suspension from the professional register for nine months. The hearing gave the trust a dilemma; should they continue to employ a member of staff who was unable to practice clinically and had been subject to heavy criticism relating to the preventable death of a baby, or should they dismiss her? Instead of rushing to make a decision that at face value might have seemed like the right and 'just' thing to do, the trust asked whether I might be willing to meet the midwife to talk through what had happened and what had been learned. I agreed to do so.

In all the years that had passed since Joshua's death, the only time I had been in the same room as any of the staff involved in his care was at Joshua's Inquest (which occurred nearly three years later) and whilst giving evidence in formal Fitness to Practice hearings. These were bureaucratic processes, determined by legal advice – cold, compassionless and inhumane.

In preparation for the meeting, I thought long and hard about what I wanted to say. I wanted to tell the midwife concerned that I didn't blame her for the mistakes made in Joshua care and that I knew she didn't intend for the outcome for Joshua to be what it was. But I also wanted to tell her how the lack of honesty afterwards had impacted on me and of my anger that Joshua's life seemed to matter so little.

When I walked into the room, after a few words of introduction by the facilitator, I was given the opportunity to talk directly to someone I thought of as caring very little about what happened to Joshua and the consequences on our family.

I only got through half of what I wanted to say that I didn't blame her for the mistakes that led to Joshua's death, but I could not get any further. The midwife broke down in tears and told me that every day since Joshua died, she had blamed herself for what happened – that she wished she had done things differently and that she would carry that for the rest of her life. It was not fake or rehearsed emotion and at that moment, the image I had in my mind of an uncaring and callous person disappeared. In an instant my anger lifted. We cried together and had a hug.

I left that meeting with a sense of healing but also profound sadness. Sadness that we weren't able to meet much earlier and sadness that on the long journey since Joshua died – somehow humanity and compassion were sucked out of the process – at the very time when kindness was needed the most.

A recent and welcome movement in healthcare is the focus on 'just culture'. If we genuinely want to make stories like Joshua's a thing of the past, we must fundamentally change the way our healthcare system responds to error and harm. These are some of the changes that I believe would make a difference:

1. Education and training for healthcare professionals relating to responding to clinical error and mistakes. Conversations about mistakes, errors and near misses in healthcare should be normal and routine and not hidden and only discussed in the shadows. This should start in undergraduate education and training.
2. Changes to ensure that the legal system doesn't act as a barrier to transparency and learning. Countries such as Sweden have had considerable success in reducing adverse outcomes in key areas by creating strong systems for rapid review and learning supported by 'no-fault' compensation systems which remove the need to prove individual or organisational 'negligence'.
3. Truly embedding systems and processes (at all levels in the healthcare system) whereby healthcare professionals involved in serious incidents and events are not fearful of inappropriate blame or punishment.
4. Implementing restorative processes to support healing and recovery after healthcare harm for both staff and patients and recognising that such processes require investment in resources and expertise.

If we get this right, the aftermath of patient harm will cease to be characterised by adversarial processes, denial and cover-up that are so toxic to learning and improvement. Instead, we can focus on the people who have been hurt and what they need to rebuild trust, to forgive and remember.

We will see a shift away from the hunt for individual blame allowing a much greater focus on the most important accountability of all – that which is owned to future patients to ensure they don't come to harm through the same mistakes happening again.

References

Kirkup, Bill: Morecambe Bay Investigation Report, 2015: published on www.gov.uk/government/publications/morecambe-bay-investigation-report

Leape, Lucian: quoted in 'Culture of blame in the National Health Service; consequences and solutions', S. Radhakrishna, *BJA: British Journal of Anaesthesia*, Volume 115, Issue 5, November 2015.

Chapter 5

Regulation and the Just Culture

Ted Baker

Contents

The Care Quality Commission (CQC) assesses the quality of care in health and social care services in England with a programme of on-site inspections. The evidence it draws on comes from directly observing care at the frontline of services and from listening to the voices of staff providing the care and people receiving the care. We correlate what we find from this with what those responsible for managing the services tell us about the quality of care they believe they provide.

A recurrent finding from our inspections has been a lack of correlation between the observed quality, or the quality experienced by staff or patients, and the quality reported by management. Faced with this, leadership teams often fall back on their governance processes and their assurance systems. They point to dashboards awash with green, to charts outlining performance indicators achieved and to audits assessing the practice as safe.

Why is this disjunction between reported quality and observed quality so common in healthcare settings? It has become clear to us that where we find this the fundamental issue is one of culture. The culture of a healthcare service must be right for its governance to be effective and the leadership must attend first to culture if it is to have assurance about the quality of care it provides. They must seek assurance about the culture of a service before they can have reliable assurance about the quality of care it provides.

For a regulator such as the CQC, this too presents a challenge. A traditional view of regulation as focusing purely on ensuring compliance with fixed standards is no longer sufficient. We need to understand and promote cultures in health services that support the provision of high-quality safe-care. We need to be able to identify and to help providers identify risks to the safety of care brought about by poor culture. We must ask not only are we observing safe practice, but also are we finding a culture that supports consistently safe practice? We need to help leadership teams understand how they can nurture the right culture within their services and we need ourselves to operate in a way that supports the right culture across health services generally.

CQC was established in 2008 with the purpose of 'encouraging the improvement of health and social care services' (Health and Social Care Act 2008). It was set up with an explicit role to drive improvement, given the conventional tools of a regulator, regulations, powers to assess services against those regulations and powers to enforce the regulations where it finds non-compliance. The assumption in this approach to regulation is that quality and safety are driven purely by the implementation of the right processes.

Regulation tends to go through a series of cycles. When there are unambiguous failures in quality, regulation is tightened. Regulators are given more powers. The systems accept, sometimes welcomes, more intrusive regulation as a way of re-building confidence. Once the failures have passed, there is a general assumption that the underlying problems are resolved and regulation becomes increasingly seen as a burden, an unnecessary overhead. This is manifest internationally when healthcare will often go through cycles of strengthening and then weakening the impact of regulation. The establishment of the CQC in England was just once such transition from a scheme of regulation build predominantly on providers of healthcare self-certifying their standards to one where the regulator had a duty to regularly assess them. The duty to assess was backed up with powers to inspect services directly.

Culture Is Critical for Quality

In 2013, a public inquiry report was published into a major failure of care at an English hospital (Francis, 2013). The report made numerous recommendations for improvement both in the hospital and in the wider healthcare system. Amongst these was a further strengthening of the regulation of healthcare with the creation of fundamental standards of care that were subsequently enshrined in the CQC's regulations. The CQC responded by strengthening its approach to assessment, introducing regular comprehensive inspections of all providers. All services were to be given a published rating ranging from outstanding to inadequate. Enforcement of the regulations would become more rigorous.

The public inquiry report certainly recommended strengthening regulation, but in its extensive and comprehensive assessment of the issues that led the failure of care, one particular theme runs through the whole report. There was a failure of culture and leadership at all levels in the system, from the frontline clinical teams all the way up to the leadership of England's NHS. This theme was taken up in an academic survey published in the aftermath of the report by Dixon-Woods and colleagues (Dixon-Woods M, Baker R, Charles K, et al, 2014). The paper reported on the culture across a wide cross section of the NHS's hospitals and found that many of the cultural issues brought to light by the public inquiry were widespread, both in the frontline providers and in the extensive system that supported them. They reported a culture that was often focused on token compliance rather than delivering fundamental quality of care. Providers often had cultures that they described as 'comfort seeking'. Quality indicators that provided reassurance were sought and valued; indicators that showed problems were discarded or explained away. Such comfort-seeking cultures tended to become defensive when challenged and when quality problems became apparent they tended to apportion blame and rationalise the quality failure as a discrete event, rather than evidence of the underlying issues. One of the features of comfort-seeking cultures was resistance to hearing bad news about quality. Staff who raised concerns were marginalised or treated dismissively, sometimes blamed for the problem or characterised as disruptive. In contrast, problem-sensing cultures were much less likely to be satisfied or self-congratulatory about their quality of care. They actively looked for problems and when they found them, they were much more likely to search for the underlying problems and ascribing failures in quality to errors by frontline staff.

To support the 2013 introduction of CQC's inspection programme, a new assessment framework was created to give a comprehensive overview of quality in a clinical service. The assessment framework was built around five key questions that were asked about every service. These were is the service safe? Is it effective? Is it caring? Is it responsive? And is it well led? The key questions were underpinned by a series of key lines of enquiry and a framework for each clinical service of the evidence that was to be examined to respond to each. Criteria were developed to assess the ratings for each key question for every service. In this way, we aimed to establish a consistent, comprehensive assessment of quality across all services.

An individual and detailed report was published for each service and each hospital, and in 2017, when they had all been inspected, overview reports were published on the findings from the whole comprehensive inspection programme (CQC, 2016; 2017a State of Care reports). The findings, the most comprehensive of their kind ever produced, essentially validated the work of Dixon-Woods and colleagues. While much good care was found, it was not consistent. Every service described safety as their top priority, but this was often not reflected in the culture in many services. In fact, ratings for safety were the poorest of the five key questions, if was often assumed but not always assured. Frontline staff often reported that they did not feel listened to and they were not confident about raising concerns, either because they thought that nothing would change or that they would be regarded as disruptive. In this first round of inspections, we rated less than one in five hospitals as good for safety and found serious safety concerns in many. The assessment framework for safety was predominantly based on assessing safety processes. We found inconsistency around how safety policies and protocols were implemented and often we found that there was a major disjunction between what leadership of services believed was happening and what we found was actually happening. Audits and assessments of safety processes were often done on the basis of seeking comfort rather than finding problems. Our approach of looking beyond reported compliance to examining actual practice revealed deep cultural problems at the heart of many services.

Our ratings for well-led key questions proved to be a strong predictor of the overall rating for a service and particularly for the rating for safety. An even stronger predictor was the scores from the national NHS staff survey reflecting the engagement of frontline staff. It became very evident that leadership and the right culture were the essential foundations for delivering high-quality care. A compliance or process-driven approach might provide comfort, but without the right culture it could not deliver quality. Recognition of this led us to revise our assessment framework for the well-led key question, strengthening the importance of culture. We launched this in 2018 together with a modified approach to inspection of NHS hospitals that made leadership and culture pivotal in our assessment of quality (CQC 2018).

Never Again

The NHS in England, like many other health systems, has a series 16 of what it describes as 'never events'. These are patient safety errors (such as wrong-site surgery or administration of a medicine by the wrong route) that are believed to be wholly preventable if the appropriate safety protocols have been implemented. Despite this theoretical preventability, they continue to occur and are not diminishing in volume. They are not common, but even the occasional failure to avoid an equivocally preventable error carries an important wider message about safety. The CQC was asked to review never events in the NHS and report about what more could be done to prevent their occurrence. There was an expectation that the answer would be better safety protocols or more rigorous enforcement of compliance with the current protocols. While we certainly found some processes that could be further improved, such as better use of technology to catch errors, the overarching lesson we drew was that the persistent recurrence of preventable errors was an indication of fundamental flaws in the safety culture within healthcare.

Healthcare is a high-risk industry like many others. As part of our review of never events we worked with experts from other high-risk industries, several of which have achieved major improvements in safety performance in recent years. What became clear was that healthcare, unlike other industries, tends to regard itself as essentially safe. England's NHS reports about two million patient safety incidents a year, approximately 20,000 of these are classed as serious. Despite this, safety events are regarded as out of the ordinary, each with a distinct cause, often a local failure of a process or by an individual. Frontline staff of course experience the reality of safety and recognise how easily errors can occur. Culturally there are barriers to openly acknowledging this. Raising concerns about safety challenges this cultural norm and is seen as disruptive or letting down the team. When an error does occur, this again challenges the assumption of safety and the response is too often defensive, denying the problem and when it cannot be denied containing it by apportioning blame. I remember reporting a never event in my hospital several years back, a wrong-site surgery. The response from the external oversight of the hospital was unequivocal. Someone must be to blame; someone must be dismissed.

The conflict between the cultural belief in the safety of care and the reality experienced by frontline staff has I believe another important consequence. Of course, they understand their own individual fallibility and yet they work in a culture where admitting error is discouraged. The cultural belief is that a competent practitioner does not make errors, but of course every practitioner makes errors. How can individuals manage the inner conflict that this dichotomy brings? This has major implications for how teams work together and the well-being and career choices of individual members of staff.

Achieving Transparency

Reports of CQC's inspections draw on evidence most heavily from what staff and patients tell us about the quality of care they experience on a day-to-day basis. As we have seen this often is discordant with what leaders believe about the quality of care. Patients and staff often applaud our reports as presenting an overdue account of the reality of quality in a service, and the leadership in contrast frequently finds the reports uncomfortable reading. The reality we have found is not the reality they want to acknowledge. Our reports are driven by a belief that transparency about quality problems is essential to driving improvement. We are challenging leaders to look beyond their performance and assurance reports to address the substantive quality problems that these often mask. As we have seen, this means moving beyond simply accentuating managerial processes to tackling the underlying culture. Many hospitals have recognised this and have achieved major improvements in the quality and safety of their care (CQC 2017b Case Studies). This is reflected in our ratings in our State of Care report in 2020 (CQC 2020). In that report, we described how three-quarters of hospital services were rated as good or outstanding in their most recent inspection.

Transparency about quality has been shown to be a major driver of quality improvement and is a central part of CQC's approach, but just as recognising error is difficult for individual clinicians, recognising quality concerns is sometimes very difficult for leadership teams. The initial reaction is often defensive and sometimes this persists. Faced with a critical report teams often feel they are being blamed for any failures. This is a challenge and concern for a regulator, and our purpose is not to apportion blame, but it is to encourage improvement. Defensive services that feel they are being blamed are unlikely to improve; indeed, they often see improvement as being about paper-based compliance rather than a real change.

As a regulator, we have a duty to take enforcement action if the fundamental standards of quality reflected in our regulations are not being met. This means applying legal sanctions to instruct the provider to take whatever steps are needed to meet the standard and to provide evidence it has done so. A hospital that is responding defensively to a critical report is likely to regard any enforcement action we take as punitive. This has the potential to create real barriers between the regulator and those we regulate. The challenge for us is to fulfil society's reasonable expectations of us as a regulator – that we will ensure that our regulations are complied with – while pursuing our aim to encourage improvement, which can only be achieved if providers of health services develop a transparent culture open to challenge.

CQC was given an extra tool in its pursuit of transparency in 2014 with the introduction of a regulation imposing a duty of candour on providers of services. This legally requires them to provide an apology and an honest explanation to patients or their next of kin when a patient safety incident occurs. The legal requirement is in addition to, but complementary to, the duty of candour that clinicians have through their professional regulation. Effective implementation of the duty of candour requires transparency about safety issues, and it has been a major step forward. However, the reluctance of staff to speak up about concerns and the defensiveness of some services remain unresolved issues.

Accountability and Blame

So a regulator can, however unintentionally, intensify a culture of blame in health systems and has to consider how to apply regulation in a way that does not promote a punitive approach. However, as outlined above, blame does not just come from regulation; it is innate within the safety culture of healthcare that does not recognise its collective and individual fallibility. Blame is indeed endemic with healthcare. So, frontline clinicians complain of their fear of blame if there is a safety incident, but they too will blame their management for failures, management will blame those higher in the hierarchy and so forth. There is no part of the system that will not find others to blame for shortcomings. Blame is a way of avoiding accountability for the fallibility all have, but many will not acknowledge it. Indeed, blame and accountability are often regarded synonymous in this context.

Separating accountability from blame is a key step that needs to be taken if we are to move from a punitive culture to one that consistently promotes safety. Blame is a barrier to safety improvement. Accountability, in terms of giving an account of a safety issue and contributing to finding a solution to it, is essential if we are to develop a culture of learning and continuous improvement in safety. This applies to an individual involved not only in a safety incident but also to a service where a safety concern has been raised. Such a concern may have been raised by a regulator, but much more often it will be raised by a member of staff. A true culture of accountability will support the airing of concerns and ensure a constructive response. It will prevent the punitive treatment of those staff who speak up.

Sir Robert Francis, who led the 2013 public inquiry, published a further report in 2015 on creating an open and honest reporting culture in the NHS (Francis, 2015). His report reflected the continuing concern at the punitive treatment of staff who had raised safety concerns and made recommendations for improvement. Yet again the report emphasises the importance of taking steps to create an open and honest culture within health services where staff feel able to raise concerns without fear. As a result of the report, the role of national guardians for the freedom to speak up was established, and there is now a network of local freedom to speak up guardians in every NHS hospital. Interestingly, the freedom to speak up initiative has revealed a variety of approaches by different hospitals, some see it as yet another process to implement, while others recognise it for what Francis envisaged it to be, a major opportunity to drive culture change within their organisation. The freedom to speak up culture in every organisation, now reported on regularly by the National Guardian's office (see, for example, their 2020 index report) is an important measure of the safety culture across the NHS. It already correlates well with the CQC's ratings for different organisations and will become an increasingly important part of our assessment of services for our well-led key question going forward.

The Voice of Patients

Staff need to feel that they will be treated fairly if they face safety issues, but patients need confidence that their safety is protected, so one more element of a true safety culture has to concern the involvement of patients. One of the problems with addressing safety issues within well-established services is that there is little challenge to group thinking. New thinking and outside challenge are important if some of the more intractable safety issues are to be successfully managed. Patients can and should provide this challenge. They are too often regarded as passive recipients of safety, rather than active participants in the safety of their care. The need to involve them in the investigation of safety incidents in which they have been involved is now recognised, but in our inspections of safety in hospitals we have found this is often relatively superficial. Patients want an apology, they want to understand what has gone wrong, they want support in managing the consequences for them and they want confidence that steps will be taken to prevent the same from happening again to someone else. The introduction of the duty of candour has greatly improved the way patients are informed about safety incidents, but too many patients are still left dissatisfied and angry. We need to go further, and the development of restorative cultures will be important in this regard.

Role of Regulators

In the CQC's review of never events I called for a radical change in the safety culture of the NHS, so that learning from other industries have paved the way, and we can achieve the level of safety we aspire to. The building blocks are in place, but there is still much that needs to be delivered. Healthcare is complex. That complexity will inevitably lead to risk. We need to accept this reality, stop asking who is to blame for the current position and start asking who can help us solve the underlying problems. Regulators, both of provider organisations and of individual practitioners, need to be a part of this solution, and they need to create true accountability without sanctioning a punitive culture. The culture must be one of transparency and honesty, it must be one that sets high standards, but recognises human fallibility and takes account of it, one where staff feel safe to speak up about their concerns and one that does not seek false comfort, but looks for problems that need action. A just culture, one where staff feel they will be treated fairly, is essential. However, we also need to consider how services involve patients as part of their drive to improve safety. Patients need to be equal partners in maintaining safety and responding to errors.

There are no simple solutions, change of culture is not straightforward and we need to learn from our experience and the experience of others, adjusting our approach as necessary. A restorative approach to responding to safety events is a welcome addition to our understanding and as it develops the test will be – does it drive a culture that delivers tangible improvements in safety. For a regulator, the lesson is clear. Those organisations with a leadership that is focused first on improving their culture are those that deliver safe and high-quality care. It is this behaviour above others that we want our actions to encourage.

References

CQC (2016). The state of care in NHS acute hospitals 2014 to 2016. www.cqc.org.uk/publications/major-report/state-care-nhs-acute-hospitals

CQC (2017a). The state of care in mental health services 2014 to 2017. www.cqc.org.uk/publications/major-report/state-care-mental-health-services-2014-2017

CQC (2017b). Driving improvement. Case studies from eight NHS trusts. www.cqc.org.uk/publications/evaluation/driving-improvement-case-studies-eight-independent-hospitals

CQC (2018). Inspection framework: NHS trusts and foundation trusts. www.cqc.org.uk/sites/default/files/20200115_Trust_wide_well_led_inspection_framework_V7.pdf

CQC (2020). The state of health care and adult social care in England 2019/20. www.cqc.org.uk/sites/default/files/20201016_stateofcare1920_fullreport.pdf

Dixon-Woods, M., Baker, R., Charles, K., et al. (2014). Culture and behaviour in the English National Health Service: Overview of lessons from a large multi-method study. *BMJ Quality & Safety*, 23: 106–115. https://pubmed.ncbi.nlm.nih.gov/24019507/

Francis, Robert (2013). The Francis Report (Report of the Mid-Staffordshire NHS Trust public inquiry). www.gov.uk/government/publications/report-of-the-mid-staffordshire-nhs-foundation-trust-public-inquiry

Francis, Robert (2015). Freedom to speak up. www.gov.uk/government/publications/sir-robert-francis-freedom-to-speak-up-review

Health and Social Care Act 2008. www.legislation.gov.uk/ukpga/2008/14/contents

National Guardian's Office (2020). Freedom to speak up index report 2020. www.nationalguardian.org.uk/wp-content/uploads/2020/07/ftsu_index_report_2020.pdf

Chapter 6

Restorative Practice and Building a Just Culture

Jill Mason

Contents

DOI: 10.4324/9781003162582-6

■ A short historic reflection on the courts and judicial system including the impact that has on what happens now in Coroner's courts.

■ Why early resolution matters and what would have to change to achieve this?

■ Legally balancing justice, accountability and learning in a healthcare setting.

Is it possible to balance justice, accountability and learning in a healthcare setting or indeed any setting? A six million dollar question!

There can be so many stakeholders, with so many separate and differing interests and perspectives involved, following the death of a patient. Clearly the patient's family and friends as well as the healthcare staff involved, the organisation they work for, the Care Quality Commission, professional regulators (such as the General Medical Council or Nursing and Midwifery Council), the Health and Safety Executive, the police, the Crown Prosecution Service could all be involved.

I therefore question whether the balance can be struck to the satisfaction of all.

It was tricky enough to try to do this up to 12 November 2020 but has been made even more complicated from 13 November 2020 following the Supreme Court decision in the case of Maughan.

This chapter will cover:

■ The numbers of and timeliness of inquests in England and Wales
■ Prevention of Future Deaths (PFD) reports
■ What an inquest is
■ The scope of an inquest
■ The case of Maughan
■ Funding
■ What happens after an inquest
■ Confidence in the system
■ Early resolution of claims
■ The importance of learning
  – Duty of candour
  – Patient Safety Investigations
  – Healthcare Safety Investigation Branch

Inquests in England and Wales – Setting the Scene

The latest Report of the Chief Coroner to the Lord Chancellor is perhaps a good starting point. This was published on 5 November 2020 and combines both the sixth and seventh such reports. It provides an assessment of the current state of the Coroner Service over the last two years.

In 2019 there were 503,857 registered deaths. Of those 40% (210,900) were reported to the Coroner. A total of 82,100 post mortems were ordered, and 30,000 inquests were opened.

There is a wealth of information in this report, but, for our purposes, it is the number of cases over 12 months old (where the Chief Coroner has a statutory duty, as set out in the Coroners and Justice Act 2009, to report to the Lord Chancellor) that are of greatest interest.

There are many reasons why inquests may remain outstanding, e.g. ongoing police enquiries, criminal investigations and prosecutions, Health and Safety Executive and Prisons and Probation Ombudsman inquiries which mean that a Coroner's inquest is put on 'hold' pending the outcome of these. However, there can also be an issue with the resources available to Coroners in some areas.

What the report shows us is that, as of April 2020, over 2,200 cases awaiting an inquest were over 12 months old. Whilst not all of these will relate to a health and care setting, it is still quite a large number (and will grow due to COVID-19 restrictions causing delays in the completion of inquests).

PFD Reports

Where an investigation gives rise to concern that future deaths will occur, and the investigating Coroner is of the opinion that action should be taken to reduce the risk of death, the Coroner *must* make a report to the person s/he believes may have the power to take such action. This is a statutory duty. These Prevention of Future Deaths reports are known as PFDs (see paragraph 7, Schedule 5 of the Coroners and Justice Act 2009 and Regulations 28 and 29 of the Coroners' (Investigations) Regulations 2013).

These are usually prepared at the end of an inquest. The Chief Coroner's Guidance (2020) specifically states that PFDs are vitally important if society is to learn from deaths. It also appreciates that a bereaved family wants to be able to say: 'His death was tragic and terrible, but at least it's less likely to happen to somebody else'. The guidance makes clear that PFDs are not intended as a punishment; they are made for the benefit of the public. The Chief Coroner is committed to learning from PFDs with a view to encouraging persons and organisations to make changes to try to prevent future deaths.

So how can such learning be timely, beneficial and improve the quality of care if there are many inquests taking over 12 months to be heard?

In addition, if steps have already been taken by an interested party then no PFD report is made and the opportunity to share lessons more widely is lost.

Whilst any person responding to a PFD report has to include in their response a timetable for the action proposed to be taken, there is no one who has a responsibility to check that this has subsequently been done.

The Courts and Tribunals Judiciary website – www.judiciary.uk/subject /prevention-of-future-deaths – contains 380 pages of PFD reports going back to 2013. These can be searched by category, e.g. mental health deaths or care home health-related deaths, but what themes are pulled from these/does anyone really study them and, importantly, share the learning nationally? The government are currently working with the Chief Coroner to consider appropriate resources to improve the accessibility of these further.

What Is an Inquest?

The office of the Coroner is an ancient one (Jervis 2019). No one is quite sure of its origins, but there is some evidence of its existing even before 1194! Back then their role was to look after cases in which the Crown was interested and to have regard to the financial interests of the King.

Fast forwarding to 2021, it is the Coroners and Justice Act 2009 which sets out the statutory duties in respect of what Coroners do and how they do it.

The duty to investigate a death arises only where the Coroner has reason to suspect the deceased died a violent or unnatural death, the cause of death is unknown or the deceased died in custody or otherwise in state detention (see s1 Coroners and Justice Act 2009). A Coroner who comes under a duty to inquire must as soon as practicably conduct an investigation which may or may not lead to a court hearing. It is that part of the investigation comprising the court hearing that is known as the inquest.

Of note is that a Coroner's investigation and inquest is a rare example of inquisitorial rather than adversarial or accusatorial proceedings. However, those who have given evidence at an inquest may be forgiven for thinking otherwise.

Lord Lane C.J. (cited in R v South London Coroner, 1982) summarised an inquest as follows:

> an inquest is not a method of apportioning guilt … there are no parties … there is no prosecution, there is no defence, there is no trial…. (1982)

Jamieson (cited in R v North Humberside Coroner, 1995) is a key case in inquest case law. There the court said:

> An inquest is a fact finding inquiry to establish reliable answers to four important but limited factual questions. The first of these relates to the identity of the deceased, the second to the place of his death, the third to the time of death…. The fourth question, and that to which evidence and inquiry are often and most closely directed, relates to how the deceased came by his death ….
>
> It is not the function of a Coroner or his jury to determine, or appear to determine, any question of criminal or civil liability to apportion guilt or attribute blame.

Courts (R v Birmingham Coroner, Ex p Benton (1997)) have also observed that:

> It is of critical importance to recognise the true purpose of an inquest. Sadly the public's perception of such purpose does not always match the reality and those caught up in the process expect much more than it can, or is permitted to, deliver thereby adding to their distress.

Scope of an Inquest

Readers may often hear reference to Article 2 of the European Convention on Human Rights in the context of inquests. This is the Article, incorporated into English law by the Human Rights Act, often known as 'the Right to Life'. It imposes duties on the state to protect life and, where there is an arguable breach of the duty, to carry out an independent investigation. An inquest can form that independent investigation.

An inquest will engage Article 2 where evidence shows an arguable case that the state or its agents committed a breach of a substantive Article 2 duty in relation to the death under investigation. In medical cases, there is room for legal argument – here there must be more than mere error or negligence, the dysfunction must be systemic, there must be a link between the dysfunction and the harm, and the dysfunction must have resulted from a failure of the state to meet its obligation to provide an effectively functioning regulatory framework.

It is not always engaged by the death of a person in the care of the state. A state's enhanced duty to initiate an investigation only arises in medical cases in limited circumstances. Allegations of individual negligence are not to be *dressed up* as systemic failings. There may be an exceptional line of cases that *went beyond a mere error or medical negligence* which concern circumstances where the medical staff, in breach of their professional obligations, failed to provide emergency medical treatment, despite being fully aware that a person's life would be put at risk if that treatment was not given (see Parkinson v HM Senior Coroner for Kent, 2018).

A death by natural causes would not engage Article 2 in the absence of any reason to believe that the state had failed to protect the life of the individual in question – such as failure to provide timely and appropriate medical care to a prisoner obviously in need of it (see Maguire v HM Senior Coroner for Blackpool, 2019).

A Coroner has a duty to ensure that facts are fully, fairly and fearlessly investigated.

The scope of an inquest is a matter for a Coroner's discretion. Issues can be divided into three categories – those which a Coroner must investigate, those which a Coroner has a discretion to investigate and those which the Coroner is not permitted to investigate (see Speck v HM Coroner for District of York & Ors [2016] 4 W.L.R.).

An Article 2 inquest cannot be approached as the ultimate public inquiry. A Coroner in an Article 2 inquest is only obliged to investigate the issues which are, or at least appear arguably to be, central to the cause of death. In particular, in this case of R (Wiggins) v HM Assistant Coroner for Nottinghamshire (2015), the judge said that it would be *wrong in principle* to go into *issues of policy and resources with which an inquest should not be concerned.*

What about previous deaths? Are the circumstances, or facts, of previous deaths capable of being within the proper scope of the Coroner's investigation and, if so, to what extent?

Although in some cases it will be perfectly proper for the Coroner's investigation to include obtaining some high-level details of previous deaths, the basis for doing so must be clear and the relevance to the scope identified. The Gosport Independent Panel report (2018) stated that

> the decision not to hold a public inquiry into the deaths at the hospital was a missed opportunity. As a result the inquests into the deaths at the hospital were not able to consider in sufficient detail matters relating to the management and history of events at the hospital dating back to 1991.

Inquests Turned on Their Heads

On 13 November 2020, the UK Supreme Court handed down judgment in the case of Maughan. This decision sent shock waves through the legal profession as it means that now all forms of conclusion in a Coroner's court (including suicide and unlawful killing) are to be on the balance of probabilities (instead of on the criminal standard of beyond all reasonable doubt).

Unlawful killing can now be recorded where all of the elements of the offences of murder, manslaughter (including corporate manslaughter) or infanticide are 'probably' made out when previously the court had to be 'sure'.

Lady Arden decided that:

■ There was no cogent reason for not applying the principle that in 'civil proceedings' the civil standard should apply;
■ Applying the criminal standard may lead to suicides being under-recorded and lessons not being learnt;
■ A revised standard of proof is more in-keeping with changing societal expectations and the changing role of inquests; and
■ The change brings us into line with other commonwealth jurisdictions.

This wholesale change in the law will have a significant impact on inquests in the health and social care sector – an area where, often because of the vulnerability of those being cared for, acts or omissions will often be a contributory factor in the death. Where advocates for the family would often argue that the particular elements of a rider of 'neglect' were made out on the facts – they will now be inviting the Coroner or jury to evaluate the scale of any failings against the criminal tests. Applying the civil standard rather than the criminal standard in this way will elevate the stakes at many of these inquests.

Commentators (see Crown Office Chambers, 2020, and Mills and Reeve on the inquest landscape, 2021) have expressed a huge degree of concern and consider it likely that interested persons faced with the potential conclusion of unlawful killing will enter into a more legal argument than they would have done before Maughan over topics such as disclosure, witnesses, scope, the application of Article 2 and whether a jury is required with a view to preventing from the outset a conclusion of unlawful killing being left to a jury or a Coroner. That will then inevitably lengthen and complicate inquests cutting into the already relatively sparse resources of the Coroner's courts. Concern has been expressed that many more inquests will have to consider evidence relating to the elements of gross negligence or corporate manslaughter.

If we take a case in which the jury is not sure that an act is so grossly negligent so as to amount to a crime, but considers it is more likely than not that it does: in a criminal trial, a not guilty verdict would be returned. In the Coroner's court, a conclusion of unlawful killing will be returned. Not only because the standard of proof overall has been lowered but, in this example, because now the goalposts on one of the elements have moved such that the element of the offence itself starts to change.

The quotes from the cases of Jamieson and Thompson (referred to above) date back to 1982 and 1995 may well need to be revisited now.

As it is now open to a Coroner's court to publicly conclude that the deceased was 'probably' unlawfully killed, it is now stretching credulity for a lawyer to tell a client that an inquest is purely a fact-finding inquiry.

On 13 January 2021 the new Chief Coroner set out his thinking on the case. His take is a little different. His Honour Judge Teague QC explained that this change must be viewed in its wider context – with fewer than 166 conclusions of unlawful killing made by Coroners or juries in inquests out of a total number of 31,284 inquests conclusions (or approximately 0.5%) in 2019.

He stated that while the decision in Maughan will probably have 'some continuing impact on the figures, the issue of unlawful killing is likely to feature in relatively few cases'. And in those cases where it does arise, the Chief Coroner would expect Coroners to take 'a well-reasoned and fact-specific approach when faced with submissions and/or decisions as to the conclusions that are open to consideration'. The Law Sheet on Unlawful Killing has since been updated to reflect Maughan.

However, where a conclusion of unlawful killing is one that on the facts is open to the Coroner or the jury, he states that the Coroner will then need to direct himself (or the jury) as to what elements need to be established for the offence(s) that may be in play and then to apply the civil standard to the facts as they relate to each element of the offence.

The Chief Coroner makes plain in his Law Sheet that the case of Maughan serves to *emphasise* that an inquest is a fact-finding exercise and not a method of *apportioning guilt*. He makes the point that where unlawful killing may be an issue, it will be important for the Coroner to explain the distinction between criminal proceedings and inquests. Further that at any inquest where a Coroner or Coroner's jury comes to a conclusion of unlawful killing, that finding has no bearing on criminal proceedings, which are subject to a 'materially higher' standard of proof – as well as entirely different procedural rules.

Further consideration will now also need to be given to how this fits with the 2018 report from Professor Sir Norman Williams which made recommendations to support a more just and learning culture in the healthcare system. It was set up to look at the wider patient safety impact of concerns among healthcare professionals that simple errors could result in prosecution for gross negligence manslaughter, even if they happen in the context of broader organisation and system failings. It covered:

■ The process for investigating gross negligence manslaughter;
■ Reflective practice of healthcare professionals;
■ The regulation of healthcare professionals.

It is worth quoting directly from his covering letter to Jeremy Hunt:

> Those of us who have never experienced the unexpected death of a family member or friend receiving healthcare cannot fully appreciate the enormous sense of loss and grief that will be inevitable in such circumstances.

What families and loved ones want in such circumstances is transparency, a thorough investigation, an explanation of what went wrong and reassurance that measures are put in place to prevent similar tragedies. If this does not happen and they are ignored or worse provided with explanations that are inaccurate in some way, then trust will be lost and concerns will remain.

It also has to be appreciated, however, that healthcare professionals go to work to alleviate suffering not to add to it. They work in complex, high-risk environments, invariably as part of a team, and when things go wrong it is rarely the result of one individual's error.

When a patient dies due to one or more errors, it has a profound effect on that healthcare professional and the entire team, both psychologically and in terms of their confidence. Such effects can then be compounded by an investigation which may seek to blame, rather than to understand the factors that have led to the tragedy so that lessons can be learnt to prevent future incidents. At all stages of any investigation the stress levels for those involved, including the professionals, can be overwhelming. For the healthcare professionals a sense of fear pervades and patient safety is jeopardised as they become cautious about being open and transparent, impeding the opportunity for lessons to be learnt.

His panel heard widespread fears from healthcare professionals and representative groups that personal reflection where things have gone wrong, and in particular written reflection, might be used as evidence against them in criminal or regulatory proceedings, particularly following the case of Dr Hadiza Bawa-Garba.

The case of Maughan, with a lower threshold relating to unlawful killing, is likely to further concern healthcare professionals.

Funding for Families

Funding for legal representation for families is an issue that has been controversial. In February 2019, the Ministry of Justice published a review on this subject. It concluded that they would not be introducing non-means tested legal aid for inquests where the state is represented. They noted that the financial implications of this would result in additional spending of between £30 million and £70 million.

The Chief Coroner has since asked that the Lord Chancellor gives consideration to amending current guidance so as to provide exceptional funding for legal representation for the family where the state has agreed to provide separate representation for one or more interested persons.

In the government's response to the House of Commons Justice Committee report on the Coroner Service, this subject was also covered. On 10 September 2021, the government stated that they remain of the view that the inquest process is intended to be inquisitorial and that legal representation should not be necessary at all inquests. However, they went on to say that they will be considering their approach to legal aid for inquests as part of its response to Bishop James Jones' report of his review of the Hillsborough families' experiences and will respond to his recommendations on legal aid then. In the meantime, they did confirm that they would be taking forward legislation to remove the means test for Exceptional Case Funding in relation to legal representation at inquests.

The case of Maughan may well mean that this current 'funding disparity' is widened if organisations who feel that the stakes have been raised are said to be 'lawyering up' (Simon Antrobus QC).

What Next?

The inquest process can be used to develop a potential civil litigation case. It is part of the overall process of establishing the existence of evidence that can be used to substantiate a claim. In some cases, however, by the time the inquest is heard such a claim is already advanced or indeed settled.

An inquest conclusion or a PFD report can also lead to a civil clinical negligence claim. A neglect finding recorded as part of a Coroner's conclusion is particularly one that might lead to a claim. However, neglect is narrower in meaning than the duty of care in negligence. It is limited in the medical context to cases where there is a gross failure to provide basic medical attention where the deceased was in a dependent position because of youth, age, illness or incarceration. There must be a clear and direct causal connection between the conduct described as neglect and the cause of death (Jamieson again).

Whether to admit liability for a civil wrong (for example, negligence) is often considered prior to an inquest by potential defendants to a civil claim.

However, in terms of both risk management and the duty of candour in an ideal world that admission (if warranted) should be being made long before an inquest.

NHS Resolution is an arm's-length body of the Department of Health and Social Care. They provide expertise to the NHS on resolving concerns and disputes fairly, sharing learning for improvement and preserving resources for patient care. Their 2020–21 Annual Report shows that they are carrying a provision of £82.8 billion in respect of claims against secondary care. The cost of harm falling under their Clinical Negligence Scheme for Trusts in 20/21 alone was £7.9 billion. These are eye-watering sums which can only emphasise the importance of early settlement and learning from incidents.

Other litigation could be criminal or there might be referrals to professional regulators, e.g. General Medical Council or Nursing and Midwifery Council.

Criminal proceedings could be in respect of homicide or perjury (and again further heightened by the case of Maughan). Whilst not common it was always something that was possible. Readers will be familiar with the prosecution of David Duckenfield, the former South Yorkshire Police Chief Superintendent and Hillsborough match commander.

Witnesses could seek to invoke the privilege against self-incrimination at an inquest, but that does nothing for the reputation of the organisation as a whole.

Families are put in the front and at the centre of inquests, but the knock-on effect of this can be that other interested persons and their witnesses may fail to attract the same degree of sympathy even though the consequences may be far-reaching.

Finally, old complaints to regulators can be reinvigorated or new evidence heard at the inquest can lead to new referrals to professional bodies.

Question?

So on the one hand we know from the Coroners Act 2009 that an inquest is focused on the Who, When, Where and How and that the scope is limited.

On the other hand we know that the standard for returning a conclusion of unlawful killing has just been changed to on the balance of probabilities so the question is – does an inquest really fit with restorative practice and creating a sustainable, just, restorative just culture?

Confidence in the System?

Reports have been published over the years that are critical of the investigations into serious incidents that have occurred in healthcare settings.

One of the most recent of these is The Report of the Elizabeth Dixon Investigation by Dr Bill Kirkup. Whilst it relates to events almost 20 years ago, it was only published in November 2020.

Dr Kirkup expresses concern that the same attitudes and behaviours (which included concealment of key facts about her death from the outset) as were evident then may still be found in places today. His commentary on the case includes the following striking points:

■ It is fundamentally unjust that the only person held formally responsible for the death of Elizabeth has been the most junior involved who also happened to be female and of an ethnic minority. Whilst she should have recognised her own inability to provide safe care there is also no doubt that she was placed in that position through a series of failures that involved people who knew that she was not qualified as a children's nurse and had no experience of infant tracheostomy care, as well as by those who commissioned the care from an organisation incapable of providing it safely.

■ Elizabeth's death should have been treated as unexplained; instead, it was treated as expected. A blocked tracheostomy tube and morphine overdose were unexplored and inadequately investigated from the outset, by the coronial service, the health authority and the private healthcare provider. This may have appeared at first to be a startling lack of curiosity, but it clearly progressed to the point that facts were wilfully ignored and alternatives fabricated. That this resulted in a cover-up of significant facts that stood for so long is greatly disturbing.

■ This is a recurring feature of health services complaints; instead of serving as a valuable warning of problems they are seen as something to be fended off with limited, closed and defensive responses, which is deeply unsatisfactory for all concerned.

■ Professional regulatory and criminal systems are based on the assumption of discrete, single events involving individual practice and are very unsuited to examining complex, multiple failures spanning different organisations.

■ Clinical error, openly disclosed, investigated and learned from, should not result in blame or censure; equally conscious choices to cover up or to be dishonest should not be tolerated.

He has recommended, amongst other things, that:

■ Professional regulatory and criminal justice systems should contain an inbuilt stop mechanism to be activated when an investigation reveals evidence of systematic or organisational failures and which will trigger an appropriate investigation into those wider systemic failures;
■ Implementation of a better system of responding to complaints must be done in such a way as to ensure the integration of complaints into NHS clinical governance as a valuable source of information on safety, effectiveness and patient experience.

Dr Kirkup calls for the Public Authority (Accountability) Bill, drawn up in 2017 following the aftermath of Hillsborough, to be re-examined. It was drafted to do many things including setting a requirement on public institutions, public servants and others to act in the public interest with candour and frankness, to assist courts, official inquiries and investigations, to enable victims to enforce such duties and to create offences for breach of certain duties. It is not currently law.

Dr Kirkup's report related to events in 2001. We do hope that things have moved on from then in healthcare settings and indeed some of the points we raise below demonstrate that.

Early Resolution of Claims

As we mentioned above, an important feature to have in mind around inquests is the timescale. In many cases, the inquest takes place many months, sometimes many years, after the death. There will have been a local investigation by the healthcare provider in most cases. The family should have been engaged in that investigation and know the outcome. The outcome may have settled in the minds of the family that real lessons have been learned, to ensure the same thing does not happen again, or at least steps to mitigate against such events happening have been introduced. This is not always the case. The family position may be disengaged from the efforts of the organisation trying to restore confidence and satisfy a family concern. The family position may be entrenched, sometimes based on erroneous information or beliefs and difficult to recover. Such difficulties are made worse by delays in completing a local investigation or a lack of openness. A lack of openness can arise from the difficulty of managing the interests of various stakeholders.

In our experience, there are many perspectives in play. The staff involved may be unsure about their future, especially so if the death has led to complaints. As Mersey Care's Amanda Oates highlights in Chapter 9, there can be different perceptions of accountability – Is that holding people to account or that people can tell their account of what happened, from their perspectives? She notes that the former creates fear, but the latter enables psychological safety.

The interests of the family and their lawyers may develop depending on how a complaint is dealt with. Typically a Coroner will identify all these different interests from long experience of dealing with them, but the ability of any Coroner to play an effective part in a restorative process is limited by the opportunity they have to engage. Delays in holding an inquest often impact further on such engagement.

Taking a unilateral approach to 'restoration', and starting with the clinical staff, the staff are pitched into an environment where they are under scrutiny. That scrutiny comes from the employer – What can they say or do? What would they like to say and do? Will they be blamed or disciplined? Are they free to say what they think? Do they have all the information they need to process what actually happened? As you will have read in this present volume HR processes and preventing similar incidents from happening again are very much interlinked. Everyone's focus must be on creating a 'patient safety dividend', as Amanda calls it. Staff need to feel safe in raising patient safety concerns, but it is understandable that they worry about the personal consequences of the blame too. It is powerful to read in the next chapter about the trust's staff side representative witnessing marriage breakdowns and physical and mental health of staff and their families suffering.

Having a no-blame (or restorative) culture is important in engaging the staff and ensuring that investigations happen quickly. Regardless of what may have gone wrong (and the staff will have views about that) getting all relevant information out in the open so that it can be discussed and considered is essential. That process will likely unearth problems and failures, as well as examples of good practice. The restorative process is about being open about all of that and giving staff the confidence to be open and forthcoming.

The staff may be concerned about opening themselves to criticism, but a no-blame culture should ensure they have the confidence to be open, knowing that whatever else happens they will be supported. This present volume highlights the Advisory, Conciliation and Arbitration Service (ACAS) statutory code of practice on disciplinary and grievances at work as well as their guidance on conducting workplace investigations.

By the time an inquest takes place, being able to refer the Coroner back to the outcome of the local investigation that has been shared with the family, and the learning that has developed and improved future care, is a really positive event. Even if a claim has emerged, it may already have been resolved, or admissions and apologies made so that the family know they are not in conflict with the healthcare provider. Also if the degree of change and restoration is such that the Coroner knows the risk of such events has been mitigated, the idea of the Coroner issuing a PFD report evaporates.

This approach to early active engagement is key to managing expectations and resolving conflict. In the absence of engagement, the staff may feel vulnerable and decline to cooperate and the family, left in the dark, may turn to lawyers to consider a legal claim – the 'golden moment' to grasp the opportunity for restoration may be lost.

All too often legal claims are planned very soon after an event that has resulted in death where there may be a reasonably clear issue that could amount to a breach of duty or negligence. The healthcare provider may have responded in accordance with the statutory duty of candour and identified the risk of such a claim but then be unsure how to manage that risk and so do nothing about meeting or mitigating a potential claim. Or they may hope that when it emerges it is less of a problem than might be expected? In our experience there is only one way to manage a potential legal claim and that is to grab it with both hands and deal with it proactively.

Learning from Incidents

Learning from incidents is key. It is important that it is done quickly and that the learning is shared within a team, within an organisation and nationally.

Risk identification, risk ownership and risk management are the building blocks needed. If the quality of incident review processes can be improved then this should lead to reduced incidents, safer care and financial savings, a triple whammy for patients, staff and organisations.

From our work with clients however we have often seen lengthy delays between the date of an incident, the date of a threatened claim and the date of a settlement. Delays in conducting serious incident investigations or poor quality investigations mean opportunities for learning are delayed if not lost altogether.

With higher quality incident reporting and this being seen as a learning opportunity and not a chore, these incidents could be seized upon. The connectivity and learning before such incidents become claims that can go a long way to developing a system of evidence-based risk management.

Statutory and Professional Duty of Candour

The statutory duty of candour came into force in 2015 (following the recommendations of the Mid Staffs Inquiry).

The intention of the Regulation is to ensure that providers are open and transparent, with people who use services and other 'relevant persons' (people acting lawfully on behalf of patients) in general in relation to care and treatment.

Openness means enabling concerns and complaints to be raised freely without fear and questions asked to be answered.

Transparency means allowing information about the truth about performance and outcomes to be shared with staff, patients, the public and regulators.

Candour means any patient harmed by the provision of a healthcare service is informed of the fact and an appropriate remedy offered, regardless of whether a complaint has been made or a question asked about it.

This general duty applies at all times.

In addition, as soon as reasonably practicable after becoming aware that a notifiable safety incident has occurred, a registered person must notify the relevant person that the incident has occurred.

For Health Sector bodies a notifiable safety incident is:

> "any unintended or unexpected incident that occurred in respect of a service user during the provision of regulated activity that, in the reasonable opinion of a healthcare professional, could result in, or appears to have resulted in death, severe harm, moderate harm or prolonged psychological harm."

When a notifiable safety incident has occurred, the relevant person must be informed as soon as reasonably practicable after the incident has been identified. The notification must be given in person, by one or more representatives of the registered person. They must provide an account which, to the best of their knowledge is true, of all the facts they know about the incident. They need to explain what further enquiries they will undertake. They must apologise. They must follow up the conversation in writing. In addition, the outcomes of further enquiries must also be provided in writing in due course. All reasonable support must be provided to help overcome the physical, psychological and emotional impact of the incident.

This is a much better opportunity for risk identification, ownership, management, learning and improving the quality of care in a speedy way and then sharing that with patients and families. And if that was not enough motivation, it is also a criminal offence not to notify a service user of a notifiable safety incident or fail to meet the requirements for such a notification.

However, the first prosecution only took place in 2020 – nearly six years after the Regulations came into force.

Regulation 20 just applies to organisations, but there is also a professional duty of candour.

Both of these should lead to speedy identification of issues, of opportunities for learning, of opportunities to communication with families to either settle claims early or avoid claims arising (as we are often told that families only bring claims because they could not get an answer/want to prevent the same thing happening to others).

The House of Commons Justice Committee report referred to above considered that health and social care bodies failed to fulfil their duty of candour to bereaved people during Coroners' investigations and inquests and recommended the Coroners' Rules be amended to make clear that this extends to the Coroner Service. The government again referenced Bishop James' report and confirmed that relevant departments and organisations are working together to carefully consider this point of learning.

NHS England and NHS Improvement Patient Safety Incident Response Framework – A New Dawn?

This is a new Framework for incident reporting. There is a phased approach to implementing it. At present several early adopter systems of healthcare providers and commissioners are testing it with a view publication of a final version in Spring 2022 and full implementation by Autumn 2022 (although that could change due to COVID-19 pressures). It would then replace the old 2015 Serious Incident Framework.

The foreword makes clear that identifying incidents, recognising the needs of those affected, examining what happened to understand the causes and responding with action to mitigate risks remain essential to improving the safety of healthcare. It heralds a new approach to incident management which facilitates inquisitive examination in the spirit of reflection and learning rather than as part of a framework of accountability.

It moves towards a proactive approach to learning from incidents and the quality of investigations is the priority. The aim is that the investigation time frame will be three months on average. There is a move towards a proactive approach to learning from patient safety incidents.

In terms of its purpose, the Framework is to support system learning and continuous improvement in patient safety rather than address individual concerns or performance management issues. It goes on to emphasise that it insulates against other remits/scope creep that frustrate safety improvement, for example, determining the cause of death (requiring coronial investigation).

Not all incidents will be selected. The strategic, risk-based approach will be to select incidents based on the opportunity for learning.

In its introduction it makes clear that patient safety incidents will be reviewed to understand the circumstances that led to it for the purpose of system learning and improvement and not to determine the cause of death or to hold any individual or organisation to account (including judgements on avoidability, preventability, liability etc.). The introduction states that separate processes must be followed when there are legitimate concerns about individual and/or organisational accountability.

In terms of preparing to respond to a patient safety incident, it requires the behaviours of an effective and compassionate patient safety reporting, learning and improvement system to reflect three main principles – openness and transparency, a just culture and continuous learning and improvement.

The Framework has a specific section on Coroners which states that organisations should provide Coroners with any requested documents, such as the patient safety incident investigations (PSII reports) or relevant supporting materials where these exist. Further, if they become aware that a Coroner is holding an inquest into someone's death they should advise the Coroner of the existence of any relevant documents they hold, even if these are not specifically requested. Having said that it recommends that organisations should request that the Coroner continues to consider the potential impact of any shared investigative supporting materials entering the public domain.

How will this be affected by the Supreme Court decision in Maughan? If staff face the prospect of a conclusion of unlawful killing will they be as open with an internal trust investigation that will end up with the Coroner?

HSIB to HSSIB (Lots of Acronyms)

The Healthcare Safety Investigation Branch's (HSIB's) purpose is to improve patient safety through effective and independent investigations that don't apportion blame or liability.

At the Westminster Health Forum Patient Safety Conference on 21 October 2020, they explained that they endeavour to look at the system and not at the person asking what can the system do to protect the environment? They seek to do what they can to make sure people feel they can be as candid as possible. They are not a regulator or an enforcement body.

They aim to see safety investigations as a whole professional pathway.

Their three priorities are – Firstly, a safety management system for the NHS as a whole (not just individual trusts) with better connections and coordinations between regulators. Secondly, Just Culture with a focus on systems. However, they experience problems when Coroners have insisted they provide transcripts or notes of interviews with staff. Finally, the involvement of patients, families and service users in all stages of investigation and implementation of recommendations.

The draft Health Service Safety Investigations Bill in 2019 was drafted to place HSIB on an independent statutory footing. It also provided for the creation of a *safe space* investigation approach (at a local level in trusts but also for HSIB) to ensure that information provided as part of an investigation will only be disclosed in certain limited circumstances or by court order.

This led to a lot of discussions, critique and comment. The charity Action against Medical Accidents (AvMA) campaigned against the proposals, calling them 'misguided and very dangerous' and in direct contradiction to the duty of candour. Whilst the government dropped plans to allow the 'safe space' in local investigations, it is to remain for investigations carried out by HSIB.

The Bill was delayed by Brexit and COVID-19, but, in February 2021, the long-awaited White Paper set out legislative proposals on a range of health and care topics including this. The thinking is set out in its 'additional proposals' relating to safety and quality. The government has now published the Health and Care Bill. The Health Services Safety

Investigations Body (HSSIB) will be established as an Executive Non-Departmental Public Body with powers to investigate the most serious patient safety risks to support system learning. The White Paper stated that independence as a concept is fundamentally important to HSSIB as it will be a crucial way of ensuring that patients, families and staff have trust in its processes and judgements.

The Bill, as currently drafted, sets out that HSSIB has the function of investigating incidents that occur in England and which have or may have implications for the safety of patients. It states that the purpose of the investigations is to identify risks to the safety of patients and address those risks by facilitating the improvement of systems and practices in the provision of NHS services or other healthcare services in England. So the remit has been extended to cover healthcare provided in and by the independent sector. In addition, the Secretary of State may direct HSSIB to carry out an investigation.

Draft reports must be shared with those who could be adversely affected by the report so that they have the opportunity to comment. If those comments are not taken into account, then HSSIB must explain why.

A final report may not include an assessment or determination of blame, civil/criminal liability or whether action needs to be taken by a regulatory body. In addition the final report may not, without their consent, include the name of an individual who has provided information to HSSIB for the purposes of the investigation or who was involved in the incident being investigated.

Reports are not admissible in proceedings to determine civil or criminal liability, before an employment tribunal, before a regulatory body or to determine appeals relating to any of these. However, the High Court can order that such a report is admissible on an application by a person who is a party to the proceedings.

The Bill, as currently drafted, also provides for the protection of material held by HSSIB. Protected material means any information, documentation, equipment or other item held for the purposes of HSSIB's investigatory function and which relates to a qualifying incident. Schedule 14 sets out several exceptions to the prohibition on disclosure. These include the following:

■ Disclosure relating to safety risks: where the Chief Investigator reasonably believes that disclosure is necessary to address a serious and continuing risk to the safety of any patient or to the public.

■ Disclosure by order of the High Court: On application by a person the Court may determine that the interests of justice served by the disclosure outweigh:
  – Any adverse impact on current and future investigations by deterring persons from providing information for the purposes of investigations;
  – Any adverse impact on securing the improvement of the safety of healthcare services.
■ Coroners: A Senior Coroner may require disclosure of the protected material. However, they must not disclose that to anyone else. Should they wish to do so they must apply to the High Court.

The government had previously committed to engaging with the Chief Coroner to understand the impact on Coroners' ability to investigate effectively deaths that may be related to healthcare, if they are unable to access information held in 'safe space' by the new body. How the case of Maughan will have impacted the Chief Coroner's view remains to be seen.

Likewise how will the Parliamentary and Health Service Ombudsman's (PHSO) ability to hold public bodies to account and to effectively investigate healthcare matters be impacted if it were unable to obtain information held by the new body in 'safe space' without applying for a court order?

It will be interesting to see how the Bill progresses through Parliament.

Conclusion

We have covered a lot of ground in this chapter moving from the 12th Century to the 21st Century and plans covering beyond.

The law and policy relating to deaths in a healthcare setting are ever changing and evolving.

The death of a patient is a tragedy for all concerned. It can set off a chain of events which can include a serious incident investigation, an inquest, complaints, civil claims, criminal prosecutions, regulatory action and, of course, distress to all of those involved.

To balance justice, accountability and learning is a big ask.

We may have been on the verge of achieving that balancing act but then came the case of Maughan in November 2020.

References

Association for Victims of Medical Accidents (AvMA) – various briefings on Safe Space

Chief Coroner's Combined Annual Report 2018 to 2019. https://www.gov.uk/government/publications/chief-coroners-combined-annual-report-2018-to-2019-and-2019-to-2020

Chief Coroner's Law Sheet (2021). www.serjeantsinn.com/wp-content/uploads/2021/01/Chief-Coroner-Law-Sheet-6-Maughan-13.01.21.pdf

Chief Coroner's Law Sheet (Sept 2021). www.judiciary.uk/wp-content/uploads/2021/09/Law-Sheet-1-1-September-2021-Unlawful-Killing.pdf

Chief Coroner's Revised Guidance No 5 – Reports to Prevent Future Deaths (November 2020).

Coroners and Justice Act 2009. https://www.legislation.gov.uk/ukpga/2009/25/contents

Courts and Tribunals Judiciary Prevention of Future Deaths. See Judiciary website for all such reports at https://www.judiciary.uk/subject/prevention-of-future-deaths/

Crown Office Chambers briefing – Innocent Until Proven Guilty November 2020.

Healthcare Safety Investigation Branch – Purpose and Values. cited on their website https://www.hsib.org.uk/who-we-are/our-purpose-and-values/

Health and Care Bill – Introduced in the House of Commons on 6 July 2021. The Bill can be read in full on the UK Parliament website at https://bills.parliament.uk/bills/3022

House of Commons Justice Committee. The Coroner Service: Government Response to the Committee's First report. 10 September 2021.

Integration and Innovation: Working Together to Improve Health and Social Care for All. February 2021.

Jervis On Coroners, 14th Edition, edited by Paul Matthews, Sweet and Maxwell, 2019.

Maguire v HM Senior Coroner for Blackpool [2019] EWHC 1232 (Admin).

Ministry of Justice Review of Legal Aid for Inquests – February 2019

NHS England – Patient Safety Incident Response Framework.

NHS England – Serious Incident Framework. See https://www.england.nhs.uk/patient-safety/incident-response-framework/

NHS Resolution Annual Report 2019/20. https://resolution.nhs.uk/2020/07/16/nhs-resolutions-annual-report-and-accounts-2019-20/

Nursing and Midwifery Council: Professional Duty of Candour. see the NMC website statement at https://www.nmc.org.uk/standards/guidance/the-professional-duty-of-candour/

Parkinson v HM Senior Coroner for Kent [2018] EWHC 1501 (Admin)

R (on the Application of Maughan) (Appellant) v Her Majesty's Senior Coroner for Oxfordshire (Respondent) [2020] UKSC 46

R v South London Coroner Ex p Thompson (1982)

R v North Humberside Coroner Ex p Jamieson [1995] 1 Q.B. 1,23-24 –

R v Birmingham Coroner, Ex p Benton (1997) 162 J.P. 807 –
R (Wiggins) v HM Assistant Coroner for Nottinghamshire [2015] EWHA 2841
    (Admin)
Regulation 20 Health and Social Care 2008 (Regulated Activities) Regulations 2014.
    https://www.legislation.gov.uk/ukdsi/2014/9780111117613
Speck v HM Coroner for District of York & Ors [2016] 4 W.L.R
The Coroners (Investigations) Regulations 2013. https://www.legislation.gov.uk/uksi
    /2013/1629/contents/made
The Gosport Independent Panel Report- June 2018.
The Life and Death of Elizabeth Dixon: A Catalyst for Change – November 2020.
    https://www.gov.uk/government/publications/the-life-and-death-of-elizabeth
    -dixon-a-catalyst-for-change
Williams Review into Gross Negligence Manslaughter in Healthcare – June 2018.
    https://www.gov.uk/government/publications/williams-review-into-gross-negli-
    gence-manslaughter-in-healthcare

Chapter 7

Patient Safety: A Political Perspective

Jeremy Hunt

Contents

Why I focused on patient safety?

When I accepted the role of Health Secretary in September 2012 I was a complete outsider to the world of health. I certainly hadn't heard of patient safety, avoidable harm or a just culture. But making the NHS safer quickly became my main focus in office, and patient safety remains a passion of mine to this day.

This journey had its roots right at the start of my time as Health Secretary. One of the first major issues I had to deal with was the scandal at Mid Staffordshire NHS Foundation Trust. As is now well known, terrible care there led to between 400 and 1,200 unnecessary and often cruel deaths over a four-year period. These issues only came to light because of tireless campaigning by the families of those who had been affected and brave whistleblowers who spoke up during the subsequent inquiries.

In responding to the Francis Inquiry that looked into this I felt the real scandal was not that failures of care happened but that they went unnoticed

DOI: 10.4324/9781003162582-7

for so long. Whilst this had happened under a previous government I wasn't convinced that I would know if similar tragedies were happening during my tenure.

The prevailing attitude within the NHS and the Department at the time was to try and address issues like this behind closed doors so that public confidence in the system wouldn't be undermined. There was also a feeling that some level of harm was just part of the business of healthcare. One of my senior civil servants said to me, 'You have to understand that in healthcare we harm 10% of patients'. When I pushed to understand how many that meant we killed I was shocked by the findings that there were about 150 avoidable deaths every single week, just in England. And yet barely anyone outside of healthcare appreciated this.

It was whilst grappling with this uncomfortable truth and with how to respond to the recommendations of the Francis Inquiry that I first met Scott and Sue Morrish. If institutional scandals were the high-profile catalysts to me taking an interest in patient safety then it was meeting people like them that turned this into a passion. They were the very first parents who came to see me in my office as Health Secretary, just a few months after I had taken up the post, to talk about their son Sam's tragic death. They told me about the countless mistakes that led to Sam's death. Their GP thought the issue was a virus, not sepsis. The phone helplines didn't work well. And as he wasn't immediately screened for sepsis on arrival into hospital, he was not given the antibiotics that could have saved him.

But it was the sadly too common reaction by the hospital to Scott and Sue's questions, many months later, that really stuck with me. They had been told that Sam had suffered from an incredibly rare form of flu with an infection so he could not have been saved. But whilst they were grieving they noticed that descriptions of his condition had been incorrectly recorded. They found out that at key moments they had been speaking to people without medical qualifications. The antibiotics Sam was prescribed weren't given to him for three critical hours. No one had mentioned sepsis.

When they tried to raise these concerns, the shutters came down. No one from the hospital was prepared to meet them. As Scott told me, 'I never wanted anyone to be fired. I wanted them all to stay, improve and learn so that other tragedies could be avoided. But the system doesn't understand that. It only ever saw me as a problem'.

I didn't really appreciate it at first, but this was my first encounter with a group of passionate patient safety campaigners, many of whom had been deeply hurt by the system I was responsible for, who didn't want to apportion blame, but who just wanted those who had made mistakes to acknowledge those errors, to learn from them and ensure they were never repeated again. It was by hearing from families like them that convinced me that Mid Staffs was unlikely to be an isolated problem for the Trust and that more should be done across the NHS to improve patient safety and reduce the amount of avoidable harm people were currently experiencing.

Mental Health

If meeting Scott and Sue taught me about the bureaucratic nightmare that some families face when questioning what happened to their relatives, then meeting Steve Mallen helped me understand how a clear ambition and steely determination can tackle some of these problems.

When I first met him Steve told me the story about his son Edward's tragic suicide. As Steve related earlier in this volume, Edward had a place at Cambridge University, had been head boy at both his primary and secondary schools, was a gifted classical pianist, was a cricketer, had good friends and was voted by his schoolmates the person most likely of all of them to become Prime Minister. By the time he died, Edward had told five different medical professionals that he was actively thinking of taking his own life. Twice he said he would be happy for his parents to be informed and involved in his care. But nobody told his parents a thing.

I had already heard tales of similar bureaucratic issues from families who had problems with the provision of physical health services – the simple mistakes that could have been avoided. The communication problems within different parts of the system meant things were missed. All of which ultimately led to tragedy. It became clear to me that patient safety issues were commons across both mental and physical health services.

But Steve Mallen, Joe Rafferty and the rest of the Zero Suicide Alliance also taught me that even for an issue as complicated as suicide we must aim high if we are to succeed in reducing avoidable harm. In trying to ease Steve's pain, many suggested that Edward's death had been a 'terrible accident' which nobody could have averted. Again this was similar to those who had told Sue and Scott that Sam's death had been 'one of those things'. But it was clear to Steve that Edward's death could have been prevented and in fact this was later to be proved by an independent investigation and the Coroner's report. That key belief is at the heart of the Alliance and gives us a crucial insight into how to tackle avoidable harm across the board.

Because in contrast to those who had told me that some level of avoidable harm was inevitable I had now met an organisation dedicated to eliminating all such harm – and in one of the most sensitive and difficult areas of mental health. Their quest for zero suicides made me realise the wisdom of Aristotle's saying that the problem is not aiming too high and missing a goal – but aiming too low and hitting it. So whilst not every suicide can necessarily be prevented, by challenging medical orthodoxy and having this ambition Joe and his team ensure we have the best chance at reducing harm and really opened my eyes to what can be done on patient safety across all types of healthcare.

Transparency Is Key but Not Enough on Its Own

Before I had really understood the importance of 'zero' as an ambition I decided to do something about one of the key drivers of unsafe care – the lack of transparency that seemed to grip the system when something went wrong. We had seen this at Mid Staffs where poor care went unchallenged for four years. But among the most persuasive people I've met on the need to create a just culture is the campaigner James Titcombe.

As recounted in this book, James tragically lost his son Joshua after a series of failures at Morecambe Bay NHS Trust. But once again it wasn't hearing about the poor care, shocking as it was, that really upset me. It was the extraordinary battle he had to go through to find out the truth about what happened to his son. It lasted six years, involved the police, the courts, the senior leadership of the NHS and me as Secretary of State for Health. James thinks he wrote over 400 emails and letters to get to the bottom of what happened. The institutional resistance to simply telling a grieving parent what went wrong with the care of his newborn baby has to be tackled.

Once the scale of this systemic cover-up by the Trust became clear, James approached me as Health Secretary to ask for an independent inquiry into maternity services at the hospital. I agreed to James' request for the inquiry and when its report was eventually published it confirmed the worst fears of many families. It listed a catalogue of failings including dysfunctional management, a board completely unaware and uninterested in what was going on, a working culture that discouraged openness and poor oversight by the wider NHS. Up to 11 baby deaths were assessed as having been preventable. Ultimately James' and Joshua's story was not about rogue staff or a rogue hospital. It was about a rogue system that I, as Health Secretary, sat on top of, one that sometimes did its utmost to stop grieving families from uncovering the truth.

So I was determined to shine a light on the standard of care throughout the service. My main tool to do this was through the introduction of a transparent and independent rating system for hospitals, GP surgeries and care homes – the first healthcare system in the world to do so. Based on the Ofsted system, the Care Quality Commission (CQC) model has worked well to drive up the standards and highlight where we fall short. By the end of my time in office, nearly three million more patients were being treated in good or outstanding hospitals, and NHS leaders were more aware of where improvement was needed the most. I also introduced regulations to ensure that NHS Trusts publish details on the number of avoidable deaths they experienced on a yearly basis.

At first this seemed like enough. You improve transparency and more people would know where poor care was happening. More resources or better management could then be brought in to turn things around. But the longer I remained in office, the more I became convinced that there was a bigger issue at the heart of our failure to really tackle avoidable harm. And that is that medicine is just not as good at learning from mistakes and sharing best practice as it should be. Whilst a lack of transparency allows poor practice to go on for too long and frustrates grieving relatives it is actually the cultural impact on the NHS as a workplace that such an approach instils that does more damage.

If an organisation's first response to challenge is to cover-up and deal with the scandal quietly, then it will never acknowledge that mistakes have been made. And if it doesn't do that then how can staff be expected to learn from these errors and that learning be shared around the system? I had shied away from culture change in my first few years at the department and instead focused on structures and incentives. But after a while I came to realise that whilst these are important they are not enough unless you have culture change too.

Support for Clinicians Is Vital if We Are to Move from a Blame to a Learning Culture

To deliver the required change, it is important to understand what drives the current culture. In both James Titcombe and Scott and Sue Morrish's cases we saw institutional resistance to sharing the truth behind what happened.

Sadly we have seen too many other examples of this in recent years. Issues at East Kent Hospitals, Shrewsbury and Telford and the case of Elizabeth Dixon have all needed independent inquiries to get to the bottom of why poor care occurred. It is important to understand why these things happen rather than just look to blame individuals for making mistakes and then trying to cover them up.

If we take the midwives at Morecambe Bay for instance, no one becomes a midwife to cover-up tragedy. But the culture of that hospital must have been so troubling that professional clinical staff were prepared to cover things up rather than admit mistakes. They must have been concerned for their jobs, their careers and the reputation of their unit and hospital. And I believe it is the current role played by our legal system that creates this fear.

It seems obvious to me that doctors and nurses fear being blamed for a mistake. They fear that they might lose their job, be struck off, be sued or prosecuted; none of which is conducive to being open about how a mistake happened and learning how to avoid it again in the future. This needs to change and clinicians need to be supported not blamed when they are open about what goes wrong. Thankfully things are changing with many great NHS leaders demonstrating that it is possible to create this kind of environment. But I think there are some big structural reforms we can look at to help with the creation of a learning culture.

The heart of the problem is that no compensation is payable unless families are able to prove that a clinician or hospital has been clinically negligent in a way that has caused injury. This is an immensely damaging charge to admit to. So from the outset patients and their relatives are pitted against doctors in an adversarial process where self-preservation rather than learning from mistakes is the top priority. This contrasts starkly with the approaches taken in Sweden and New Zealand where compensation levels are lower, but it is easier to get as you only have to prove that something was avoidable. Sweden in particular has a much safer maternity system as a result.

Such a change would indicate that our main priority after a tragedy was to learn from it and share that learning. There must always be justice and fairness for anyone who suffers because of a medical error – but there also needs to be justice and fairness for other families for whom the same heartache could be avoided. The real crime is not ordinary human error but failing to learn from it and failing to support clinicians to be open enough to undertake that learning.

Chapter 8

Supporting Organisational Health through an OD Approach

Joseph Rafferty, Amanda Oates and Joanne Davidson

Contents

DOI: 10.4324/9781003162582-8

So What Is Organisational Development

In its simplest terms, Organisational Development (OD) recognises the organisation as a human system. Later in this book, we will discuss in detail what OD seeks to deliver. Here we need to know that it exists as a discipline to identify systemic issues and solutions that impact the ability to maximise human potential to the best advantage. At Mersey Care, we describe OD as Organisational Effectiveness (OE). This is because at Mersey Care we expect OD to take a strategic, proactive approach that underpins a culture of prevention, continuous improvement, high performance and transformation, plainly speaking, making it more effective – hence the term OE. Equally and critically, where this desired culture does not exist, OE is often associated with providing remedial intervention and restorative approaches to support mitigation of manifesting risk.

As the Chief Executive described in Chapter 2, this terminology change was part of the trust's commitment to openness in its development. Semantics are important, and we wanted absolute clarity of intent. Our evidence and our ambition led us to be clear that we had to improve organisational effectiveness and our organisational health.

In healthcare, the work of Organisational Effectiveness practitioners may be confused with that of their colleagues in Human Resources, Learning and Development or Quality Improvement. All are essential to the delivery of a high-quality People Strategy for any organisation. And whilst an OE practitioner's toolkit draws from these other professions it has been important to recognise OE as distinct in their own field and their work as a key dependency for organisational health.

How Does This Fit with our Restorative Just and Learning Culture Progress?

Mersey Care's aspiration for Perfect Care articulated clear and audacious goals for clinical practice and an ambition to become both a provider and an employer of choice. The transformation required was significant. Any organisational effectiveness plan had to be designed to recognise that this level of transformation cannot be achieved through a technical solution alone. This type of change needed to be socially constructed. Mersey Care's strategy needed to recognise the organisation as a human system which was emotional, unpredictable and rich with invaluable untapped knowledge, skills and expertise potential.

As the organisation began this change, we recognised that we needed to develop a different relationship with our workforce. We needed to re-establish trust. We needed to give full attention to the psychological contract and the things that were impacting people's ability to do their best work.

We recognised the importance of the alignment of personal values and beliefs to those of the organisation if we were to harness both the emotional and intrinsic engagement that draws people to a career in care. For some of our workforce, we knew that we would need to create a shift from apathy, learned helplessness and a fixed mindset, to one of belief, ambition and commitment to continuous learning and improvement. This growth mindset is evidenced by Professor Carol Dweck's research at Stanford University (Dweck, 2006). We needed to facilitate the alignment and mindset shift at both individual and corporate levels to ensure the effective balance between engagement, psychological safety and accountability.

We were well aware that this would require a very different style of leadership in the trust. A new approach required new skills, behaviours and enhanced levels of emotional intelligence. We needed collective, compassionate leadership with the ability to inspire and translate our vision and to effectively re-engage and develop safe, high-performing teams.

The academic rigour of a number of experts in the field provided good grounding. Several of them, and indeed the experiences of a number of people with lived experience, provided us with a robust approach to teamwork that, as leaders, we wanted the organisation to take. Their work and their testimony is rightly part of our 'journey' and recorded in this volume.

Listening, Engaging and Taking Collective Action

In 2014, organisational effectiveness was new to Mersey Care. In fact, it rested with one dedicated practitioner. The Board recognised the need to invest in the development of the resource to support the delivery of a co-produced, evidence-based plan and systems approach. We recognised it was a high-level skill set, but one that would have a significant and positive impact on our organisational health. Once services began to see the benefits of the approach, they were keen to fund OE posts to support specific projects and transformation programmes. Additional practitioners have subsequently been recruited to the team bringing a varied experience set from differing professional backgrounds as well as the desired skill set.

Our insight began with a comprehensive programme of engagement events to hear the perspective and reality of the workforce. As described in Chapter 2, our first Perfect Care Senate in 2013 had asked clinicians of all professions to tell us what the barriers to delivering perfect care would be. Surprisingly, people did not say money or expertise; instead, there was agreement that the real barriers to achieving perfect care were values, mindsets and behaviours, the calibre and style of leadership, how people and teams work together and the organisational culture.

Critical to this is the full support and understanding of the Trust's Board of Directors. With their confirmation, we led a huge engagement campaign that we branded 'Your Voice Your Change'. This included a series of 'mega conversations' with staff and service users, patients and carers representing all areas of the Trust. We asked some very simple questions:

■ What would help our organisation to provide best care?
■ What could we do to enable our people to do their best work?
■ What action should we prioritise and take together?

The themes that emerged were consistent. They supported the accompanying data and drivers for change to inform an organisational diagnostic. From this, we agreed a plan of improvement priorities and strategic objectives:

■ Culture, values and behaviours;
■ Change fatigue, engagement and involvement in improvement and innovation;
■ Leadership;
■ Teamwork;
■ Capacity, capability and potential of the workforce.

The themes confirmed our belief that it was imperative to nurture a culture of decision-making on the front line. We needed to create the conditions, mechanisms and relationships that would encourage and enable this. And it was very clear that this would need to be a culture of trust and psychological safety built on teamwork.

Translation into Our Trust Strategy

By 2015/16, these programmes of work were firmly established and demonstrated that our strategy had placed our people at its core. There was an emerging corporate recognition that the sector is a human system, where there must be congruence between culture, structure and process in order to achieve the organisational health required to deliver organisational performance. The two are intrinsically linked and support the ability to manage complexity whilst sustaining quality.

Our ambition to create a Restorative Just and Learning Culture and apply organisational health concepts addresses the risk to safety. We know they will improve outcomes for patients, lower levels of turnover and increased levels of well-being and commitment within the workforce. This culture had to be underpinned by a comprehensive programme of engagement. This had to be far more than the traditional organisational 'listening exercise': it would facilitate a continuous process of dialogue that challenges our thinking, informs our strategic priorities and reinforces our shared accountability for quality and organisational culture.

We have developed a suite of evidence-based programmes and interventions that underpinned organisational health, clinical excellence and patient safety. All of these are effectively operationalised for leaders, teams and the wider workforce. The plans and interventions were and are designed to create a culture of enthusiastic cooperation, teamwork and support within and across organisations, taking responsibility for improving quality, learning and developing better ways of doing things.

Our chosen methodology deliberately aims to embed inclusion. This approach encompasses the recent refocus on anti-racism which is a primary driver in the review of the Trust operating model and employee life cycle. We have introduced systems that identify aspects of work where safety and efficiency have been impaired, aspects that ultimately erode staff resilience and engagement. We recognise that our ability to deliver the best care is also dependent on the capability of our workforce and believe that investing in developing capability today is proactively creating the capacity to deliver services tomorrow.

Our interventions and methodologies are designed to be culturally feasible to ensure they become systematised, embedded and sustainable across differing services to truly underpin continuous improvement in organisational performance. These programmes are now well established, and evaluation demonstrates triangulation to improvement in quality and reduction in costs.

Psychological safety has been continuously created through open and honest dialogue, creating a sense of inclusion and belonging in team-based working plans, safety in speaking up and out, mutual respect, civility, cooperation and accountability through our leaders and teams. Psychological safety is cited as a fundamental requirement for learning and improvement. At Mersey Care, we recognise that it is fundamental to the effectiveness of the Trust's Four Step Process in relation to the degree of honesty the staff member feels able to share in their account of when things do not go as planned.

Through this OE approach, we create a line of sight to Restorative Just and Learning Culture (RJLC), a golden thread through our people, systems and processes, providing a compassionate environment that supports Perfect Care and high-quality, safe services.

Summarising the Drivers for Change

■ **Significantly improve standards and outcomes for our patients, service users and communities through innovation and creativity.** There was a spectrum of attitudes to mental health learning disability care, from passion to frustration and most dangerously, apathy. The lack of ambition and belief perpetuated unacceptable outcomes and risks for patients and impacted staff.

■ **Combat 'change fatigue', recreate the narrative, inspire and reconnect the workforce to the aspiration of the vision, collective values and the work.** Best quality, compassionate care is highly dependent on our ability to tap intrinsic motivation, reignite the passion, elicit understanding and instil belief in our ability to achieve our goals and that 'we can do this together'.

■ **Re-establish the trust and relationship with our workforce, demonstrate care and compassion.** Providing care is relational. The quality of healthcare is significantly impacted by how well engaged and supported the care providers are. It is the people who are closest to the work that have the expertise to make the decisions. In order to achieve this, we knew we would need to create a culture of psychological safety, collective learning and continuous improvement to support sustainable high performance and quality. The most successful organisations cultivate cultures of inclusion, trust, psychological safety, teamwork, continuous learning and support. To do this, our staff had to feel understood and cared for when things did not go to plan.

■ **Combat apathy and learned helplessness.** In order to empower people we needed to shift the mindset to create and align collective commitment to achieving the ambition. We created the conditions, mechanisms and relationships that encouraged and enabled confidence. This meant enabling greater safety for our people through safety management systems and processes, creating the conditions for staff to raise concerns, challenging cultural norms and creating greater alignment with 'work as done', as opposed to 'work as imagined' (Wickens, 1997).

- **Reframe integration and the importance of team or inter-team working in the delivery of care.** Healthcare teams are multidisciplinary. They must often 'team' rapidly with individuals across traditional boundaries that they may or may not know to respond to emergencies. (Edmondson, 2012) This supported our ability to mobilise teams effectively with local partners during the pandemic, where people in different systems, of varying expertise and status, working in extensive geographical areas came together quickly to address a new and urgent situation.

- **The need for a different leadership style, approach and capability.** Formerly in Mersey Care there was little collaboration or sense of 'team' across the leadership community. The Trust was hierarchical. Its style of management traditionally was mostly command and control. We needed collective, compassionate, inclusive leadership and personal and collective accountability for behaviour, contribution and outcomes for the organisation.

- **The need to maximise and align our capacity, talent and capability to the Perfect Care strategy.** We knew we had to harness the wealth of talent and expertise within the organisation and within our delivery partners to enable us to innovate and transform clinical standards and practice.

- **The need for a new operating model that achieves congruence between strategy, culture and new ways of working.** We recognised that our infrastructure did not enable sustainable high performance and consistent standards of operational excellence, alignment and maximisation of resource, cross-boundary teamwork and equity for patients. We asked ourselves:

'To what extent does organisational or system design facilitate or inhibit psychological safety, inclusion, learning and restorative practice? What are the design principles we should apply (and also avoid), in order to design the work in a psychologically safe way to ensure sustainable high performance with the right 'hardware and software'?

- **Creating collective accountability to make it sustainable.** Reframing the narrative to help people recognise that quality and efficiency are intrinsically linked. Providing quality first time is less expensive and resource intensive. We needed to articulate this for successful engagement with our clinicians to empower their active support as opposed to the traditional top-down approach. We needed to articulate the improving approaches for staff and patients alike and created a safety dividend for both, reinforcing in healthcare that 'quality without efficiency is unsustainable, efficiency without quality is unthinkable' (The National Quality Board, 2017. Shared Commitment to Quality) was to become a mantra for us.

- **Enhance performance and employee experience throughout the employee life cycle through the application of best practice people management and development.** Truly meaningful engagement is achieved through every interaction with an employee, where the impact on their psychological contract and how they really experience the organisation becomes truly valued.

- **Authentically listen and learn when things do not go as expected or to plan.**

  Operating in a healthcare human system, we must acknowledge that our people operate in difficult and complex environments still. We know that things do not always go as intended or planned. In those moments we aspire to always listen to understand. So if something did not go as we had planned, either at the organisational, divisional, service, team or (rarely) to one individual level, we must learn from it.

As we have described, often staff engagement, leadership, team and culture development activity are often seen as lesser priorities within some organisations. They are fundamental to an organisation's caring obligations. Public enquiries such as those regarding Mid Staffordshire and Morecambe Bay, and reports from the Care Quality Commission, from healthcare organisations that have been rated as 'Inadequate', have sadly all recorded this (Morecambe Bay Investigation Report, 2015).

Whilst they sit in a context of other factors, too often those issues described above are cited as major causes that manifest in risk to the safety and quality of care patients and staff experience. Their consequences are a matter of public record and indeed distress.

Culture Change Activities and Interventions – What We Did

1. **We sent out a call to action, aiming high, reframing the narrative, articulating the ambition and enabling collective delivery of strategy**

Mersey Care set out, with a level of ambition we had not aspired to before, our ambition to deliver the very best standards of care, continually improving, compassionate care: *Perfect Care*. We recognised that our staff were experts in their field and would influence and shape the future of care. This was a call to action to embrace this opportunity on behalf of our patients and to share the accountability for our collective action and leadership for making this happen.

The Trust has a detailed engagement plan. It incorporates more routine or seasonal activities that are planned around the financial year and also activities linked to significant organisational changes and programmes. These all provide opportunities for staff involvement in informing and operationalising the strategy and annual operational plan.

2. **We listened to our people and our staff side voices like we never had before**

We had to listen and understand the hurt and emotions around our people and patient safety processes. This gave the Trust a dialogue with staff side representatives and an understanding that went beyond the traditional engagement approaches. We started the restorative approach without even realising it, attempting to address the hurt, create safety and re-engage and collaborate with some previously hurt or disengaged staff.

3. **We expanded our organisational effectiveness team to support the redesign of our organisation and people systems and processes**

Previous approaches had led to severe mistrust in some parts of the organisation. There were staff who were at best disengaged and at worst damaged by their experiences. As mentioned previously, once services began to see the benefits of an OE approach, they approached us to include OE activities in transformation and workforce plans, acknowledging and supporting the requirement for additional resources and practitioners. This work has been critical not only in implementing continuous improvement initiatives but also in a way it helped Mersey Care support the acquisition of organisations, which themselves bore the scars of damage.

4. **We reviewed our policies and processes**

The approach we took with our HR processes is documented elsewhere in this volume. Simply speaking, we took an OE approach to examining our people management policies and processes in action. This meant that we did not just look at the data; we spoke and engaged with our people through focus groups, forums and team-based working. Collectively we changed and developed methodologies side by side. As we progressed, we also reviewed many other HR and safety policies and processes, including, but not limited to, our grievance and disciplinary policy, our Managing Attendance policy, our incident reporting processes and complaints procedures.

It is worth describing how such changes are done in partnership. Our trust policies concerning bullying, harassment and grievance policies were re named as Early Resolution, Respect and Civility. Not only is this a new name but there is a new focus on offering resolution at an informal stage for staff to raise concerns and have them addressed sooner. This change was completed in partnership with HR, staff side, operational colleagues and staff networks. These are kept under regular reviews, again in partnership. The approach also includes the use of Trust's Respect and Civility 'jigsaw', an illustrative tool devised by trust staff to guide difficult conversations. Along the way, our approach and tools picked up significant national commendations in the *Business Culture* and *Health Service Journal Awards*, against submissions from public and private sector organisations. More importantly, there has been approximately a 60% reduction in what would have been formal bullying and harassment cases in our trust.

Other key considerations included the following examples. The list isn't exhaustive and is in no particular order of precedence, but we consider these worth describing in some detail:

■ Staff's annual appraisal was redesigned to align effort and resources to shared purpose and goals and the cascade of objectives showing a line of sight between every individual's contribution to the patient, regardless of their role. This values-based appraisal emphasises the importance of assessment and development of behaviours alongside competencies and performance.

- Career conversations are included as part of the appraisal process and preceptorship programmes. Conversations in the appraisal process inform the Trust talent and succession planning process (Maximising Potential). Each process places emphasis on the individual's well-being and capability and importantly, the impact every person has on our culture and the quality of care. These processes ensure that the Trust is proactively developing the capability required to deliver its priorities and ensuring alignment of effort and resources to the delivery of the strategy. This has enabled us to develop a direct dialogue with all our BAME staff regarding a lack of representation in trust leadership positions.

- A deep dive into the value of Respect was carried out using input and feedback from our Staff Networks, data from our NHS Staff Survey and in-house culture surveys. A dialogic approach was used as we facilitated conversations about respect at Manager Forums, in our Leadership Development Programmes and in focus groups. The accumulation of all this information led to the creation of our Civility and Respect framework in 2018 which was influenced by the work of Dr Chris Turner and his colleagues 'Civility Saves Lives'. The development of the framework included a review of the language, asking whether the words we used in our official documentation were pejorative or assumptive, when they should be impartial or neutral. This continues with ongoing work taking place in HR team meetings, staff side meetings, staff networks and focus groups to revisit trust documentation where word choice may reveal other micro-aggressions or inequalities.

- A new Director of Patient Safety was appointed and new policies and procedures embodying our Restorative Just Culture (RJC) principles were created. We are embracing the momentum towards Patient Safety II (see Hollnagel et al., 2015) and developing practices about learning from incidents in a psychologically safe way, such as a new complaints' policy and practices inclusive of RJC principles ensures that lessons are put into practice when a complaint arises from a situation where something hasn't gone to plan.

- Our corporate induction processes were refreshed using feedback from new recruits as well as best practices from other organisations. Our approach now weaves the RJC message in right from the start, including respect and civility with clear expectations and role modelling of desired behaviours by the Chief Executive, his team and other senior leaders.

■ Our Trust's values are embedded into every point of the employee life cycle. From our values-based pre-employment programmes, recruitment processes and apprenticeship schemes to our bespoke leadership development pathway, we embed our values and the principles of our Restorative Just and Learning Culture into everything we do. Leaders on our development programmes participate in 360 feedback where they receive feedback from team members, colleagues and their managers about their performance against our values. Our employee and team recognition scheme creates a space for people to be thanked and nominated for an outstanding performance against the values. They really do live in the organisation, and this was evidenced in our 2020 NHS Staff Survey results where we received above-average scores for colleagues feeling respected by others.

5. **Mindsets and Alignment; Embedding Values, Intrinsic Motivation and Engagement**

Our values are our brand at Mersey Care and they underpin our culture. We knew that the importance of aligning personal values and beliefs to those of the Trust was pivotal to emotional engagement and cultural shift.

This process of alignment began with the process of co-producing our trust CARES values. Individuals from across all areas of the organisation were invited to take part in numerous activities and events, sessions and conversations that all looked in detail at the meaning and the intent of our existing values (Continuous Improvement, Accountability, Respect and Enthusiasm). The result of the sessions and the activities listed below was the recognition that there was a gaping hole in our values around our new RJC philosophy of supporting and nurturing those who had been involved in an incident or a situation that hadn't gone to plan. The resulting action was that a new value of support was added that explicitly covered the behaviours people wanted to see in this space. Activities then took place to share this idea and seek feedback. These included:

■ Engaging and warm 'Welcome to Mersey Care' sessions for incoming staff, with both mandatory induction items and presentations on our RJC, reputation and the tone of how we communicate as an organisation;

- Service user feedback sessions;
- Inclusion in forums for operational managers, senior leaders and the Trust;
- Informal 'Birthday Breakfast' sessions which are open to all staff to meet executives;
- Break-out activity in leadership programmes;
- Focus groups with representation from all clinical and corporate services, Staff Networks and governors;
- Email feedback from Non-Executive Directors;
- Online surveys;
- Trust communication channels such as intranet pages, newsletters and, more recently, a well-received private staff Facebook group.

Our accompanying Staff Charter was then also reviewed and updated following the value refresh, and a Civility and Respect framework was created. These were then translated into our people management and development policies, practices and programmes (as described above). The Values and Staff Charter serve to guide staff, their managers and our organisation as a whole to our expected style of communicating, behaving and decision-making. They are also embedded intrinsically in our Team Based Working (TBW) approach that we adopt to support and develop all teams.

From the beginning, we aimed to create a shift in mindset and recognized the importance of the growth mindset in learning organisations. We prioritized staff engagement, and plans are regularly reviewed and amended to reflect local and system needs, with ongoing listening and learning events at Trust and local levels to ensure that all staff have a voice, can speak up and see visible changes when they do. The CARES values and our Restorative Just and Learning Culture also underpin the NHS's wider Freedom to Speak Up strategy. This provides a safe space to alert concerns and risks which were outcomes requested by Sir Robert Francis (both his 2013 report and 2015 review) as well as expectations from Dr Bill Kirkup and the Morecambe Bay investigation (Morecambe Bay Investigation Report, 2015).

As Mersey Care's system and structures change around us and mergers, acquisitions and the integration of services continue, we recognise that our partner providers have their own values and core drivers of care. Built into our processes as the trust expands, our Restorative Just and Learning Culture retains its prominence and primacy. The Trust is clear in its expectations of staff to model behaviours, initiate values-based conversations and share learning and reflection. This means provider partners can access, learn and benefit from our approach. We see this regularly in both informal inquiries from other organisations who may have seen our work at a conference or on social media and also more formal requests for support or training. We do also experience challenges when working with others who do not work in an RJC way. In this space, we continue to share our learning, give feedback and role model the principles and behaviours we aspire to.

6. **Compassionate, collective leadership**

We knew that achieving our ambitions and the desired cultural shift would be highly dependent on the calibre and behaviours of our leaders. As with most organisations, leaders' skills and styles varied across the Trust and the role and expectations of leaders going forward changed significantly.

In 2019, the NHS Long Term Plan set out an ambitious future for the NHS and the political and national focus has only intensified in the challenging times since then. Leadership culture has been cited in the NHS People Plan as one of the most fundamental issues to be addressed nationally, regionally and organisationally. Alongside the importance of teamwork, it has been recognised that leadership behaviour, culture and patient safety and quality are intrinsically linked. The research demonstrates that a leader's capability and behaviour and their propensity to engender compassion, inclusion and belonging and to create psychological safety all are factors enabling a Restorative, Just and Learning Culture.

In addition to the emerging national and regional picture, the Trust's vision of a Restorative Just and Learning Culture and NHS Patient Safety II strategy is also influencing how leadership capability and competence is defined, assessed and developed. In Mersey Care, we see leaders as the blueprint for culture in their teams. They are accountable for their team's culture and for what's promoted and permitted. Every decision and every interaction, every day, influences the extent to which we develop a culture of belonging, high-quality, continually improving and compassionate care.

Our leadership model and bespoke programmes have been specifically designed to facilitate an RJC at various levels of the leadership structure. Leaders new to the Trust complete RJC training as part of their managerial induction, our 'Arrive' programme. We help leaders understand the impact that they have on their teams, the quality of the outcomes that they achieve and the environment that they create. We know that providing care is all about relationships and that the best care is delivered through great teams. Our ability to create a culture of compassion, learning, improvement and innovation is highly dependent on people feeling safe, supported and valued. We know that psychological safety in the workplace is highly dependent on a person's relationship with their leader and with their team. Our Leadership Development Programmes ('Strive' and 'Thrive') place emphasis on a leader's ability to develop high-performing teams and create a climate of honesty, trust and collaboration. Our aim is to leverage the capability, passion, energy and leadership strengths of all staff.

Our leadership development model is inclusive of everyone and our offer is a full pathway from aspiring to strategic leadership capability. This work has been purposely and strategically aligned to the Trust's vision for Perfect Care. It recognises the balance between engaging, compassionate, values-led leadership and robust performance and business management.

The COVID context has reinforced the importance of supporting leaders' resilience and their ability to create psychologically safe teams, to have greater emotional intelligence and to instil a sense of belonging in everyone. The pandemic has alerted us to sensitivities of diversity in ways that perhaps had not been afforded levels of care or scrutiny until very recently. Managing agile teams and environments requires high levels of skills and techniques. Never before has managerial excellence been more important to ensure people are clear and supported, services are delivered efficiently and effectively and precious resources and capacity are maximized. In response to the increased needs of managers through COVID-19, we added to our Leadership Development Programmes by facilitating short 'Leading in a Crisis' sessions online. The purpose of these sessions was to support our leaders through this challenge and to develop a set of resources in line with RJC and our values that would offer insight, practical tools and expertise from respected and credible sources. These sessions and resources helped our leaders to maintain resilience and effectiveness during these uncertain times. Mersey Care's take on the global 'Be Kind' messaging played its part here and helped our managers to support our remote workers, helping them cope in this new care context, with the groundwork already laid in respect and civility.

Psychologically Safe, Resilient High-Performing Teams

The NHS Patient Safety Strategy (2019, updated 2021) and the work of Suzette Woodward (Woodward, 2020, Implementing Patient Safety) informed and strengthened Mersey Care's own developing commitment to widening the thinking around patient safety. This is more than just addressing when care does not go as planned (Safety I) but must now look at what regularly works and works well as planned (Safety II), building on the foundations of Just and Learning Culture. Safety II defines safety as the ability to succeed under varying conditions, not just focus upon the exceptional. It is also about understanding routinely delivered safe and effective care. In the Safety II construct, the focus is on making systems safer by understanding day-to-day care better. Care goes as planned with good outcomes most of the time, and by studying and understanding what happens most of the time, the conditions which support safe and effective care can be identified, replicated and strengthened. The focus on safety is intended to support the development of learning within teams, focusing on:

■ Reflecting upon and analysing routine care to better understand how it works day to day; use positive language to describe circumstances;
■ Recognising the exceptional as a platform for addressing when care does not go as planned; this instils optimism and identifies the good work of others and creates positivity in the workplace;
■ Recognising what can be done by the team and act to ensure inclusion, collaboration and empowerment;
■ Taking a multiple professional cross-system perspective to introduce new views and potential solutions to problems.

At Mersey Care, we know the positive impact that effective and resilient teams have on patient outcomes and mortality. We see this in our CQC inspection results and our own internal quality review processes. With a vision to aspire for Perfect Care, Mersey Care recognises the reality of clinical frontline teams providing care for individuals with complex needs. We therefore provide proactive and planned support for teams to maintain and grow their resilience. This is essential to maintaining effective teamwork during times of significant pressure. From the beginning we have an integrated approach to leadership and team development, recognising that the two are intrinsically linked. Our systematic, planned approach to Team Based Working (TBW), as set out by West et al. (2001), using evidence-based methodology enables the principles of restorative Just and Learning to be applied widely, not just when reviewing incidents and safety from the patient perspective.

For ease of application, we have synthesised the research behind Team Based Working (ibid, psychological safety (Edmondson, 2019)) and

Restorative Just Culture (Dekker, 2016) to create our Team Canvas. The Team Canvas tool is fully aligned to clinical excellence and PSII to support the systematised implementation of an evidence-based, high-performing team framework.

Invariably when teams are in need of support (deliberately not using the term 'in difficulty'), the basic principles of Team Based Working are missing, and risk manifests into risk to patients and staff safety. Usually there are accompanying high levels of sickness and attrition. Providing intervention for a team in need of support takes time and is costly. Investing in Team Based Working is equally about the prevention of avoidable harm as it is about improvement. This framework is our mechanism to systematise improvement at the team level and is accompanied by a digitised toolkit and support offer. Team assessment criteria have been developed and embedded within our clinical quality assessment and Team Accreditation processes. These have demonstrated that the improvement of team-level engagement and people metrics, triangulate to innovation and improved outcomes for patients and service users.

The Learning

We have documented – publicly on many occasions – our journey. It has been an open process to firstly understand and then secondly take actions to improve how we deliver care, the care environment and the relationship with the people who receive and those that provide it. This has been a continuous process of learning and it has never been easy. Whilst we have developed a reputation for the significant impact of this work to create a Restorative, Just and Learning Culture, there's no complacency: we have so much more yet to do.

The next phase of the RJLC work will further align culture, safety and improvement to be part of PSII and the concept of *work as done versus work as imagined*. This will place particular emphasis on psychological safety, learning in teams and organisational design. We recognise that the initial focus of our RJC work was clinical practice. We omitted to include an audacious RJC goal for our workforce.

We thought that we knew our culture, but the reality for some staff was very different to that of our espoused values and aspirations for patient care and staff support. We had not applied an OE approach to some of the most powerful and emotional processes an employee might experience. These are the policies and processes that are instigated when things do not go as expected. This had caused significant hurt and mistrust and was continuously undermining the proactive people and cultural development described in this chapter.

Instead of attempting to facilitate cultural and behavioural shift through a suite of interventions that were applied separately to service and practice redesign, we fully recognise that culture and behaviour change is the result of a redesign of the operating model. It's not a stand-alone process or programme of work. There has been shared accountability across the executive portfolio and our progress to date is the result of collective ownership and leadership.

Progress against delivery of our strategy and feedback from our regulators (such as the CQC noting and naming our culture change in their 2019 report) gave assurance that we were delivering great work and improving. We were achieving some exceptional outcomes. However, we recognised that the level of progress and impact systematically across our workforce was hindered as the organisation continually changed in nature, scope and size. The sequence of acquisitions of other organisations and services presented additional risks and challenges and often brought disengaged, sometimes aggressively resistant workforce members. Limited OE resources would be diverted from transformational programmes and realigned against new priorities and risks which affected the improvement and sustainability of our workforce and culture change programmes. OE plans have needed to be dynamic, continually reviewed and adapted to continually align the workforce to the organisational strategy.

'Every system is perfectly designed to get the result that it does' is a quote often attributed to the American engineer and statistician W. Edwards Deming. Whatever its provenance, what is required is a systems approach. We have recognised that when you change one part of the system it has an impact on other parts of the whole. Plans need to incorporate the entire workforce, not just the newly acquired workforce. In an operating environment like the NHS, attention and limited capacity usually shifts to where there is considered to be the most risk and assumptions can be made that the existing, more stable, engaged workforce will be okay.

In comparison to enterprise-wide, corporate or enabling functions, clinical services are perceived as the most important and higher risk. Such assumptions can have adverse consequences both operationally and in relation to the relationship with staff and their perception of being valued.

The organisation can be likened to a patient with multiple, complex needs such as new models of care, structures, processes, workforce, culture. That patient is being treated by a number of different practitioners, all of whom may be specialists in their own right. However, without a 'care package' and a multidisciplinary team approach, the patient may receive treatment, but their health fails to improve and worsen, and they die of shock.

For some time, we failed to coordinate the organisational care package. On paper, we were doing all of the right things to improve various aspects of care within the organisation. However, through the lack of a systems approach and coordination, we were unknowingly creating incongruence and misalignment within our own microsystem. This has required an honest, collaborative, aligned leadership approach to create a systems approach that gives equal attention to culture, structure and process. Constant communication about our plans and progress against delivery of strategy helps explain and provides reassurance, but we know action speaks volumes and engenders belief, trust and motivation.

Workforce Mindset and Alignment Needs Constant Attention and Care

Strategy must be aimed at creating a growth mindset, a key requirement for a Restorative Just and Learning Culture. As the workplace and teams become more complex, alignment becomes much more difficult and much more of a risk.

Getting the Basics Consistently Right

In an organisation properly committed to psychological safety, people are managed fairly and supportively. Psychologically safe organisations prioritise good people management and development. Mersey Care has a reputation as a thought leader, an innovator, a change catalyst. Through innovations like our Centre for Perfect Care and our digital developments (both before and during the pandemic), the organisation has a track record for operationalising strategy and delivering transformation. Yet like every organisation, we still have leaders who do not manage to support people and service well.

We seek to improve and to systematise this through all leaders and all teams in our next phase of development.

Culture Change Is Not a Process; It Is a Strategic Long-Term Endeavour

When seeking to create a cultural shift, it must be recognised that there has to be a strategic endeavour. Many organisations seek to apply the interventions described above without designing them for context, or without aligning to an overarching strategy.

Resilience, Persistence and Leadership Alignment

Culture change is a journey with highs and lows and is one that at times can be painful. Part of the strategy must create the resilience, passion and belief and most important of all, aligned and committed leadership.

Capability and Capability

On a practical level, consideration must be given not just to the planning of the work to support these interventions. There must be the creation of the capability and capacity to deliver. This may require investment and resourcing. If Boards are paying equal attention to organisational health and organisational performance, time and resource must be fairly distributed.

Getting It Right for the Workforce Means We Are Now Translating Our Practice Further into Our Clinical Practice

All Mersey Care's comprehensive portfolio of people and clinical programmes, processes and interventions have been mapped against the restorative triangle from prevention, intervention to restoration and reintegration.

We continue to explore and expand this offer; more recently incorporating the development of Restorative Practice Nurses to provide dedicated intervention when things do not go as planned and specialist support for well-being in stressful situations. Part of this new role will be to explore and develop the use of Restorative Circles within the Trust.

Impact of OE Interventions

Over the last five years, as Mersey Care has acquired other organisations, we fully expected that some of our initial success of embedding RJC into all aspects of our organisational health, performance and life would be eroded as we shifted our focus onto new areas of the organisation. Despite this, we have always strived to measure this impact and seek out the data that signals our progress in this space.

We have accepted that direct triangulation of comparable data has proven difficult because of the organisation's continually changing size, complexity and growth. However, the data demonstrate the relationship between interventions, levels of staff engagement, team cultures, quality care and patient outcomes.

In 2018, we undertook a more formal evaluation of the relationship between the clinical assessment outcomes (the Quality Review Visit (QRV)) and the levels of engagement within teams that had had dedicated OE support and intervention including leadership and team development as described in this chapter. Our evaluation indicated that:

- There was a triangulation in those teams that received OE support, the level of team engagement and the safety and quality of care assessment via the QRV process;
- All teams who demonstrated a high engagement with OE team interventions were also high-performing teams, based on QRV outcomes; and
- A positive relationship exists between teams showing positive Culture of Care Barometer (CCB) team engagement survey results and a facet of the 'well-led' domain relating to leadership culture.

1. **Employee relations activity**

Despite an increase in the workforce of 135% between 2016 and 2020, we saw a decrease in disciplinary investigations of 79% and a decrease in suspensions of 86%.

2. **Staff turnover**

The Trust has remained below target for 'staff turnover in month' for a number of years. The target is 0.91% and as of 30 April 2021 it was 0.84% and in April 2020 it was 0.70%. The overall target vacancy rate is 7% and as of 30 April 2021 it was 3.79%, a further improvement from April 2020 when the rate was 6.9%.

3. **RJC training**

Approximately 500 of our managers had attended our RJC internal training prior to our most recent trust acquisition in June 2021. Frustrated by the impact of Business Continuity Planning and the wider impact of COVID-19, our training plan is to have trained 1,000 managers by March 2022 therefore building a solid base for the continued roll-out of RJC.

In addition to this, by July 2021, 79% of our workforce have completed the Respect and Civility e-learning module. We are on a trajectory to reach 100% by the end of the financial year.

4. **Team performance and team-based working**

The Team Canvas was established as part of the Trust team-based working methodology from April 2021 as a means to scale up team-based working across all teams. Prior to this, significant work was carried out using the Affina OD 'Team Journey' model with over 100 teams completed prior to the pandemic. Up to this point, at any time, around 20% of teams in the Trust were participating in Team Based Working activities. Over 50 staff including clinicians as well as corporate and support staff were trained to use the Affina methodology between 2014 and 2019. Results of a 2018 evaluation of 46 teams who participated in this Team Based Working activity showed a clear correlation between OE interventions, improved levels of engagement and performance outcomes against the Quality and Safety Framework.

In addition to the implementation of our Team Canvas, all teams who demonstrate the evidence-based criteria set out in our internal quality review process for outstanding teams have been awarded 'Excelling' in the Trust's Team Accreditation process and are rated as Outstanding against CQC criteria.

5. **Leadership development**

Between April 2018 and March 2021, 300 Band 6,7 & 8 Leaders completed Leadership Development Programmes, the content of which included a significant focus on leading in RJC cases. Each of those leaders subsequently returned to their teams to share this message and embed a Just and Learning Culture. This represents the beginning of a social movement designed to spread the culture and embed the RJC practices. If each team had just ten team members, this would represent 3,000 members of the workforce touched in some way by the message, almost 40% of the workforce at that time.

6. **Staff engagement during COVID improved**

Mersey Care's in-house culture pulse check tool is run quarterly throughout the year and has been in place since 2016. The Culture of Care Barometer results (CCB) showed that in May 2020, at the height of the first wave of the pandemic, 75% of staff said that they felt well informed about what was happening in the Trust, in comparison to 57% in May 2019. This result reflects the emphasis placed on effective and honest communication, enabling staff to feel connected. Feedback via the CCB provided praise for the supportive style and tone of messaging. We included advice-themed around aspects of restorative justice and specifically kindness each week during the height of the 2020 lockdown. These used videos of familiar staff and practical resources aimed at those newly homeworking or not meeting their teams in the workplace as had been the norm.

7. **Staff survey**

According to the 2020 NHS Staff Survey, Mersey Care is second in the country for staff stating that they feel safe to report a concern of bullying and harassment. There was also a 16% improvement in reported scores from the NHS annual Staff Survey question relating to whether staff would feel secure raising concerns about unsafe clinical practice; this figure rose from 62% in 2016 to 78% in 2020.

The NHS Staff Survey 'overall staff engagement' score measures the ability to contribute to improvement, the willingness to recommend the Trust as a place to work or receive treatment and the levels of employee motivation. Mersey Care has seen a year-on-year increase in staff engagement scores since 2016 despite substantial organisational change and redesign. In 2018, when Staff Survey 'Theme Scores' were introduced Mersey Care scored 7.0 for Overall Staff Engagement. This rose again in 2020 with a score of 7.2.

In terms of patient safety questions, the 2020 NHS Staff Survey tells us that 79% of staff feel that the Trust takes action to ensure that incidents do not happen again. This is a 6.1% improvement on the previous year and is 5.2% higher than the comparable national average. Also, 71.3% of staff report that they are given feedback on the changes following an incident or error. Again, this is significantly higher than the national average of 64.7% and a marked improvement on Mersey Care's 2019 score of 64.6%.

8. **Performance appraisal compliance**

Mersey Care is pleased to see an increasing trend for the completion of annual performance appraisal from 2017 (82%) to 2018 (88%) to 2019 (84%) as psychological safety increases and (we believe) people are feeling the real benefit of an honest conversation with their manager as part of this process.

All clinical and professionally regulated staff groups are contractually mandated to complete eight weekly episodes of supervision to ensure staff are consistently reviewing and updating their skills, knowledge and expertise within a supportive restorative Just and Learning, psychologically safe network of practice within teams, through regular discussion with their line manager/supervisor. The completion rate is above target at 90% completion (2021) and has seen significant increases in compliance since 2018 (70%). Again this is viewed as a symptom of growing psychological safety amongst teams and with team managers.

9. **Induction (new starters' programme)**

Hundred per cent of new starters are receiving awareness of RJLC and specific training on the CARES values and Civility and Respect and civility awareness.

10. **Economic**

- The salary costs averaged over two fiscal years were reduced by £4 million per year, coinciding with the introduction of a Restorative Just and Learning Culture in 2016.

- Mersey Care achieved around £1 million in saved legal and termination expenses; conservatively half of these savings have been attributed to the introduction of a Just and Learning Culture itself, and the other half to non-related factors.
- It is estimated the total economic benefit of restorative justice in the case of Mersey Care NHS Foundation Trust to be about £2.5 million or approximately 1% of the total costs and 2% of the labour costs. Something between 1% and 2% of our trust's turnover can be attributed to restorative Just and Learning practices.

11. **Single Oversight Framework**

Mersey Care has a culture of continuous improvements which can also be demonstrated by the regulatory NHS Improvement Single Oversight Framework (SOF). Metrics from 2017/18 show that there were 11 out of 25 key performance indicators that were consistently not meeting the national target of 56% of SOF metrics on target. As at February 2022, the trust was achieving 25 key performance indicators, which is 92% of metrics. This is the highest reported number of metrics achieved within the NHS oversight framework to date.

Conclusion

The work undertaken to date has created fertile ground for further cultural transformation which is ongoing in Mersey Care. This is embedding, and changes are being evidenced in our staff survey and employee relations data. By the very nature of our services, geography and rapid growth over a relatively short period of time, we acknowledge that Mersey Care is a complex system, constantly in transition and development and we absolutely acknowledge and accept that there are pockets of the organisation, where the impact of the interventions have not been realised or had the desired impact. Of course, there is more we must continue to do, to listen and to understand and ultimately to act with the intention for impact. Consequently, we intend to maintain momentum, continue learning and further develop the model in line with the needs of our people.

Each of these culture change activities and interventions has been an important feature facilitating a cultural shift to a sustainable Restorative Just and Learning Culture. They ensure that it is explicitly woven into the DNA of the organisation, people management and patient safety practices. This enables a safety culture to thrive across all areas of the trust, leading to a measurably more engaged workforce, improved care and safer outcomes for our patients and their families.

Psychological safety has been continuously created through open and honest dialogue, creating a sense of inclusion and belonging in team-based working plans, safety in speaking up and out, mutual respect, civility, cooperation and accountability through our leaders and teams.

Strategy and dedicated work to facilitate psychological safety precede the level of honesty and, therefore, the effectiveness of the Mersey Care Four Step Process.

Through this approach, we are creating a line of sight to the Restorative Just and Learning Culture at every development conversation and learning opportunity providing a golden thread through people, systems and processes, providing a compassionate environment that supports Perfect Care and high-quality, safe services.

Mersey Care will continue to act as an 'anchor institution', supporting partners in the Health and Social Care System to develop shared language and behaviours.

As our workplace is volatile, uncertain, complex and ambiguous (VUCA), the RJLC strategy keeps a focus on our people as our greatest asset who deserve compassionate, safe, respectful leadership and team-based relationships.

Progress against RJLC principles and values are measured at regular intervals. This allows for continual improvement and accountability for plans and interventions that keep alignment to the trust's common purpose as a compassionate, listening, inclusive, responsive employer and culture. This is evident in key performance indicators for RJLC that measure employee engagement with work plans and employee relations metrics that look for continually improving trends. Alongside this we continue to identify, through triangulation of data and OE diagnostics, some teams in difficulty who will require additional support. The Team Based Work project plan and the Leadership Development offer will be our vehicle for co-delivering the RJLC into those teams.

In partnership with staff, stakeholders and communities, we will continue to co-design, develop and continually improve a healthy, positive, safe and compassionate culture for our people. We want them to be the best version of themselves whilst working with our patients and service users. These plans remain dynamic and highly contextual. This is especially so following more than two years of pandemic and the trust's additional acquisitions and reconfigurations.

References

Affina Organisational Development (2021). www.affinaod.com/team-tools/affina -team-journey

Care Quality Commission (2019). Routine Inspection of Mersey Care. www.cqc.org .uk/provider/RW4/reports

Dekker, Sidney (2016). *Just Culture: Restoring Trust and Accountability in Your Organization*, Third Edition. CRC Press.

Dweck, Carol. (2006). *Mindset: The New Psychology of Success.* New York: Random House.

Edmondson, Amy (2019). *The Fearless Organization: Creating Psychological Safety in the Workplace for Learning, Innovation and Growth.* Wiley.

Edmondson, Amy (2012). Teamwork on the Fly. *Harvard Business Review.* https:// hbr.org/2012/04/teamwork-on-the-fly-2

Francis, Robert (2013). The Francis Report (Report of the Mid-Staffordshire NHS Trust public inquiry). www.gov.uk/government/publications/report-of-the-mid -staffordshire-nhs-foundation-trust-public-inquiry

Francis, Robert (2015). Freedom to Speak Up. www.gov.uk/government/publications /sir-robert-francis-freedom-to-speak-up-review

Kirkup, Bill (2020). The Life and Death of Elizabeth Dixon. https://assets.publish- ing.service.gov.uk/government/uploads/system/uploads/attachment_data/ file/938638/The_life_and_death_of_Elizabeth_Dixon_a_catalyst_for_change _accessible.pdf

NHS Long Term Plan (2019). www.longtermplan.nhs.uk/

NHS Patent Safety Strategy (2019, updated 2021). www.england.nhs.uk/patient -safety/the-nhs-patient-safety-strategy/

NHS Staff Survey (2020). https://www.nhsstaffsurveys.com/results/

Morecambe Bay Investigation Report (2015). www.gov.uk/government/publications/ morecambe-bay-investigation-report

Hollnagel, Wears, & Braithwaite (2015). From Safety-I to Safety-II. https://www .england.nhs.uk/signuptosafety/wp-content/uploads/sites/16/2015/10/safety-1 -safety-2-whte-papr.pdf

West, M., Borrill, C. S., Carletta, J., Dawson, J., Garrod, S., Rees, A., Richards, A., & Shapiro, D. (2001). *The Effectiveness of Health Care Teams in the National Health Service.* Birmingham: University of Aston.

Wickens, C. D. (1997). An Introduction to Human Factors Engineering. www .researchgate.net/publication/239060793_An_Introduction_to_Human_Factors _Engineering

Woodward, S. (2020). Rethinking Patient Safety. https://suzettewoodward.org/2020/11/

Chapter 9

Restorative Practices in Context for Improving Our People Processes, or People Processes the Restorative Way: Putting it into Context

Amanda Oates

Contents

DOI: 10.4324/9781003162582-9

Introduced by Peter Cheese

Chief Executive of Chartered Institute of Personnel and Development

People in any job or role are part of a system. A system of processes, practices, policies, technology, structure and culture. Of course, people are also fallible and will make mistakes, but so often the mistakes and failures have their roots in other aspects of the wider system. Perhaps it was a lack of training, or lack of support, or confusing processes or conflicting rules, or not having learned from previous errors, or individuals who are overly stressed, or even the mistakes of others somewhere else in the system.

In other words, human errors are rarely deliberate or premeditated, or the result of a single person's action of omission or commission. That seems obvious, but too often we see cultures of blame. When things go wrong, the energy is spent on finding the 'guilty party' and apportioning blame. This is what a retributive culture is – there are rules, and if you break them, then you will be held to account and the one to blame.

The healthcare system is not only vastly complex, but it is also under almost constant stress, particularly in these challenging times. Systems under stress will usually reinforce and reflect their bad or good cultures of behaviour. Positive cultures work with an understanding of the whole system, see mistakes as vital opportunities for learning and improvement – what the well known American psychologist Carol Dweck described as 'growth mindset', versus a fixed mindset that treats everything as fixed and rule based.

Behavioural science evidence over many years shows that people respond best to positive support and encouragement, but with clear purpose, objectives and accountabilities so they can understand their role in relation to others and the system as a whole. It is also true that we tend to remember and learn most from our mistakes, but unless mistakes are shown to be deliberate, they should also be treated as an opportunity to learn and to grow.

The essence of a positive restorative culture as this chapter clearly lays out is a culture where there is a sense of psychological safety – where not only can individuals recognise their mistakes, and whilst being held to account, can learn and improve as a result. This culture of safety also helps people feel they can speak up when they see things that have gone wrong or need to change, without being overly judged themselves or being seen just to blame others. Such cultures therefore are also fundamentally about trust – trust from leaders and managers in their people, but also trust in leaders and managers from the people and in each other.

In healthcare as much as in any work environment, positive mindset in the carers supports positive patient outcomes. When the carer feels supported and trusted, their own levels of stress reduce and their wellbeing is enhanced. Now more than ever we need to ask who is caring for the carers.

Mersey Care has worked hard to take on these principles. HR has a huge role to play and has led from the front. Beginning with a clear understanding of the prevailing culture, how management and staff work together, whether trust is there, and the extent to which employees at all level feel safe and supported. The HR team then developed a clear four step programme of change, with specific interventions to enable change across the system, including policies, practices, learning, and support with strong input of evidence of what works. They also had to be honest about themselves, and the role that they had played in the past, and their own mindsets and beliefs. In other words, to be the change that they wanted to see.

This chapter explores all of these ideas, bringing evidence and experience to bear. It covers legal guidance and precedent, particularly through disciplinary processes which is where so often the real tests of cultures become evident. It encourages us all to understand the evidence of what is happening and how our practices, processes and behavioural cultures are really working. Restorative cultures really are human centred, and remind us all of the *human* in human resources.

The first thing we must acknowledge when considering people processes in healthcare and social care settings is that our people and teams operate in a complex system which can be inherent with risks associated with patient safety. Such risks may come about from any number of factors. They may arise through mechanical error, flawed systems, the varied responses to medication and treatment or through the lived experience of family members. All of these may be seen through a patient's own ethics and lifestyle choices. The National Health Service (NHS) Patient Safety Strategy (2019) quantified the costs of these 'risks' to patient safety, suggesting that a possible 11,000 lives are lost annually, and further treatment needed as a result of incidents may cost £1 billion (NHS England, 2019; Hogan et al., 2015.

In managing such risks, we are mindful of the old view of so-called human error in people processes and the general tendency towards person-centred attributions (Dekker, 2002). This view held that the safety of the system and the care of patients are best protected by the removal of unreliable people or 'bad apples' through punitive and retributive approaches (Holden, 2009). Too often in healthcare systems and in the National Health Service (NHS), our people processes have adopted a blame-centred approach, seeking to denounce individuals rather than taking system-centred approaches to consider all relevant factors. In many instances, this approach has been inadvertent and unintentional; the belief that good process confirms neutrality has been at the centre of this.

Our healthcare staff are amongst the most trusted in society but they are human. From time to time, they will get things 'wrong' or provide care that comes within undesired – even unacceptable outcomes. We cannot simply reset an undesired outcome as we would do on a computer. Healthcare is at the furthest point from the pressing of *control and Z* on a keyboard to simply and effectively undo something assessed as being in need of change. There are decisions and interpretations of judgement to be made. There are judgements. These can ripple in many dimensions and affect wider variables than are in the control or management of one clinician or one clinical process.

In the vast majority of cases, the risks encountered in a healthcare setting are managed with professionalism and care while balancing heavy workloads, fatigue, stress and burnout to achieve the desired outcomes (McNally,

2019). Of course, experience and the motivation of vocation play their parts, not withstanding a significant amount of science in medicine of course, but most clinicians will confess, or celebrate, that there is art too. There is no one correct way of looking at an incident or event: people have multiple perspectives. Each individual will act to some extent within these perspective choices.

This is important and it is not the same as partiality or prejudice or even unconscious bias. As human beings in a system we are not the totality of the system but add further complexity to it as socially constructed beings. We work in a system into which we bring our own emotions and current state of well-being which can be affected by everyday events such as our emotions about the day's politics or rush hour anxieties. We must acknowledge that our people cannot completely leave all their perspectives and emotions at home. We put on our professional garb and our professional attitude and we rise above it all. But we remain nevertheless human beings and the extent to which our individual perceptions, feelings and experiences impact our ability to do our job and the decisions that we make should not be underplayed. We are organic beings. We are naturally fallible. We react to circumstances in ways that whilst they have prescriptive limits, are varied and not wholly predictable. As Dekker (2017) observes with irony, the system would be fine were it not for a few unreliable humans in it. Herein, we find the domain of 'human error', the space where unaccountable outcomes or places of risk start can emerge. Risk can form either a concern or begin an innovation, or sometimes even both.

Dekker makes an important distinction between 'bad people in safe systems, or well-intentioned people in imperfect systems', which can be used to examine our people processes. In his book *The Field Guide to Human Error Investigations* (2017), Dekker articulates the simplicity of Bad Apple Theory as opposed to Learning Theory, the former creating the organisational climate for bad systems which blame good people, the latter recognising that people do not come to work to do a bad job. There is a need for organisational people processes to be able to distinguish between the two. Organisations which have adopted models for people processes which focus on human error, or people as bad, or having done a bad thing, will consequently have a higher proportion of disciplinary investigations, suspensions actions and sanctions. Such organisations will also be places with many rules and low levels of systemic organisational learning or change. If this feels familiar, then it is a clue that something really should change for your people and your people processes.

Too often people processes have embedded the person-centred approach that when things do not go as expected, then our response is to blame our people, creating a platform for the creation of more hurt (NHS England, 2019). In modern societies, the workplace shifted from dealing with an incident or adverse event through summary justice or lashing out to approaches that are more heavily formalised and legislative, designed to safeguard all parties. However, where these approaches remain person-centred, the resulting hurt experienced by a healthcare worker may become even less obvious or even unintentional. It is ironic that the very people processes that are designed to keep staff safe and legally protected are often the vehicle with which we do the most harm to our own people. Just as in the practice of medicine where the idea of iatrogenic harm is well described, so it is in HR. We need to be aware of similar phenomena generated by our own processes.

This disconnection between the intended outcomes of our people processes and staff experiences of people processes is a telling sign. It suggests that rather than feel supported and protected to deliver safe and continuous care, they feel hurt and blamed. In other words, what staff actually experience is a very good example of an old and simple observation: how people *think* that work is done on the front line and how work *is actually done* are two different things!

People processes are often perpetuated by a lack of understanding and discontinuity most often at the corporate level of organisations. This becomes a significant contributor to the way accountability is shaped, applied and meted out in many organisations. Most often accountability as we think it happens can be enacted out in practice in an entirely different way. This was also the case in Mersey Care. Revisiting the point of 'work done' versus 'work imagined', the journey of exploration into our own people processes found that operationally the very policies and processes that were put in place to protect our staff can, in practice, hurt them. Looking at our people process through a restorative just culture lens, Dekker (2014) has described forward-looking models of accountability based on trust and learning, instead of blame. These can facilitate a critical way of reflecting on the ways in which our organisation's people processes are geared up to generate accountability.

Ask yourselves: do your people processes view accountability as 'holding people to account' for that which we as HR practitioners perceive to be the errors that were made? Or does accountability mean that your people can tell their account of what happened, from their perspectives? The latter enables psychological safety and allows for a safe space where subjective and biased people processes are managed and negated where possible and appropriate. The former creates fear and blame which are likely to limit the opportunity for learning. Here, in an effort to protect themselves from the retributive people processes, people may cover up and hide from telling the truth as they simply do not trust you with the truth to treat them fairly and well. These behaviours will not be isolated and specific to the event. In Mersey Care, we found a whole alternative narrative about a blame culture, passed from staff member to staff member. What does that do for our duty of candour? What might it do for individual, team or organisational learning from failure? And at its very worst what does that do for creating the right environment to prevent similar incidents occurring, again and again? How could we possibly hope to see continuous improvement at the heart of our culture?

People processes are central to the development and support of individual and team-level psychological safety. They seek to mitigate as much as possible the negative impacts to healthcare worker's well-being and patient safety as a result of carrying out their work (Edmondson, 1999; Edmondson, Kramer and Cook, 2004). In moving the focus of our people processes from retributive to restorative, we can start to repair, heal and support our people's psychological safety and well-being, enabling them to give their account and their story because they feel safe to trust in the people processes that you are now operating. The meaning and wider importance of psychological safety are discussed in more detail later in this volume.

The results however of a restorative psychologically safe approach are ultimately better patient experiences and better levels of care: smaller details do not disappear, people do not cover up or change the reality and they no longer leave out critical information. Operationally, it is possible to close care gaps more rapidly and accurately. This approach also has to be better for our people, the caregivers. If our caregivers feel safe to tell their account and feel supported in doing so, accountability such as this will embody true organisational learning. It creates a patient safety dividend of transparency and honesty. Importantly, it does *not* create a culture of zero blame or an organisation without accountability. Indeed quite the contrary, it creates the culture in which compassionate support and learning can thrive. In this culture, accountability is widely discussed; transparency is an ally, not an enemy.

The call for people processes that are restorative and forward-looking rather than retributive and backward-looking has been noted by a number of key healthcare, social care and research organisations. In a September 2020 report from the King's Fund, 'The courage of compassion: Supporting nurses and midwives to deliver high-quality care', eight recommendations emphasised the importance of colleagues being supported in the workplace. They stated that every layer of our system should be built on fair and psychologically safe cultures to promote fair, equitable and reflective outcomes. The report also recognised the commitment this required before COVID-19 and the impetus now needed to address long-standing problems exacerbated during the pandemic.

The NHS Patient Safety Strategy (NHS England, 2019) and the 'We are the NHS People Plan 2020/21: action for us all', also acknowledged and adopted the premise of just and learning cultures that are supportive and restorative as part of their central strategy. These reports highlight the cost to patient safety resulting from healthcare teams that do not feel supported to carry out patient care.

The NHS paid £2.4bn in clinical negligence claims in 2019–2020, according to NHS Resolution's annual report. That is around 2% of NHS England's entire budget. More than this, NHS Resolution must also account for claims likely to be received in the future. The *British Medical Journal* (BMJ; 2 March 2020) puts the figures in stark simplicity: 'Now standing at £83.1bn, the amount "set aside" for such claims is among the most substantial public sector financial liabilities faced by the UK government, second only to nuclear decommissioning (£131bn)'.

The BMJ goes on to note that though those most affected by harm are the patients and their families, 'every pound spent on clinical negligence is a pound that cannot be spent on care' – often 4% of total trusts' income and this has tripled since 2009. In 2018–2019, NHS organisations paid just under £2bn into the Clinical Negligence Scheme for Trusts. The BMJ observed that, but the estimated cost of the liabilities incurred was over four times the amount paid in.

The article concludes that the best way to control costs is to improve safety so that both patient harm and subsequent litigation are reduced. We are clear that teams that feel safe and who are supported to become effective teams are the ones that deliver safe and continuous care and can operate without this negligence and subsequent litigation.

Acknowledgement of the need for people processes that are restorative and not focused on blame also came from NHS England and NHS Improvement (NHSEI) in a May 2019 letter to all NHS chairs and chief executives. The document 'Learning lessons to improve our people practices' asks them to review their people processes. It reminds leaders of the suicide of a staff nurse in February 2016 which came after an HR disciplinary process (described in the NHS Provider Bulletin on 5 June 2019). An advisory group was established by NHS Improvement to consider what extent the failings in the case were unique to the trust involved or were more widespread across the NHS and what learning can come from it. Within this letter, each Trust was to ask of itself:

■ Are the issues sufficiently understood to justify formal action?
■ Would formal action be proportionate and justifiable?
■ Will it be given sufficient resources to be fair, effective and objective?
■ What will be the likely effect on the health and well-being of the individual and their wider team?
■ And can all this be applied to all current cases too?

The letter asked if these questions had been asked in each recipient's organisation yet and what were the answers? The challenge was to ask what had the organisations changed and adapted as a result of those answers, and if they were to ask these questions again would the organisation be happy with the answers or is there still a need to change people processes?

Reflecting Back on Mersey Care's People Processes

The tragic case described in the letter is made more awful by the realisation underlined in the last bulletin point. It was not an isolated instance.

Looking back at Mersey Care's own people processes from 2014 to 2016, it is important and unsettling to note that we could potentially have been in the same position. Indeed, staff side had raised their concerns about the impact of these processes on people's mental health. When Mersey Care began the Just and Learning approach, approximately 4% of staff faced disciplinary investigations every year. This figure excludes the former organisations that Mersey Care has subsequently acquired, and if they were, this number would be considerably higher.

Over half of these investigations found that 'there was no case to answer', almost alluding to the impression that we could have flipped a coin with people's fate dependent on which side the coin landed. The most questionable impression we are left with is the lack of acknowledgement that our staff suffered as a result. They were not only hurt as individuals, but as part of wider teams, and there were impacts outside of the organisation such as the effects on their families. Some staff were suspended for long periods of time, subject to rumour and 'no smoke without fire' gossip. Exonerated and non-exonerated staff have all reported hurt during the process. This is expressed through their lack of psychological safety and that of their colleagues, some physical or mental health problems and even a perceived or real impact on their careers.

Some of the accumulated 'hurt and staff pain' was documented in a powerful film released in April 2018 which details the 2016–2017 of Mersey Care's journey (Search YouTube for Dekker Mersey Care). Although Mersey Care supported the film's production, it was made independently by Sidney Dekker, with the CEO's request to 'tell it as it is'. Few in the trust can fail to recall the sense of distress as we saw the initial cuts of the film one afternoon in our conference room. It was a moment of paradigm change.

We felt the staff's pain; tears were shed and our immediate collective response was that there was no going back on our journey, no matter what the challenges were. As a trust with a strong tradition in mental health, it was clear from the film we had missed the need to care for the mental health and well-being of our staff. On the contrary, some of our processes, investigations and management of harmful events actually damaged the mental health of our own staff. Continued action was needed to support urgent change given that the hurt staff experienced was essentially cumulative in its impact a situation that simply and effectively eroded psychological safety.

Sadly this situation is not unique to Mersey Care or the NHS. An article in *People Management* in June 2019 entitled 'My brother took his own life after being suspended from work. He didn't need to die' (Sheridan, 2019) highlighted the story of a man who died by suicide after being suspended from work. In it, the author, under an assumed name, gave a heartfelt plea to all employers to change the way they handle disciplinary processes and for this to start with their HR and people processes: 'I know the people who suspended my brother did not want him to die', she concludes. Whilst a just and learning culture needs to be led from the top, every staff member has to be the guardian of the culture they want to create if it is to thrive. It needs to embed in all processes, not just HR and people processes. Indeed, organisations have to ask themselves a series of questions. They must be rigorous and become detailed conversations at Board level:

- How do you know your people processes and systems support the organisational culture they aspire to achieve?
- Do your people processes focus on 'who' or 'what'?
- Do they acknowledge harm or perceived harm? How?
- Do your people processes encourage accountability of all your stakeholders? How?
- Do they identify and address systemic issues? How?
- What is the gap between the intended work outcomes for your people processes and what is happening? How do you know?
- How does your culture live and breathe within your organisational context? Is that the same everywhere or are there subcultures which are visible?
- What is the impact on all of the above on your people? How do you know?
- How do you work with staff side, freedom to speak up guardians and wider stakeholders as partners to improve all the above?

The Informal versus Formal Approach – What Does ACAS Say?

The Advisory, Conciliation and Arbitration Service (ACAS) is a non-departmental UK government body, established by the Employment Act (1975), with a statutory function to assist parties reach a resolution in disputes and to promote the improvement of employment relations. Over recent years, ACAS has put much focus into how to manage disputes inside workplace, including identifying creative, early and non-legal solutions to managing conflict in response to the increase in individual disputes in the form of claims to the employment tribunal systems (Dix and Barber, 2015). However, the approach of ACAS invites further questioning.

It is worth considering the ACAS statutory code of practice on disciplinary and grievances at work (July 2020). This provides guidance to employers, employees and their representatives, and it sets out clear principles for the handling of disciplinary and grievance situations in the workplace. The guidance does not rest solely on an explanation of formal action; it explains steps to handling issues informally.

HR practitioners and union representatives often base their organisation's policy on this code. This is to be expected given the authoritative and respected status of ACAS as a Crown body which was affirmed a robust place in industrial relations following the significant employment regulation developments of the 1970s. Yet the question covered by that organisation's guidance on Conducting Workplace Investigations (June 2019) that we have to ask ourselves is: Do we gloss over the organisational preparation in answering the question 'Is the investigation necessary?' The question is posed, however in our experience it is not considered fully enough. Indeed the default scenario of triggering investigations is that we leap into establishing terms of reference and commencing an investigation before we have truly answered or reflected on whether a formal investigation is needed in the first place. This is duly observed in the early bullet points of the NHEI Providers' letter.

ACAS does state that some incidences may arise and can be resolved quickly without due process. They also highlight that preliminary information and data gathering are appropriate and could indeed prevent the need for commencing formal investigations. Further, in a paper by ACAS on 'Fairness, justice and capability – repositioning conflict management' in 2019, the importance of improving conversation and skills for managers and leaders is highlighted, and that new approaches and alternative methods are needed to manage conflict more effectively. The balance between handling the informal and the formal is not always a simple task but we have an obligation to consider the informal resolution before instigating formal investigations, because of the impact this has on our people. We must ask if our people have the skills to deal with issues and investigations in new ways that advocate fairness.

What If There Are Criminal or Safeguarding Proceedings?

As a healthcare organisation, we have safeguarding proceedings which require us to inform external authorities such as commissioners, councils or regulators in certain circumstances. There are also occasions where criminal proceedings are required. As an employer, we may have to decide to continue or pause our investigation or part of it until the criminal proceedings have concluded. In reaching these decisions, we have to consider what is reasonable to the organisation, to the staff member and to wider communities. We have a duty of care to all of our people – who we care for and the caregivers. As Dekker notes, those who have deliberately acted in a manner which take us into the realm of sabotage, criminality or terrorism would require different interventions and formal investigational route, whilst restorative approaches will also frame these formal approaches, such acts take us beyond the scope of this book.

Non-prejudicial Action – It's Not That Simple

ACAS accepts in certain situations that employees may have to decide that suspension is necessary while information is gathered either informally or formally. This includes where:

- Working relationships have broken down;
- The employee could tamper with evidence;
- There is a risk to an employee's health or safety;
- Property or the business of an employee or the organisation may be damaged;
- The employee is subject to criminal proceedings, which may affect whether then can do their job.

As described, in healthcare we also have the additional safety risks to our vulnerable patients and service users.

The ACAS Guide (2020) highlights the risk of suspension and the impact this could have on individual's health. It states that 'suspensions can leave individuals feeling prejudged, demotivated and devalued', in other words feeling the very opposite of being a non-prejudicial action.

Mersey Care now formally recognises that stating that a formal investigation or suspension is a 'non-prejudicial action' does not feel like that to the member of staff concerned. However obvious it may be, this was not admitted until very recently. It is an indication of the sort of disconnected hierarchy that allows leaders to imagine one outcome when frontline staff experience another. The realisation means that staff in HR now work with real focus and purpose alongside operational managers and unions to keep investigations and suspensions to an absolute minimum. Our staff side colleagues speak of this in this book as a real shift from *saying* we work together to *actually being* partners. Our Board leaders see and discuss the data relating to employee relations' (ER) activity.

This is really important for all staff involved to maintain their psychological safety and well-being. The effects of this realisation go wider. Consideration needs to be given to the occupational health model and also to staff support systems and associated interventions.

Top Tips for Understanding Your People Processes

1. What is your data telling you? Look at staff survey data, people metrics, numbers of investigations, suspensions and associated costs.
2. What are your people telling you? Ask people who have previously been subjected to your people processes what it felt like for them. This must include a proper appreciation of what staff side colleagues are saying as well.

   NB: Ask the same two questions again through a protected characteristic lens as their maybe further evidence regarding disparities (Being Fair, 2019).
3. How can you be assured of the consistency in the application of your rules or decision-making processes?
4. What is the cognitive framing within your policy framework? Look at the language you use: Is it framed against the employee or supportive of the employee?
5. How are you distinguishing between causal effects and contributory factors in your people processes?
6. What practical steps has your organisation taken to ensure your people processes are restorative?
7. How are you assuring yourself that you are really applying restorative just culture in action (*if you believe you are already on this journey*)?
8. What are your HR teams and operational managers' mindsets about this new approach?
9. Where is the learning now and how is it captured?
10. What do you think will be the critical steps in making progress to a new way for restorative people processes?

    (You can see these points set out on Mersey Care's website – we suggest downloading it and spending time as senior leaders on each point: Search online Mersey Care Just Culture Journey and links to our Just Culture 4 e-learning modules.)

Improving People Processes – It's within Our Grasp

We are at a point where employment law and restorative just culture share similar aims. UK employment law principles compliment restorative just culture people practise very well. Indeed, the UK legal framework operates in accordance with the principles of reasonableness and fairness which are embedded in the concept of restorative just culture approaches in the workplace. Case law also highlights the importance of full and proper approaches and understanding of all the circumstances surrounding an event or incident. Therefore, there is no reason for employment law to inhibit the application of restorative people processes in the workplace. In fact, it should be seen as an enabler to keeping organisations and employees safe at work and removing some of the traditional employee relations issues.

The HR Challenge – Keeping the Human in Human Resources

So can all organisations apply restorative just culture approaches in people processes and practices without commencing an investigation? This is a critical question – the answer to which any team implementing this approach will need to be able to handle. In many aspects, the investigation itself is a form of litmus test for the integrity of any local implementation of restorative just practices. Almost certainly those who are still evaluating the concept - never mind the practice - will have many questions. We hear them from time to time: 'Has a formal process become informal?', 'Are we now just letting people get away with things?', 'Are we too soft on people now?' And of course: 'In my day you would have been sacked for this'.

Trusts have to acknowledge that if disciplinary cases become a way of shifting blame onto colleagues, we miss the systematic or organisational contributing factors. Worse, we inhibit the learning. The UK GMC's independent review 'Gross negligence manslaughter and culpable homicide: working together for a just culture' (2019) highlighted this very concern: why should the lessons about one individual carry the blame for what they considered to be wider systemic failings which contributed to some individual errors. If organisations find themselves asking why does this keep happening, you have to ask are you merely attempting to defend your position by saying this one is slightly different to the last one. Yet if we step back from it, if it looks the same and feels the same, are we really being open to the opportunity of learning? The consequence of not being really open to the learning is that we unintentionally disinvest in preventing further incidences occurring or at worst reoccurring. This is the patient safety dividend.

To have patient safety as the optimum goal of any health organisation, the care givers have to feel psychologically safe first. If our people feel too vulnerable to raise a concern about system pressures which lead to errors, then we are not truly being open to the wider implications for patients and indeed our care givers.

As described in Chapter 2, working collaboratively with our staff side colleagues and operational managers, Mersey Care held the mirror up to ourselves about how our people processes (HR and patient safety processes post-incident) were barriers, both perceived and real, to achieving our trust's aspirations to deliver the best care possible. In Mersey Care terminology, this is our ambition for 'Perfect Care'.

This new process began with a pilot in the trust's Secure Division. This part of the organisation supports patients who present a significant risk to themselves or others and are detained in secure healthcare facilities under the Mental Health Act (1983). These locations are some of the most challenging places to deliver care and therapy. In these highly complex settings, there had historically been periods of adversarial employment relations and breakdowns in relationships with unions which had led to incidents of industrial action and employment tribunals.

At this stage, we were modelling the earliest form of the culture change, still called 'just culture'. Prototyping and adapting our approach we started to ask ourselves what was going wrong when incidents occurred rather than jumping to apportion blame. This process required an investment of time and effort. The result was that we saw a significant reduction in the number of disciplinary investigations and suspensions.

Investigations and Suspensions in Mersey Care

Through further staff engagement and co-production with unions and managers, Mersey Care formally launched our new process in April 2017. This meant awareness-raising across the whole of organisation, staff communications, meetings and roadshows. We sought to mobilise this in our diverse services. It could not be just top down. We appointed staff ambassadors, people working in wards, services, in all the kinds of roles the trust provides. Many of these ambassadors had personal experiences of our former people processes. We were making the first steps in our journey to reducing the hurt.

This broadening out to all parts of the Trust took time. It occurred as the organisation itself was evolving in other ways. Mersey Care was taking on new services and acquiring other, previously independent organisations. The trust was to double in size (see Figure 9.1). That process of expansion brought its own challenges as new cultures, and indeed new instances of serious harm and hurt to people emerged.

Throughout this, trust continues to aspire to a position that allows for all parties to discuss how they have been affected on all occasions and collaboratively decide what can be done to repair the harm. This recognises that there are multiple perspectives at play. We remain on our journey and continue to learn through application along the way.

At the beginning of 2021, the Trust saw a spike in formal disciplinary investigations. This was something we had suspected may occur, but we remain confident in our methodology and approach. That does not infer complacency. We have made use of these events to learn, review and refresh our material with our partners, including HR, operational manager's and staff side representatives. We have also ensured transparency by taking papers to our board committees to provide comparative data in our activity

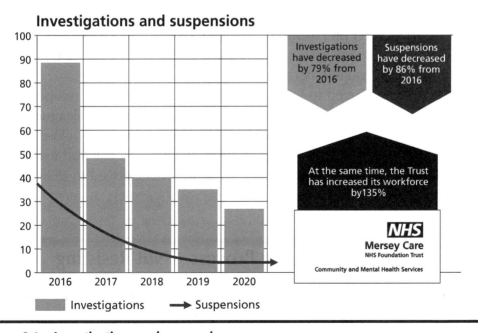

Figure 9.1   Investigations and suspensions.

levels, explanations and learning. Transparency, continuous learning and the review of our approaches and practices with stakeholders are critical to our continuous learning approach.

The Right Approach for Us

The application of a restorative just culture approach to support and manage people practices will help organisations establish if an investigation is actually needed. In reviewing the most appropriate approach for the application, we reviewed ACAS guidance, CIPD literature and factsheets on discipline and grievance at work, 2020. We also considered Professor Dekker's literature and research and that of other academics on just culture. Most recently, we have made good use of Dekker's Restorative Just Culture Checklist (2018) and the NHSI (*A Just Culture Guide*, 2018 tool) and Kirkup (2019) criticism of NHSI's Just Culture Guide: good intentions failed by flawed design (*Journal of the Royal Society of Medicine*, 2019) and Woodward's Implementing Patient Safety (2019).

From this review early in our own journey, and as we progressed in years that followed, we found Professor Dekker's work gave the most thorough focus on the conversations between managers and staff involved in the incident/event to understand and make sense of the restorative aspect of Just Culture. It was that approach we believed most appropriate in a clinical setting. We had been practising restorative justice with some of our patient groups but had not extended its application to our workforce, not considering it could apply equally there too.

As the trust continued to learn and adapt, we have now developed our own four-step restorative just culture process working with colleagues from Northumbria University. This has come about by working very closely with operational managers, HR, staff side representatives and just and learning staff ambassadors, in a listening exercise which was pledged to deliver a meaningful and functional outcome.

Leading Restorative People Process – Not Resisting

Mersey Care's four-step process further develops NHSEi's guidance on just culture and Professor Dekker's own restorative just culture checklist – critically its asks:

Step 1 – trigger point – every adverse event or incident has a trigger that could have caused or did result in harm to people or groups of people. This can include psychological harm and feelings of hurt, or physical harm even or damage to property.

Step 2 – covers pointers on what people always need to remember re-stabilising the situation and covering questions of hurt, understanding and resources.

Step 3 – is our gateway, this step might not always be required but it asks key questions before an investigation into anyone's individual actions occurs, and is only warranted if all the statements are deemed to be true.

Step 4 – gives prompts and asks questions about restorative goals being achieved.

Whilst there are four steps, it is clear that this needs to remain a fluid process, and whilst Steps 1, 2 and 4 have to be completed, Step 3 only needs to be completed if required. However, there may be a need for some other steps to be revisited and returned too more than once, because you do not always achieve restorative practice in one attempt.

We had been endeavouring to unite our own learning deliver and incorporate NHSI's guidance and Dekker's checklist, in our four-step model. The resulting four-step process enables our managers, staff side colleagues and HR practitioners to focus on the immediate here and now issues, triggers and responses to stabilise circumstances as appropriate. It supports the needs of patients, families, staff and colleagues. The four-step process allows for multiple accounts of personal truths and quite effectively moves organisations away from jumping into individual action. Critically it also gives emphasis to repairing the trust and relationships damaged after the incident. This step is crucial and in our experience is, sadly, often missed and misunderstood. One of the ways to bring to life the fundamental shift in mindset that is possible is to compare and contrast the experience of an HR colleague with that of a staff side counterpart (see the case studies from colleagues which conclude this chapter).

This four-step approach is our framework, our methodology for our people processes. It avoids applying a fixed 'incident tree approach' which focuses on the 'who' and not the 'what'. Rigid incident decision trees tend not to address the human aspect of compassion. As Dekker (2014) observed, there is little evidence that organisations which have implemented culpability decision trees produce more learning, indeed he adds that you can't proceduralise compassion. In fact, decision trees sometimes encourage a climate of risk secrecy and still very much focus on 'who' did something and not 'what' occurred. They also ignore the impact of the bias which could inhibit how the incident decision tree is navigated through and the impact that is has on individual outcomes.

Our experience of having a framework is extremely positive. We know it is necessary to have a freedom within the framework, so it has to be underpinned by good training and people management. Cognitive framing is critical. Mersey Care took some time to look at the language we were using – the word choices that imposed judgement too soon in the process ('*You* are being investigated' and so forth). We simply speaking started to destigmatise the language of failure. We also became aware that there was a danger of falling into semi-religious definitions of right and wrong, good and evil, and indeed it brought up concerns as to who was able to offer clemency. Hurt, forgiveness, harm – these are all very big concepts. Forgiveness is a word bound up with religious connotations.

Our people come from different places and cultures. They bring multiple perspectives and inclinations of judgements. All this can complicate how an event is dealt with post-incident. We wanted to strip it back, look at the hurt and address it. We must prevent it getting adversarial or cloaked in pseudo-religious rites of who may be allowed to be the arbiter of forgiveness. People need to feel safe to do this, to have free space within the framework, but actually having that framework to guide us we have found very extremely helpful.

Within this framework, we have ensured that specific cultural sensitivities are addressed and considered. Concerns about behaviours experienced by colleagues with protected characteristics are regularly prominent in the NHS Staff Survey. Being Fair (NHS Resolution, July 2019) and workforce race equality data show that across the NHS, BAME staff are disproportionately more likely to be involved in disciplinary investigations than their white colleagues. There are other indications of power discrepancies and inequalities. In July 2019, the NHS Workforce Race Equality Standard (WRES) national team released a publication entitled 'Fairness for All' to highlight the importance of closing the ethnicity gap in rates of disciplinary action across the NHS workforce.

Mersey Care's four-step process enabled the Trust to reduce hindsight bias as much as possible. We are reviewing the potential for cultural sensitivities before investigations begin. Investigations involving all staff and therefore BAME staff are now lower in the trust than before. However, we cannot in absolute terms yet defend our position with this, since comparing the numbers of BAME staff to white staff entering the process still shows disproportionality. So whilst I may have said that in a certain year, 'only' X number of BAME staff members had entered into a formal disciplinary investigation, as our numbers are so low, we have to acknowledge the disproportionality experienced by BAME staff remains and we cannot make excuses to defend our position, rather we have to step back and understand in order to address the disparities. So, we are continuing to learn more about this. Moreover, the inequalities exposed by COVID-19 have given extra impetus to understand the effects on different populations and our people. Our trust's existing studies of the effects of incivility and disrespect (as opposed to the desired civility and respect) in the workplace have led us to expand the brief and our future focus on zero acceptance of racism, discriminatory and disrespectful behaviours has begun.

Since the annual NHS staff survey is confidential, we are frustrated in our ability to understand the details of what lies behind reported incidents of bullying, intolerance or other negativities. People sometimes tell us in confidence that they have endured mistreatment because of a characteristic but we do not get the specifics, and therefore we don't have opportunity to address the individual issues. Mersey Care's approaches have sought to reach into these areas, but we still have more work to do.

As we have seen, a restorative just culture does not ignore staff responsibilities or accountabilities for preforming their duties. Instead, with a restorative approach, an account is something we give or expect those involved in incidents to give. This contrasts with the conventional notion in a retributive system of having to pay an account. The objective being to enable organisational learning by increasing our understanding of the impact of the incident and how to put things right. Over the years of our journey, we have found professional bodies' approaches have become more akin to the notion and application of Just Culture.

People processes should not fall into the trap of using 'accountability' as a way to address a perceived failure as it will inhibit learning and psychological safety. Even more importantly HR professionals have to *unlearn* previous reactions to perceived personal failure. Ideally, they even have to learn to start to de-stigmatise the language of failure. Thereby shifting mindsets to understanding the impact of multiple perceptions and varied professional viewpoints and how it impacts reactions and responses to real and perceived to failure (maybe by reframing the language to a response to when something did not go as planned or expected). Through the application of restorative just culture techniques to people practices, organisational learning may be identified. Here we focus on distinguishing between causality and contributory factors. We have to remember that there may still be some occasions where individual needs will need to be identified. These range from reflective practices, supervision, training, performance or behavioural needs. Indeed, restorative just culture approaches in people practices should embody fairness, learning and accountability.

We find that formal action may still be required in exceptional cases, but this should never be an organisation's preferred or default choice. Indeed, our experience has shown us that some organisations use the terminology just culture merely to distinguish between acceptable and unacceptable performance or between good and bad apples: this is not the just culture approach we advocate. Retributive approaches inhibit candour and transparency, which is the critical platform to enable the demonstration of remorse, the seeking of forgiveness and the identification of organisational learning to prevent similar recurrences. If you and your organisation do not adopt a restorative approach, the real risk is the prolonging of hurt and pain or even causing further hurt.

There are other unseen costs for retributive people approaches within organisations that are often not considered. These may include the carrying of vacancies, turnover, actual costs of formal disciplinary investigations, suspensions and legal defence. This issue will be explored more later in this book.

HR Practitioners and Hindsight Basis

In *The Field Guide to Human Error Investigations*, Dekker (2014) describes the importance of how HR practitioners react to failure. This is important in determining how people processes are designed, developed and applied. Let us first look at what we mean by hindsight and bias, and together hindsight bias?

Hindsight – the understanding of a situation or event only after it has happened or developed

Bias – the inclination or prejudice for or against one person or group, in particular when you know or think you know something.

Hindsight bias – knowing the outcome of an event or incident increases people who are outside that incident to convince themselves they would have handled the incident differently, made different decisions or some other variable, which would have prevented the outcome.

Dekker describes four possible reactions to failure which HR functions may want to consider from an investigatory people process perspective:

(a) Retrospective disciplinary investigations – the investigator as an outsider observer thinks they know more about the incident or sequence of events than the people who are caught up in it.

(b) Counterfactual disciplinary investigation – the investigator as an outsider may fall into the trap of explaining what people should or should not have done, when they already know the outcome, causing the investigator to make judgements about people's actions and behaviours. This is even more dangerous if the people giving explanation do not fully understand the clinical/technical skills required or the environment in which the incident occurred.

(c) Judgemental disciplinary investigations – the investigator judges people for not knowing what you think they should have known at that time, or not doing what you think they should have done, or not mitigating the risks, that you can now see clearly, but where not aware of before. In other words, it does not try to understand the behaviour of people in the context of the environment they are working within.

(d) Proximal disciplinary investigations – the investigator focuses on 'going right to' the people closest to the incident, event or near miss – focusing on the who, as appose to systemic reflections and concerns.

Lessons on Our Journey

■ Different perspectives on an incident or event are commonplace. As an outsider with hindsight, you have the knowledge of the outcome and the impact, both perceived and real. From the insider's point of view, you do not know the outcome or the impact at that time.

■ Avoid falling into the trap of discussing an event in a way that never actually happened, i.e., they should have, could have, if only they did a, b and c.

■ Do not be fooled that just because something has not gone to plan on this one previous occasion that the same actions and behaviours will not reproducibly deliver good outcomes – our people often triumph in the face of adversity.

■ Do you understand what occurred through the lens of the person or people involved in the incident? Have you attempted to make sense of it from their perspective, in the environment in which it occurred, and on that particular day?

■ Consider how people's conscious and unconscious choices and actions are 'heavily conditioned by strongly reinforced norms and other constraints, some of them deeply institutionally and historically patterned' (A multi-site ethnographic study. Sociology of health and illness, 2016). Organisations and teams can normalise approaches to how things are done in their own sub-systems, despite what the rule book says. Consider how work is actually done on the ground compared to how work is imagined from a removed position.

■ Finally, and most importantly, focusing on the 'who' as opposed to the 'what' fails to look at the incident in a truly holistic way, i.e., in the whole organisational context and potential for various contributory factors.

Reflecting on former HR practices, Mersey Care and, we strongly suppose, other organisations often readily fall into the four possible reactions to failure Dekker describes. Alongside operational investigatory managers, HR practitioners have a tendency to look back at an event and target terms of reference and investigatory questions around what you or someone else *should have done*. Then bias naturally follows. Phases such as, 'well they should have done this or that' arise often without any knowledge or limited understanding of people's roles and the context and environment in which things occurred. In the previous system, all too often one of the first reactions to failure was to jump to the trust's disciplinary policy and scroll down the list of misdemeanours and ask which one was committed or not done. It was a process-centred approach, not a people-centred one. If the 'act' wasn't clearly defined within the procedural framework, it could be caught in the general 'other' section. More often than not, that would lead to a policy review and amendment to capture the misdemeanours not actually reflected at that time, thereby reinforcing a very real impression of a policy-centric approach to 'catch people' out, or simply speaking putting policies before your people and not one that embodies fairness, encourages accountability or learning. It was a defensive and blinded approach to honesty and transparency: it reinforced a power imbalance and left people feeling unsafe. Without any hint of irony, the HR professional can often respond to rules being broken by writing more rules, which will themselves inevitably be broken!

It's also often missed the point. It failed to make sense of actions. This is not about whether it makes sense to you, rather this is about understanding whether it made sense to the person who made the decision or thought on their feet and enacted in that way on that day. This should be about people before process, every time.

As an example and an aside, albeit a significant one, Mersey Care's Director of Finance recalls vividly the day – and what he was doing – when he was informed of a major fraud which lost the trust £900,000. This was of massive significance, as any loss of public money rightly should be and was widely reported as a 'fake invoice scam'. But the approach taken to the investigation and understanding of what happened was immediately one of restorative just culture. No one in Mersey Care had set out to be part of the aberrant behaviour. The fraudsters were the offending parties, not our finance staff. We asked what had happened. And, as the incident was reported formally there was a moment of realisation, sitting in the board-room, hearing the Director of Finance, non-executive Directors and Chair asking restorative questions – what happened, not who did it. This was a real moment of impact and showed that the culture change had landed at a time when corporately we were very visible. The cultural change was being role modelled and the behaviours we wanted to see were being lived and breathed. In a moment of humour, we joked that our job was done. It wasn't but the journey not only had senior-level support, but it was tested publicly in extremis and found to be embedded.

Aftermath – Unresolved People Processes

The research study completed in 2018 (Roberts reference) and other researchers' papers (ACAS, Disputes and their management in the workplace: a survey of British employers, 2020) demonstrate that people processes are ubiquitous features within all organisations.

The aftermath of an incident, even in an organisation which purports to embody a restorative just culture, is that the potential for incidents to spark adversarial relationships or let them fester is still profound. As Berlinger (2005) argues, what happens in the aftermath of an incident is that adversarial relationships can grow as we go into a self-protecting, defensive position either as an individual, a team or as an organisation. So critically, if after an incident or event we can address the hurt, through the ability to give our account of what occurred, offering apologies where appropriate, this will reduce the need for self-protection. When in self-protection mode, candour and learning is inhibited. We do need to be aware though that whilst this may make the conditions for forgiveness possible, it never eliminates the need or guarantees the outcome.

What If Forgiveness Cannot Be Achieved?

Extensive literature looks at seeking forgiveness from a patient perspective. We have heard in Chapters 3 and 4 in particular about the human impact of hurt and harm to patient's families. This is also an issue for the care givers as we have seen and casts concerns about terminology that bring us close to the ethics of religious forgiveness. In any people process, this is the most difficult facet as the link between true restoration and forgiveness is profound.

In the non-sacred world, enforcing apologies and seeking forgiveness cannot be mandated. Berlinger rightly highlights the conditions for which forgiveness is more likely to be achieved; however, we must recognise that for some this may never be possible or only partially so.

Creating the conditions to achieve forgiveness in our people processes may include some of these practices. There will be many others:

- Inviting all involved to give their account – first victim, second victim and wider communities and teams;
- Meeting contractual or legal obligations for first and second victims;
- Involvement of those above in the learning, and improvement and next steps needed, actions to be enacted and so forth;
- Learning reflection, clinical supervision, safe places to share and explore personal and teams' reactions to incidents and explore joint responsibilities;
- Supporting the hurt, learning how to improve psychological safety;
- Staff support or psychological interventions, supporting people who feel guilty or vulnerable for any contribution to hurt of others;
- Not forcing apologies or forgiveness;
- Giving people space to heal and time to do so;
- Organisational learning – discuss it, change practices, protocols, offer of authentic apologies, compassionate and proportionate responses;
- Full acceptance or partial acceptance and preparedness to move on, draw a line, have a new beginning, or agree new ways of working, or how relationships will be managed in the workplace, or how care will be managed;

- Not forcing victims to interact with each other, where no wish to do so from one or more party, for staff this may include redeployment or patients it may include access to care from another service or other providers – all with involvement and engagement, so done together not imposed;
- Restorative reconciliation where appropriate or mediation with patient and staff and staff and management, or staff with other staff;
- Development of civility and respect conversations, team norms;
- Refreshing policies, protocols where necessary;
- Authentic apology and/or expressions of remorse (whether accepted or not).

More about Forgiveness

Forgiveness alone is insufficient to enable an organisation or individual to have closure and move on.

Forgiveness is not a simple act, and sometimes people don't feel able to forgive or reconcile with the person who hurt them. However, neither is forgiveness similar to a judicial pardon or justification for the hurt, nor is it excusing away inappropriate behaviour or action, expecting or assuming it is forgotten. In a human system, it is (or should be) a grave disappointment then relationships cannot be restored, it is one of deep regret. One has to acknowledge we don't always get the outcome that we want and we continually get asked if we mean everything at Mersey Care embodies just and learning. Simply, do we now get it right all the time? Our response is equally succinct: things still do not go as planned or as intended today, people still do get hurt today. But the organisation is in a much better place today than yesterday: the difference today is we are transparent and open, we apologise and engage in a conversation and fundamentally we are ready to learn from it.

In Summary

The alternative to restorative just culture people processes is the traditional way. No matter how challenging or thought-provoking, the invitation to create improved people processes is too great an opportunity to miss.

The correlation between staff safety and patient safety is well researched and evidenced. Therefore how we treat and support our people through people processes at the most difficult of times gives us all insight into organisations safety culture and staff and patient experience. Restorative just culture people processes give organisations real leverage in improving fairness, accountability and learning and halt often over- proceduralised ways of dealing with the 'who' rather than the 'what'. In more recent times, we have seen the creation of safe spaces that have has supported resolution and meant we are more proactive in our response to all our people.

In healthcare, and indeed beyond, restorative just culture is a valuable approach before the formal engagement of any kind of formal people process. ACAS and the letter from NHSI say this. Mersey Care's experience goes beyond confirming that approach. We have seen that what remains can be much hurt, harm and distrust which remain in the system from before such approach was taken seriously. We have also learnt continuing with a preoccupation with what happened before or harbouring resentment can only serve to hurt all our people more. In a restorative just culture we should not have a desire to hurt anyone, but to focus on healing, learning and collaboratively planning how we put that learning into practice and action to benefit our patients and staff alike.

Traditional retribution ways or partial retribution ways still focus on the who. They minimise the opportunity for learning and at worse they don't expose risk and don't allow candour. They may even allow for the recurrence of further harm.

HR and its processes must not be what we do to our people, they must be fully about engaging with our people and including our people. We must therefore make certain that our policies are for our people, and in particular that the relational side of HR in creating psychological safety is paramount. As has become clear, we have to appreciate what is going on under the surface and any implications of bias and power to help and enable full restoration.

Mersey Care's reflection on this is that it is right and normal that in a workplace there are differences of opinion and challenges in relationships. There are risks beyond the actions of our people in delivering complex care, and we must build in, with due diligence, the knowledge that there will be 'human error' (perhaps *human frailty* is a better description here). And it is how you respond to those fallibilities that is critical. We now want to see an informal resolution first before we impose sanctions or disciplinary processes.

Our four-step approach is more effective in resolving both minor and major issues and reducing conflict, including the formal and ultimately destructive tussles that occurred between management and unions. That collective trust in the new approach between HR and our staff side colleagues has itself become a positive development of our wider journey.

The fundamental question about sense-making and understanding multiple perspectives (wearing someone else's glasses) creates a platform for autonomous learning and reducing the climate of fear about formal HR processes. We have a general acceptance that some things can and will go wrong (or reframed to 'not as expected'), but now our approaches deal with them very differently. Without that psychological safety in place, vulnerabilities will be exposed and the blame game starts all over again. This is not a task that is completed, but a consensus exists of where our journey is headed.

Personal Reflections

Mersey Care's Associate Director of Workforce Lynn Lowe Says:

Having been an HR professional for more than 30 years and leading a team of operational HR practitioners, I felt we were all greatly invested in employee relations practices. I can now see that these practices were filled with hindsight bias, were too heavily reliant on policy and process and concentrated on what individuals had done 'wrong' and what rule they had broken.

The practices of the time were leading to the trust instigating a very high level of investigations (143 during 2014 out of a workforce of 3,500). The terms of reference were too large and vague in some cases. At worst, we suspended staff (55 in 2014) because we *believed* they were guilty and did so *before* we actually told them what they were guilty of. And yes, that word 'guilty' may itself be part of the problem.

We heavily relied on the understanding that suspension was a non-prejudicial act. We did not realise or even consider the impact on the individual. Whilst we had a range of wrap around support for staff, including occupational health and staff support services, they were used just as part of a process: we missed the fundamental issue of psychological safety and the care giver. It was neglected as we concentrated on undertaking the employee relations process and ultimately put this before our people.

It could be considered that there was a lack of transparency in what we were doing and why. This consequently created a cloud of secrecy and confusion that never actually needed to be there. For some HR practitioners, because this was the way we did things and how we had been trained, we continued down this route and did not push back. Practitioners did not always question decisions by managers. We accepted their decision. On the rare occasions when we did question them, it was easy to back down. It might almost be considered that we had colluded with the manager to take an individual through a process. It was also easy to say that HR had supported and approved this approach, absolving the manager of any responsibility around this process.

What was also uncovered was that some staff were lying to us but we did not know why. If we go back to our HR professional training, we are taught that the employer/employee relationship becomes untenable as the lie has been told. We never asked ourselves why staff were lying, it never entered into our sphere, we automatically assumed guilt because something had happened and actually we never thought to ask them for reasons.

Looking back at the way we used to do things, we never thought about the impact our processes and delays had on the individual. We were too focused on completing the investigation but not always in a timely way. We concentrated on finding the evidence to confirm the guilt without any consideration to the individual being put through a process. There was no apology for the hurt caused. It became a frustrating process for all involved and often ended with 'no case to answer' and ultimately a damaged member of staff.

When Amanda Oates, Executive Director of Workforce, started to talk to me about just culture and trying something different, I felt a whole range of emotions. It began with anxiousness about changing my HR practice but I was upset and angry that I had not considered the impact on or hurt caused to others. I was also excited at the prospect of trying something new and making a real difference to how we treated our colleagues. This was an opportunity to really understand their experiences and how we could restore relationships in order to make the organisation a better place to work. I was determined to be part of this journey

It takes time to change mind set and we could not do it on our own. As a HR team, we started discussions in partnership with our staff side colleagues to find a new way of undertaking the process. Their story is also recorded in this chapter.

Initially, we developed our own incident decision tree to give structure to managing the process as we all felt that we needed a framework to adhere to. We asked different questions at the start of a process but soon realised that the incident decision tree focused on the 'who' not what had not gone as expected. The language in it was still relatively punitive. At a very early stage and jointly we agreed to discard the decision tree.

I began a programme of work with my HR practitioners to help them understand their role and responsibilities, informed by the Trust's Just Culture approach. Doing this with honesty and depth was a challenge: it was difficult and it was emotional. I underestimated the energy and resilience I personally needed to lead the HR team through this. But we all had a genuine desire for change and for supporting our people in a compassionate way. Despite a few stumbling blocks along the way we had a commitment to learn and cascade our new approach.

Immediately, we started to see a reduction in the number of disciplinary investigations and suspensions. As Associate Director, I took time to meet employees and ex-employees to hear directly from them and understand their experience of our processes and policy interpretation. I still do this. It was a significant step in helping to formulate the HR offer for Just Culture. It allowed me to appreciate the impact and hurt, both emotional and psychological that we put our staff through, intended or not. It also allowed me to share this learning with the wider team.

Since April 2017, all HR practitioners in the team have been fully involved in the development of our approach. As have our staff side colleagues. They have tested it out, sharing the learning and supporting each other. This enabled them to familiarise themselves with the approach and supported the development of our restorative just culture model. There is appropriate challenge, discussion and reflection and an aspiration to ensure that we truly treat our employees fairly and with compassion.

Without doubt, I can honestly say one of our greatest achievements has been the development of our Four Step process. This was developed in partnership with staff side, HR and managers in 2019 and completely encompasses the approach we now have in place. The four-step model is used as soon as an incident happens. It enables the organisation to understand from the individual's perspective why did it make sense for them as well as asking who is hurt. This process has given us further confidence that we are only formally investigating if there is no other way. It has also helped answer some individuals concerns that the new way is too 'light touch' and 'you can get away with anything in this new Just Culture'. The new four-step process has helpfully enabled us to focus on providing assurance regarding fairness, consistently and proportionate responses. It has also helped us address concerns particularly regarding values and behaviours. It enables us to challenge or investigate matters that, without this clearer framework, might not have been formerly investigated. It was important in this transition, that we did not worry if we saw a small peak in investigations since the introduction as we now had the new methodology to stand by. We also need to recognise that there may be a point when we will not continue to see a decrease in the number of investigations. For me, it's not just the number of them, it's the experience and support that is critical too. Behind every number is a person and consequently there are also wider teams and communities which need consideration.

A further reflection is at the beginning of our journey (prior to the four-step framework introduction), we probably did not investigate some things we should have investigated. Alternatively we conducted learning reviews or cultural reviews instead, to avoid the hurt often triggered by formal processes. In the absence of the four-step process, we can see this wasn't always the best option and did not always avoid the hurt. On reflection, we would now do this differently. We are continually refreshing our approach as HR practitioners and utilise the learning to improve work on restoring and re-integrating individuals.

As a HR practitioner, I can truly say this has been the highlight of my career and I am extremely proud and passionate of our journey. Working in a restorative just way is a message that I endeavour to spread across the HR community.

Lynn Lowe
Associate Director of Workforce – Human Resources

Mersey Care's Former Staff Side Chair Mandi Gregory Says:

During my career of 35 years working for the NHS, with 25 years experience as a Trade Union representative for Unison, I have found that I have at times loved and hated this great institution it in equal measure.

We were and are still taught to be advocates for the service users we cared for and speak up for those who may not be able to do so for themselves. There were couple of incidents that occurred quite close together where I found myself asking the question 'who speaks up for the staff?' A colleague became the target of a bully and was relentlessly undermined for having a disability. And because I stood up for her I then also became a target. Then another colleague was accused by a service user of stealing money. She was off duty at the time and was suspended immediately over the phone. All she was told was that an allegation had been made against her and she was not to come to work pending further investigations under the disciplinary policy. This was the only information she was given. Both situations left the staff absolutely devastated.

At the time we did not know who to turn to for support. The perception and belief amongst the staff was that HR were there to support the managers and could not be trusted. We worked in some of the most challenging services provided by the NHS and it felt that no one was prepared to listen or indeed have our backs as employees.

We believed the only option available for us was to turn to our trade union, Unison, for assistance. They became the voice I needed for support. I eventually undertook workplace representative training and became an active advocate for Unison and the staff as a whole within our Trust.

Historically through my representation work, I've witnessed many occasions when situations did not go as expected or incidents happened. Too often the first reaction was to look to blame the staff – they must have done something wrong. Suspensions, investigations and disciplinary action, all became the norm. It was just a process that was applied without any further thought or considerations for the impact on the staff member or their family.

We as Trade Unions should have been victorious. We won countless cases on behalf of our members, many with no case to answer. We had to go to Trust board appeals and we were winning them as well. But were we really?

I had become the Staff Side Chair for our organisation. My staff side colleagues and I personally witnessed the impact and devastation of these lengthy disciplinary processes. Some cases took well over a year to complete, coming back at hearings with no case to answer. We witnessed marriages breaking down, families being affected with children's physical and mental health particularly suffering. Ultimately our members, who worked for a mental health trust, were having mental health breakdowns caused by the stress and anxiety they were experiencing from the processes applied to them.

Teams were being affected. Mistrust and a lack of confidence grew as staff watched how their colleagues were being treated. It created at times a 'say nothing, do nothing situation' with the old adage 'don't put your head up above the parapet as you'll be next'. It also led to staff fearing to be honest around errors and how situations had occurred. They feared that even if they told the truth that the circumstances would not be taken into consideration.

I knew we needed to change; we couldn't carry on as a trust doing the same things and expecting different outcomes so I approached workforce Director Amanda Oates.

Mandi Gregory
Former Staff Side Representative and Staff Side Chair

I warmly endorse Mandi's comments. We have seen real change over the last few years with the need to support people, of all backgrounds, remaining as important as ever. Maybe even more so now. I've been able to play a key role in this approach and in Mersey Care's dedicated workstream about enabling respect and civility. Those qualities are always needed but when health services face the unique challenges of recent years, they are absolutely vital. The partnership of staff side and trust leaders, I am pleased to say, continues to everyone's benefit.

Ian Raven
Staff Side Chair and Branch Secretary Unite the Union.

References

Being Fair. NHS Resolution, 2019. https://resolution.nhs.uk/resources/being-fair-report

Berlinger, N. "After Harm. Medical Error and the Ethics of Forgiveness." Blackwell/Johns Hopkins University Press, 2005.

Darlington, Ralph, Gill Dix, and Brendan Barber. "The changing face of work: insights from Acas." *Employee Relations* 37, no. 6 (2015).

Dekker, Sidney W.A. "The re-invention of human error." *Human Factors and Aerospace Safety* 1, no. 3 (2001): 247–265.

Dekker, Sidney "Reconstructing human contributions to accidents." *Journal of Safety Research* 3 (2002): 371–385. https://1stdirectory.co.uk/_assets/files_comp/9c9cd60c-7935-4323-9f64-c361b517b168.pdf

Dekker, Sidney. *The Field Guide to Understanding Human Error.* Routledge, 2014.

Dekker, Sidney. *The Field Guide to Human Error Investigations.* Routledge, 2017.

Dix, G. and Barber, S. B. "The changing face of work: Insights from Acas." *Employee Relations* 37, no. 6 (2015): 670–682. https://doi.org/10.1108/ER-03-2015-0056

Dix, Gill, Keith Sisson, and John Forth. "Conflict at work: the changing pattern of disputes." *The Evolution of the Modern Workplace*, 176–200. Cambridge: Cambridge University Press, 2009.

Dweck, Carol S. *Mindset: the New Psychology of Success.* New York: Little Brown Book Group, 2017.

Edmondson, Amy. Psychological Safety and Learning Behavior in Work Teams, 1999. https://journals.sagepub.com/doi/abs/10.2307/2666999

Edmondson, Amy C., and Josephine P. Mogelof. "Explaining psychological safety in innovation teams: Organizational culture, team dynamics, or personality." *Creativity and Innovation in Organizational Teams* 21 (2006): 28.

Edmondson, Amy C., Roderick M. Kramer, and Karen S. Cook. "Psychological safety, trust, and learning in organizations: A group-level lens." *Trust and Distrust in Organizations: Dilemmas and Approaches* 12 (2004): 239–272.

Hogan, Helen et al. "Avoidability of hospital deaths and association with hospital-wide mortality ratios: Retrospective case record review and regression analysis." *British Medical Journal* 351, (2015). https://www.bmj.com/content/351/bmj.h3239

Holden, Richard J. "People or systems? To blame is human. The fix is to engineer." *Professional Safety* 54, no. 12 (2009): 34.

McNally, David. "Special Measures, Burnout and Occupational Stress in National Health Service Staff: Experiences, Interpretations and Evidence-based Interventions." PhD diss., Bangor University, 2019.

Roberts, Dale, "The Digital Social Workplace, People over Process." *PM World Journal*, July 2018. www.pmwoldjournal.net

Sheridan, C. "My Brother took his own life after being suspend from work. He didn't need to die." People Management, June 2019: www.peoplemanagement. co.uk

NHS England. Provider Bulletin, 2019. www.england.nhs.uk/2019/06/provider-bulletin-5-june-2019/#improving-our-people-practices

NHS England and Improvement. The NHS Patient Safety Strategy. Safer Culture, Safer Systems, Safer Patients, 2019.

Woodward, S. *Implementing Patient Safety. Addressing Culture, Conditions, and Values to Help People Work Safely*, Routledge, 2019.

Chapter 10

How to Implement a Restorative Just Culture and Learning Reviews in a Conservative Industry

Kick Sterkman and Sidney Dekker

Contents

Introduction

The energy sector is generally known for its relatively conservative approach to safety. Cardinal rules (or golden rules, or life-saving rules), for instance, have seen widespread adoption across the industry. These rules require unconditional compliance all the time, sometimes under the threat

DOI: 10.4324/9781003162582-10

of personal sanctions for violations. In other words, if people are 'caught' not following one of the rules, they can risk being fired or denied further work on the contract. After an initial hausse, the effects of such rules (and their consequences for people's employment) have appeared to be wearing off (Dekker & Pitzer, 2016). There are now concerns that the retributive mechanism they embody is giving rise to cultures of risk secrecy, in which the open, non-jeopardy discussion of obstacles, constraints, goal conflicts and difficulties of work is hampered. This is further connected to a preoccupation with injury and incident numbers as the industry's dominant putative safety metric (Lofquist, 2010; Muller, 2018). Keeping these numbers low (or even bringing them down to 'zero') is incentivized in various ways – in part by *dis*incentivizing the open disclosure and honest treatment of injuries and incidents (Hopkins, 2015). This has led to practices and industry-wide learning disabilities which have been connected to various large-scale disasters in recent times (Baker, 2007; CSB., 2016; Hopkins, 2010).

In this chapter, we present a brief case study that details the development and adoption of a Restorative Just Culture and the practice of Learning Reviews in one energy company. We review not only what needed to be done to make these approaches a reality but also detail what the policies look like today. First, we introduce the setting for the case study. We then discuss the obstacles that had to be identified and, where possible, overcome to create the conditions of possibility for conversations about a different approach to justice and learning in the organization. We conclude by reflecting on some of the necessary, if temporary, compromises that may need to be made to be successful at introducing 'just and learning' cultures to a conservative industry.

The Case Study

Neptune Energy

Neptune Energy is an international independent energy exploration and production company, with a regional focus on the North Sea, North Africa and the Asia Pacific. It operates both onshore and offshore assets. Like many others in the industry, Neptune Energy has maintained a zero-incident vision, which should translate into ambition and commitment to create and ensure safe work. Neptune rejects the idea of a zero-incident vision as a target or a goal, instead of embracing it as a commitment to those who do its frontline (and other) work.

The Need for Change

In 2019, Neptune found that its safety results were not improving at the same rate as before. This effect was also observed in overall industry results. Neptune runs an integrated incident management system. That means that the incident reporting tool is connected to the incident investigation tool and that the 'root cause' database is shared. During a discussion, it was suggested that it seemed meaningless to use an investigation to connect each incident with a selection of root causes from a database. Would it not be more effective to eliminate all root causes and never have an incident again?

Although the latter suggestion unfortunately remains impossible, the discussion did lead to the insight that Neptune may have an opportunity to improve its results by better understanding *how* it arrived at a root cause. While this may sound obvious, it actually meant that Neptune had to move away from a focus on the outcome and work to understand actions and decisions in place and time. In a technical world, dominated by engineers who prefer clear pathways between cause and effect, this signified a serious cultural change.

Neptune Energy is now actually no longer looking to drive the number of incidents to zero, if it ever had that ambition for real in the first place. Rather, it believes that it needs a constant flow of reported incidents to maintain awareness and provide learning opportunities. On one of the company's automated dashboards, it publishes the so-called reporting frequency. This is a key performance indicator (KPI) that is calculated by the number of reports per million man-hours. In sharp contrast to more traditional thinking in the industry, this KPI is considered healthy when it is high.

The Process of Changing

When looking for a philosophy to anchor the necessary cultural change, Neptune arrived almost naturally at a Restorative Just Culture. Neptune previously had a so-called 'No Blame' culture. This ensured there hardly existed a reluctance to report, whereas it was also difficult to drive learning with an eye on forward-looking accountability (Sharpe, 2003). Neptune didn't want people to take the blame, but it did want people to take responsibility – in their roles – for setting their employees up for future success. There seemed to be little in a 'No Blame' culture that aided these conversations and this process of forward-looking accountability.

The change started on the annual Neptune Energy Health, Safety and Environment (HSE) day. This is an event where the top 100 leaders of the organization gather to share insights on HSE-related topics. That year, 2018, the entire day was dedicated to a workshop on Restorative Just Culture. The day became a memorable event and a turning point in the organizational culture. The day was dominated by heated and passionate discussions and debates but was wrapped up at closure by the Neptune Energy Executive Chairman and the Neptune Energy CEO firmly stating that Restorative Just would be part of Neptune.

From there, two main projects were launched. The first project was aimed at anchoring Restorative Just in all relevant processes and governing documents. This was in fact the easy part, working down from the Neptune Energy HSE policy, creating a Restorative Just Policy and embedding the concept in the incident management systems and Learning Review guidelines and systems.

The second project was a bigger challenge. This project entailed the further clarification and implementation of Restorative Just in the wider organization. For some organizations, moving from a variation of a blaming culture to Restorative Just, this may meet limited resistance. For us, however, coming from a No Blame culture this required some serious convincing. The project was structured around facilitated group sessions in which the concept was explained in theory and clarified with examples. This approach was limited in its success until we experienced a rather severe incident on one of the operated assets. An intensive Learning Review followed of which the results were published in an animated video. The video explained how the review had been conducted, to which conclusions it had and led. It also demonstrated what the contribution of the individuals involved in the event had been to restore the situation. Especially the latter marked the start of the acceptance of Restorative Just in Neptune's organization. It turned out that, as with many things, the proof is in the pudding and convincing people across an organization depends on actions more than words.

By now, Restorative Just has become an integrated part of Neptune's culture. As a concept, it is hardly mentioned anymore – which is perhaps the clearest indicator of internalization. Learning Reviews are conducted with an emphasis on understanding local conditions, drivers and constraints, and corrective actions are often aimed at influencing these factors. Giving an open account of actions and decisions under all circumstances has become the norm and is considered a key enabler of success in Neptune Energy.

Current Processes and Policies

In this section, we present some highlights from the relevant processes and policies that are currently adopted and in use. These can be used as inspiration (perhaps also of what occasionally not to do or write when implementing these things…!). We first run through some aspects of the policies and processes around Restorative Just Culture and then those for Learning Reviews.

Restorative Just Culture

The first step in anchoring Restorative Just in Neptune's systems was by embedding it in the HSE policy. This is a one-page document, signed by the CEO, in which the organization commits itself to several HSE aspects in ten commitments. In commitment number 5, Neptune has anchored Restorative Just Culture as follows:

- Together, we will facilitate a Restorative Just Culture that promotes trust, learning, and accountability.

The Restorative Just Policy itself emphasizes that Neptune uses a Restorative Just Culture to learn from safety incidents. Its policy then reads:

> This policy clarifies how Restorative Just Theory helps us to make it safer to work at Neptune, as a key part of our safety culture and a cornerstone of our mission to continuously improve how we do things safely. We're using Restorative Just Culture to draw on the latest, cutting-edge thinking to learn from incidents. Instead of just establishing the technical facts of what happened, we're asking why it happened, so we can understand the full context behind the decisions and actions that led to the incident. Following this step, we work to restore the situation in an open and just manner. Through this approach, we will focus on learning from our experiences and using that knowledge to make it safer to work here.

The Restorative Just Policy is approved and signed by the CEO and gives clear guidance on how to apply this cultural element. For further implementation and acceptance in the organization, some of the original Just Culture nomenclature was changed. Where the original version asks the question

'Who is hurt?', the Neptune Version talks 'Who is impacted?'. Neptune doesn't use the word 'victim' but 'impacted party' and uses 'reconciliation' instead of 'forgiveness'.

Next in the document hierarchy is Neptune's Global Operational Integrity Management Standard (GOIMS). The standard contains 14 elements. Restorative Just Culture is covered in Element 7 on incident management, which elaborates all relevant aspects of Restorative Just Culture. Any negative trends and incidents related to operational activities are systematically managed, with the primary aim to prevent incidents from happening. The secondary aim is to learn from past incidents and facilitate performance improvement. Incidents and near incidents are identified, documented, managed and retained in an incident management system. Incident management shall be handled in accordance with the Restorative Just Culture Policy. This is spelled out as follows:

1. Training and instruction shall be provided in a structured manner so all personnel can identify and report incidents, near incidents and observations.
2. An incident management system shall be in place to allow the classification of all incidents and near incidents in terms of actual and potential severity. Severity shall be assessed an individual event basis. Effective management of incidents and near incidents shall be based on incident severity rating and frequency of occurrence.
3. Incidents, near incidents and observations shall be classified and registered in a database with an appropriate set of metadata to allow effective queries and trend analyses.
4. Periodic analysis of the incident database shall be performed to ensure the identification of emerging trends and potential system weaknesses.
5. A structured and consistent Learning Review (investigation) process shall be in place. This process shall be facilitated by a common methodology to ensure consistent and comparable results across all activities. Any Learning Review shall be proportional to the severity, or potential severity, of the incident.
6. All Learning Reviews and subsequent reporting regarding the cause of incidents, near incidents or negative trends shall be conducted in accordance with the Restorative Just Culture Policy.
7. Actions or activities shall be assigned to address identified improvements. Timely implementation and closeout of follow-up actions is mandatory and shall be documented.

8. Safety alerts and lessons learned from incidents and near incidents shall be distributed appropriately for reasons of prevention and to facilitate performance improvements.

These requirements were further clarified in Neptune's Learning Review Guideline as well as the Restorative Just Policy.

Learning Reviews

Learning Reviews in Neptune Energy are regulated and conducted in the same manner across the organization. This creates consistency in results. The principles are written down in the Learning Review Guideline. The guideline defines Learning Reviews as:

> A Learning Review is a systematic approach to understanding the causal elements of an incident by focusing on why, and how, decisions and actions that formed a part of the chain of events came about. The underlying assumption is that a learning culture requires an analytical approach to understand behavior in context. All learning reviews in Neptune Energy are to be conducted in line with Restorative Just Theory.

To be allowed to perform a Learning Review, reviewers are trained in the use of the review software and methodology and inducted in the Restorative Just Culture. A selected group receives Lead Reviewer training which teaches review planning and interview techniques at a more advanced level.

What Neptune is continuously looking for is reduction of the probability of severe events and it believes that Restorative Just Culture is one of the main enablers of its capacity to achieve this. In its Learning Review Guideline, it describes the following reasons for the deployment of Restorative Just Culture:

■ Bringing awareness to the importance of reporting incidents for a culture of learning.
■ Understanding and ensuring the workforce understands incidents are not individual or shameful, but systemic information about and for the organization as a whole.
■ The primary difference between a safe and unsafe organization is not in how many incidents it has, but in how honestly it deals with incidents.

- Debriefings are critical. They maintain morale, maximize learning and reinforce the basis of a just culture.
- A Restorative Just Culture is organized around complete inclusivity and impartiality.
- People must not be motivated to act out of fear of retribution. They must be motivated to act out of ownership and participation in the change process.
- Freedom-in-frame is important in creating inclusivity, engagement and empowerment. Involving employees in the outline and content of their professional discretionary space empowers them and makes them naturally more willing to uphold their responsibility.
- Understand and own the fact that the industry operates in a complex and high-risk environment and all who work there have to remain attentive to this fact.
- We are all responsible for identifying problems, making them known and being willing to assist in preventative recommendations.

Conclusions

In this chapter, we have discussed the introduction of 'just and learning culture' concepts into a conservative industry. As can be seen, some compromises and sacrifices were made in order to facilitate the initial transfer and adoption of the basic ideas of a 'just and learning culture.' These compromises relate to both language and practices that enjoy considerable legitimacy in the industry, such as 'risk management,' 'root cause,' 'control of work process' and 'accountability.' Levering known concepts and terms is a way to accelerate acceptance of new ways of thinking – even if they do, of course, point to epistemological and ontological commitments that might belong to a Safety I, as opposed to a Safety II, world. These include the ideas of definitely determinable cause–effect relationships, a lingering focus on 'who' is responsible, and the suggestion that all risk might be manageable if only there is a good, well-controlled process that people comply with. The relinquishing of such control and its replacement with trust, autonomy and self-organization are of course among the longer-term ideals of Safety II. But getting 'just and learning' and Safety II ideas into a conservative industry may require the use of such 'Trojan' terms and practices. There is, of course, an aspiration that, over time, these terms too can become supplanted or elided.

References

Baker, J. A. (2007). *The report of the BP U.S. refineries independent safety review panel*. Retrieved from Washington, DC. https://www.hse.gov.uk/leadership/bakerreport.pdf

CSB. (2016). *Investigation report Volume 3: Drilling rig explosion and fire at the Macondo Well, Deepwater Horizon Rig, Mississippi Canyon 252, Gulf of Mexico, April 10, 2010 (11 fatalities, 17 injured, and serious environmental damage) Report No. 2010-10-I-OS*. Retrieved from Washington, DC. https://www.bp.com/content/dam/bp/business-sites/en/global/corporate/pdfs/sustainability/issue-briefings/deepwater-horizon-accident-investigation-report-executive-summary.pdf

Dekker, S. W. A., & Pitzer, C. (2016). Examining the asymptote in safety progress: A literature review. *Journal of Occupational Safety and Ergonomics, 22*(1), 57–65.

Hopkins, A. (2010). *Failure to learn: The BP Texas City refinery disaster*. Sydney: CCH Australia Limited.

Hopkins, A. (2015). *Risky rewards: How company bonuses affect safety*. Farnham, UK: Ashgate Publishing Co.

Lofquist, E. A. (2010). The art of measuring nothing: The paradox of measuring safety in a changing civil aviation industry using traditional safety metrics. *Safety Science, 48*, 1520–1529.

Muller, J. (2018). *The tyranny of metrics*. Princeton, NJ: Princeton University Press.

Sharpe, V. A. (2003). Promoting patient safety: An ethical basis for policy deliberation. *Hastings Center Report, 33*(5), S2–19.

Chapter 11

Psychological Safety

Sidney Dekker and Amy Edmondson

Contents

Psychological safety is the shared belief held by members of a team that the team is safe for interpersonal risk-taking, and that members can challenge, question and disagree without suffering consequences to their image, reputation or career. The term stems from the work by Schein (1992) and was investigated in teams by Amy Edmondson of Harvard in the late 1990s (Edmondson, 1999). Psychological safety research pulls together several insights about team effectiveness, resilience and organizational learning. As you will likely surmise by the end of this chapter, a climate of psychological safety is critical for building a restorative just culture.

Where teams face uncertain situations and when members' decisions, viewpoints and actions are interdependent, it is critical that contradictory and dissenting voices are heard. This is not easy. Without knowing it, team members can exert downward pressure on openness, honesty and innovation. Members often surrender to the desire to maintain a sense of harmony, and they typically want to avoid risks to one's own reputation and status in

DOI: 10.4324/9781003162582-11

the team. This can override their desire to speak up and disagree, or voice a question or uncertainty about what the team is doing, as they

> may believe they are placing themselves at risk; for example, by admitting an error or asking for help, an individual may appear incompetent and thus suffer a blow to his or her image. In addition such individuals may incur more tangible costs if their actions create unfavorable impressions on people who influence decisions about promotions, raises or project assignments.
>
> **(Edmondson, 1999, p. 351)**

Teams often consist of members of varying seniority. This can help raise some voices over others, just as members' backgrounds, knowledge or personal factors can. And as Edmondson identified above, it can also actively squelch junior voices, particularly when aspects of their future depend on the opinion of senior members of the team. Yet even if a member is not beholden to other, more senior, members for career, promotion or graduation chances, one's own standing in the team is important. Asking for help, admitting errors and seeking feedback are the kinds of behaviors that could undermine one's face or standing in the team. When facing potential threat or embarrassment, team members' behaviors bend toward the safe and agreeable teams. As worded by Edmondson (1999):

> Image costs have been explored in research on face saving, which has established that people value image and tacitly abide by social expectations to save their own and others' face. (pp. 351–352)

The collective insight from this research is that course corrections, learning and changing by a team, and by an organization, all depend on psychological safety. Its examples are often counterfactual, yet just as intuitive (see Figure 11.1).

The Voice from Below

When their teams lack psychological safety, organizations detect and correct fewer errors; they learn and innovate less (Argyris & Schön, 1978). And they can get into more trouble. The recognition of a lack of psychological safety (though it wasn't called that back then) has been fundamental to

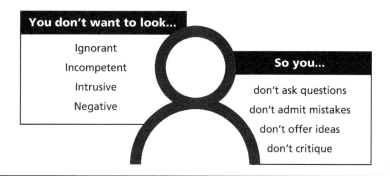

Figure 11.1   You don't want to look.

the development of crew resource management in aviation, for instance. From the 1970s onward, airliner accidents were increasingly attributed to the inability of junior crew members to speak up and voice their concerns about a chosen or unfolding course of action (Maurino, 1996; Wiener & Nagel, 1988). The majority of accidents occurred when the senior pilot was flying the plane, and the junior was the one supposed to be monitoring him or her (Fischer, Orasanu, & Montvalo, 1993). Legitimating and amplifying what Dietrich Bonhoeffer once called the 'voice from below' (Plonz, 2004) has become an effective, if unending, struggle against the perceived risks to one's standing, promotional chances, career and team harmony (Salas, Wilson, & Burke, 2006).

Groupthink

A very similar research insight has come from yet another angle. In the 1960s and 1970s, sociologist Irving Janis tried to understand how teams of smart people could generate glaring policy failures. His work has become an important contribution to our thinking about team effectiveness and its links to honesty, openness and learning. Janis relied on forensic case material for his data. His focus was on the small group dynamics that gradually help congeal a really bad decision as the most logical, legitimate and desirable thing to do. His poster child was the 1961 Bay of Pigs invasion, in which a CIA-sponsored paramilitary group of some 1400 Cuban exiles launched a botched attack on the south coast of Cuba. It lasted three days, until the invaders surrendered and mostly ended up in Cuban jails. But other cases drove his theorizing as well, including the escalation of the Vietnam War and the Watergate scandal. He also used contrast cases in which policy makers produced good outcomes, such as the ending of the Cuban missile crisis of 1962 and the making of the Marshall plan, which helped Europe recover from World War II (and prevent recurrence of armed conflict there).

Groupthink, at its heart, is a theory about how cohesive teams develop informal norms and intra-group social dynamics that aim – as if driven by a hidden, non-explicit, unwitting agenda – to preserve harmony and team relations.* This can lead to the identification and solidifying of a single policy option as the one that everyone agrees on to the expense of any other (and often better) options. While the team settles onto a decision, and more and more psychological, reputational and time commitment is sunk into it, alternatives become ever more difficult to bring up. The symptoms of groupthink as identified by Janis are below. They are cast in the slightly normative and judgmental fashion that is common to this type of study. Yet it might help you identify important phenomena that call for more investigation and greater understanding in your own workplace.

- *Incomplete survey of alternatives.* It is difficult to say, of course, what a 'complete' survey would be. But Janis did observe a striking paucity of alternatives generated in homogeneous teams (even though certain policy-making situations actually often have very few alternative options).
- *Incomplete survey of objectives.* Discussing policy options often took precedence over agreeing on the goals these policy decisions were meant to achieve. And even if that was present initially in discussions, cohesive teams could quickly start taking knowledge of and agreement about their objectives for granted.
- *Failure to examine the risks of the preferred choice.* This is of course easy to say in hindsight (when the risks of a failed approach are all too apparent), but Janis often didn't even see conscious, let alone systematic efforts to try to identify or enumerate the risks of the preferred choice.
- *Failure to reappraise initially rejected alternatives.* Once a policy choice was, or seemed to become, the preferred one, these cohesive teams had no way to go back to square one. Their social dynamics would have in fact discouraged any member of the team from initiating such a return.
- *Poor information search.* Once a policy decision had (and often even before it had) become obvious as the preferred one, teams

---

* Others before Janis, or contemporaneous to him, were also interested in group dynamics in general, and this phenomenon of cohesiveness and 'group think' specifically, and studied it within fields of social psychology and political science, including Kurt Lewin, Philip Tetlock, Stanley Schachter, Hans Morgenthau, Arnold Wolfers, Phil Zimbardo and Raymond Aron.

paradoxically stopped investing in finding out everything about it. Whether this was an unconscious decision to avoid coming up with contradictory data, or a logical choice to invest effort in planning the execution of the decision now that it seemed all but taken, crucial aspects of the situation were often left unexamined.

■ *Selective bias in processing information at hand.* Whatever information seemed to support the preferred policy direction was generally deemed just, moral and reliable.

■ *Failure to work out a contingency plan.* In a sign of confidence that the decision (to be) taken was the right one, and wouldn't fail precisely because it was the right one, cohesive teams often expended no energy on working out a plan for if it were to run into trouble or fail after all.

The subtle intra-group pressures through which these symptoms played out and became visible would seem to be highly dysfunctional. But of course, cohesiveness does have things going for it. Research during the 1950s and 1960s had shown that:

> Other things being equal, as cohesiveness increases there is an increase in a group's capacity to retain members and in the degree of participation by members in group activities. The greater a group's cohesiveness, the more power it has to bring about conformity to its norms and to gain acceptance of its goals and assignment to tasks and roles. Finally, highly cohesive groups provide a source of security for members which serves to reduce anxiety and to heighten self-esteem.

> **(Dorwin Cartwright (1968), as quoted in Janis, 1982, p. 4)**

And indeed, diversity – in socioeconomic background, race, gender – was not generally regarded as a necessary virtue during that time. The interacting social dynamics that Janis gleaned from his casework were as follows:

Overestimation of the Group's Power and Morality

■ An illusion of invulnerability, shared by most or all the members, which creates excessive optimism and encourages taking risks.

■ An unquestioned belief in the group's inherent morality, inclining the members to ignore the ethical or moral consequences of their decisions.

Closed-Mindedness

■ Collective efforts to rationalize in order to discount warnings or other information that might lead the members to reconsider their assumptions before they recommit themselves to their past policy decisions.

■ Stereotyped views of out-group people as too evil to warrant genuine attempts toward engagement, or as too weak or stupid to counter whatever risky attempts are made to defeat their purposes.

Pressures toward Uniformity

■ Self-censorship of deviations from the apparent group consensus, reflecting each member's inclination to minimize to himself the importance of his doubts and counterarguments.

■ A shared illusion of unanimity concerning judgments conforming to the majority view (partly resulting from self-censorship of deviations, augmented by the false assumption that silence means consent).

■ Direct pressure on any member who expresses strong arguments against any of the group's stereotypes, illusions, or commitments, making clear that this type of dissent is contrary to what is expected of all loyal members.

■ The emergence of self-appointed mindguards – members who protect the group from adverse information that might shatter their shared complacency about the effectiveness and morality of their decisions.

On the basis of his and others' research, which allowed him to formulate initiatives to counter the kinds of dynamics generated by groupthink, Janis suggested that teams and leaders do – among other things – this to prevent it from happening:

■ The leader of a policy-forming group should assign the role of critical evaluator to each member, encouraging the group to give high priority to airing objections and doubts. This practice needs to be reinforced by the leader's acceptance of criticism of his or her own judgments in order to discourage the members from soft-pedaling their disagreements.

■ The organization should routinely follow the administrative practice of setting up several independent policy-planning and evaluation groups to work on the same question, each carrying out its deliberations under a different leader.

■ Each member of the policy-making group should discuss periodically the group's deliberations with trusted associates in his or her unit of the organization and report back their reactions.

■ One or more outside experts or qualified colleagues within the organization who are not core members of the policy-making group should be invited to each meeting on a staggered basis and should be encouraged to challenge the views of the core members.

■ At every meeting devoted to evaluating policy alternatives, at least one member should be assigned the role of devil's advocate.

The contribution from Janis to a just learning culture is probably fairly obvious, even though his work was focused on policy makers in political settings. The sorts of countermeasures he suggested might well have been considered as useful in a number of accidents and disasters that followed his work.

Psychological Safety, Trust, Leadership and Accountability

For the most part, Edmondson (1999) reminds us the beliefs about whether a team is safe for personal risk-taking are tacit. Psychological safety implies an unspoken sense of confidence that the team will not embarrass, reject or sanction a member for speaking up or disagreeing. Trust and respect lie at the basis of this. If you have trust inside a team, you have the expectation that future actions (or reactions) by other team members are good for you and that they will do good by you. That makes you willing to be vulnerable in the face of those (re-)actions. Trust is of course easy to break and hard to fix. Other team members' actions and reactions are key in this. If sanction, however subtle, follows an admission of disagreement or error, then that may have a chilling effect on future (and others') willingness to speak up. Trust is bolstered or broken by the reactions that team members get when they make themselves vulnerable (read: accountable) to others.

The role of leadership in creating the trust necessary for psychological safety would seem intuitive. It is known that team leaders attract more attention to their actions and attitudes than team members do. Their reactions set the tone about what is normal and expected, and what is allowed or not.

Leaders can influence the psychological safety of their teams in the follow-ing ways (ibid., 1999):

■ *Accessibility.* Being available and personally involved in the decision process of the team helps create the conditions for psychological safety. Showing an interest in, and commitment to, the success of the team is important. Not making others feel stupid when they come with ques-tions or disagreements is also important.

■ *Acknowledging fallibility.* Team leaders who show that they too can make mistakes and need team members to keep them honest and accountable are usually strong in creating the conditions for psychologi-cal safety (Vincent, 2006). The role that error has in learning has long been acknowledged (Rasmussen, 2003). Leaders who say, 'I need you to tell me, because I'm likely to make mistakes' explicitly invite learn-ing and encourage psychological safety. They put their humanity and humility out there for the team members to see and work with. I recall flying on the Boeing 737 with some captains (and many in this group were female) who did this brilliantly. One female captain would come into the cockpit after doing the walk around external inspection of the aircraft on the platform, sit down and say: "So, Sid, we're going to fly this thing down to so-and-so, and then back up. If there's anything you don't like about my flying, you tell me. And I will do the same with you."

■ *Empowering lower-status team members.* In teams with power differ-ences, the tendency exists for team members to not share the unique knowledge they hold (*if* they even recognize that they have a unique perspective or information that others lack). As a result, group discus-sions may consist primarily of going through jointly held information, or affirming that which the leader is believed to think or have concluded. The onus on leadership to open up the discussion for wider views – and diverse views – is huge. This involves explicitly empowering lower-status members, not just by asking them to speak up, but also by acknowledging their inputs and evidently taking them and their ideas seriously.

The examples above show that psychological safety doesn't suggest a care-less sense of permissiveness nor an unrelentingly positive affect among all team members (Edmondson, 1999). In that Boeing 737 cockpit, I was going to be held accountable, after all: I had been explicitly instructed and encouraged to speak up when the captain did something I didn't like. This amounted to a form of social–professional contract to which I could be held. Still, some bristle at the idea that they should give their team member a free pass to admit their uncertainties, errors, disagreements and questions – or to be too liberal at pointing out the errors in others' judgments and actions. Should they, and their team, not be inspired to pursue perfection, to strive for excellence, to show their best side rather than reveal their brittleness and anxieties? Shouldn't team members be accountable for their performance and show good results?

Psychological safety blossoms in a climate where not just everything goes. Psychological safety goes hand in hand with accountability, because psychological safety and accountability are not each other's inverse. A team with high psychological safety is not a team without accountability, and vice versa. They are, she suggests, two separate dimensions. Accountability and psychological safety are two different aspects of what a team is and does. The most effective, innovative team that is most ready to learn new things is the one that is both accountable and psychologically safe. The relationship between psychological safety and accountability can be categorized like this (Edmondson, 2008):

- *Comfort zone*: Team members really enjoy working with each other, but they may not feel particularly challenged to deliver (exceptional) results. As a result, they may not work hard, and won't challenge each other to do so either.
- *Apathy zone*: Team members in this zone tend to jockey for supremacy and better positions in the team. This is not a climate in which team members are willing to share what they know because it may be a disadvantage to their advancement goals. They are not likely to be held accountable for a lack of results because what matters is that they are in favor of whoever leads the team at that time.
- *Anxiety zone*: Team members here fear to ask questions or offer tentative ideas. They won't try new things or take much initiative. Instead, they will wait for the leader to do so, because there is no safety in doing so themselves. At the same time, team members in this zone will be held accountable for results (or rather, for failures to achieve results important to the leader or the organization).
- *Learning zone*: Team members in this zone have committed to collaboration, learning and making themselves vulnerable in the service of high-performance outcomes for the team.

Finally, a team is of course not effective and doesn't produce great results just because it is psychologically safe. Team composition and the distribution of expertise are important too, as is a setting that ensures the availability of information and resources to take appropriate actions with (Norman, 1993; Rasmussen, 2003).

References

Argyris, C., & Schön, D. (1978). *Organizational learning: A theory of action perspective*. Reading, MA: Addison-Wesley.

Edmondson, A. (1999). Psychological safety and learning behavior in work teams. *Administrative Science Quarterly, 44*(2), 350–383.

Edmondson, A. C. (2008). The competitive imperative of learning. *Harvard Business Review*, July/August 86(7–8), 60–67.

Fischer, U., Orasanu, J. M., & Montvalo, M. (1993). *Efficient decision strategies on the flight deck*. Paper presented at the Seventh International Symposium on Aviation Psychology, Columbus, OH.

Janis, I. L. (1982). *Groupthink*, Second Edition. Chicago, IL: Houghton Mifflin.

Maurino, D. E. (1996). Eighteen years of CRM wars: A report from headquarters. In B. J. Hayward & A. R. Lowe (Eds.), *Applied aviation psychology: Achievement, change and challenge* (pp. 99–109). Aldershot: Avebury Aviation.

Norman, D. A. (1993). *Things that make us smart: Defending human attributes in the age of the machine*. Reading, MA: Addison-Wesley Pub. Co.

Plonz, S. (2004). 'The view from below': Some approaches from a German perspective. Paper presented at the Bonhoeffer Lectures on Public Ethics, Washington, DC, 11–13 October.

Rasmussen, J. (2003). The role of error in organizing behaviour. *Quality and Safety in Health Care, 12*, 377–385.

Salas, E., Wilson, K. A., & Burke, C. S. (2006). Does crew resource management training work? An update, an extension, and some critical needs. *Human Factors, 48*(2), 392–413.

Schein, E. (1992). *Organizational culture and leadership*, Second Edition. San Francisco, CA: Jossey-Bass.

Vincent, C. (2006). *Patient safety*. London: Churchill Livingstone.

Wiener, E. L., & Nagel, D. C. (Eds.). (1988). *Human factors in aviation*. San Diego, CA: Academic Press.

Chapter 12

Evaluating Just Culture and Restorative Practices: The Business Case

Robert J. de Boer and Nico Kaptein

Contents

DOI: 10.4324/9781003162582-12

This book has established that restorative just culture is 'a culture of trust, learning and forward-looking accountability' (Dekker, 2017) and is presented as an alternative to a traditional (retributive) just culture, 'where behaviours of carefully selected and trained individuals and working under supervision is unfortunately compared by analogy to behaviours of criminals intending to cause harm' (Bitar, Chadwick-Jones, Nazaruk & Boodhai, 2018, p. 281). A restorative just culture aims to achieve moral engagement of all stakeholders, reintegration of the caregivers into their community of practice, emotional healing of those affected by an incident, and organisational learning and improvement (Dekker, n.d.). Anecdotal evidence suggests that there are clear economic benefits to applying a restorative just culture. For instance, De Boer (2021, p. 16–17) reports how a restorative approach towards a road worker that 'illegally and seemingly frivolously' had crossed a multi-lane freeway amidst oncoming traffic enabled the identification of malfunctions deep in the system that would have remained hidden if a more traditional approach had been adopted.

Mersey Care NHS Foundation Trust was one of the first organisations globally to attempt an organisation-wide application of restorative just culture from late 2015 onwards. Inspired by the devastating effect on individual staff members caused by disciplinary investigations, the executive director of workforce Amanda Oates turned to Dekker's writings to seek an alternative (Ross, 2019). With support of the trust's CEO Joe Rafferty, she was able to pilot an approach to reduce the number of formal investigations, remove retributive and legal language out of HR policy documents and shift from a focus on blame to addressing wider problems.

In 2018, a previous study was executed to investigate the qualitative and economic benefits of this approach at Mersey Care (Kaur, De Boer, Oates, Rafferty, & Dekker, 2019). This study found that the goals of restorative justice were being achieved. (We call these 'qualitative' benefits to differentiate from the economic impact and economic benefits that might also result from restorative just culture). The same study estimated the annual economic benefits of restorative just culture to be about £2.5 million or approximately 1% of the total costs and 2% of the labour costs at Mersey Care after corrections for inflation, acquisitions and anomalies. These savings were composed of a reduction in salary costs by £4 million per year and another £1 million that were saved in legal and termination expenses, and of which half were attributed to the introduction of restorative just culture. However, the study was executed shortly after the introduction of the restorative just culture. The authors recommended that a follow-up study investigates whether these results would prove to be sustainable and to compare results with other studies that may have become available in the meantime.

The objective of the current longitudinal study is therefore to report on the qualitative and economic benefits that have been realised at Mersey Care after implementation of a restorative just culture, looking back over several years (from 2014 to 2020). In comparison with the previous study, we will be able to investigate whether the benefits have proven to be sustainable. We will also be able to compare divisions within the trust as there have been three acquisitions over this period that have implemented a restorative just culture later in time. As in the previous study, we will first ascertain the existence of non-economic (qualitative) benefits of a restorative just culture: these are of value in their own right and are considered the cause for any economic gains that are identified.

The practical contribution of the current study is that an understanding of the financial impact of the introduction of a restorative just culture, besides the qualitative impact, is an important input for decision-makers in organisations that consider the adoption of a restorative just culture. The identification of qualitative and economic benefits may help overcome the hesitation to implement a restorative just culture, thereby avoiding the pitfalls of a traditional just culture. These pitfalls include (Dekker & Breakey, 2016, p. 192) the following: it is not adequately victim-oriented; does not encourage practitioners to recognise their contribution to the (potential) harm caused and does not treat them as potential (second) victims; does not involve all relevant stakeholders in rule-development and in the processes of restoring trust; is not based on dialogue, participation and collaborative decision-making; and it does not tackle deeper systemic issues. Since the traditional approach does not address harms, needs and causes, it can hardly be considered respectful to all parties. In many organisations, the reluctance to introduce a restorative just culture may be due to time pressures of managers and supervisors, but more often blaming others helps to distance oneself from the event and to absolve oneself of guilt (Cook & Nemeth, 2010). This is even valid for complete departments or organisations, and who can absolve themselves of further damaging investigations by directing attention to an isolated human action. The thought that an individual is responsible for the adverse outcome further maintains the illusion of control in an orderly, rational world – rather than accepting that things are uncertain, and disaster can therefore strike again without warning. We believe – even expect – that there must be someone to blame that either caused the event or failed to prevent it. Hopefully, the business case for a restorative just culture will overcome any hesitations to start its implementation.

In the rest of this chapter, we first introduce Mersey Care and operationalise a restorative just culture to ensure that any qualitative benefits can be ascribed to this intervention rather than general improvement initiatives. We then describe the qualitative benefits that are predicted after a restorative just culture is implemented. Finally, we suggest the economic benefits that might be expected. Following this introductory section, we describe in the next section in more detail the methodology that we applied and then the results that we have found. We present a section in which we discuss the findings, and recommendations for other organisations wishing to define the business case for a restorative just culture. The conclusion summarises the key messages from this chapter.

Restorative Just Culture Operationalised

Restorative just culture derives from restorative justice that has been implemented in the latter half of the 20th century in certain western jurisdictions for relatively minor crimes (and even before that in many traditional tribal civilisations). Rather than aiming for retribution to be pronounced by an independent arbiter, restorative justice aims to put key decisions into the hands of the victims of the crime, thereby making justice more healing and transformative and so reducing the likelihood of future offenses (Zehr, 2014). Dekker (2017) builds on the descriptions of restorative justice by Zehr and others to describe how such an approach might be adopted in organisations to avert blame and retribution for the professionals that are involved in an adverse event. He describes a restorative just culture that aims to repair trust and relationships damaged after an incident allows all parties to discuss how they have been affected, and collaboratively decide what should be done to repair the harm (Dekker, n.d.). The application of restoration in businesses is even more meaningful than in society at large because many of the assurances that a legal system offers (like independence of rule writers and judges, opportunities for appeal, professional support for defendants) are not available in organisations.

Several authors have listed the attributes of a restorative just culture. Zehr (2014) gives the 'signposts' for a restorative justice but these are given in the context of crimes, not unintentional adverse events. Thorsborne & Blood (2013, pp. 63–66) present a checklist for change readiness for schools wanting to implement a restorative just culture that can be adapted to other organisational settings and that includes restorative attributes. However, this listing is oriented more towards the results that are being achieved than the actions that can be evidenced.

Based on an extensive review of the literature, Turner, Stapelberg, Sveticic and Dekker (2020, p. 576) have listed the following hallmark signs of a restorative just culture:

1. Promoting the healing of trust, relationships and people;
2. Empowering first victims (those suffering the direct consequences of the event without having played an active role in its cause) and second victims (practitioners involved in an adverse event who feel personally responsible and suffer as a result of this);
3. Moving away from asking who did something wrong and what should be done about them, to what was responsible for things going wrong and how this can be addressed;
4. Recognising that staff are accountable for being part of the healing, learning and improvement process after an incident;
5. However, at the same time, recognising that they too may have needs for support and ensures these needs are recognised;
6. Action orientation: assigning roles and responsibilities for all who have a stake in the event;
7. Advocating forward-looking accountability (for the implementation of safeguards and improvements) rather than backward-looking account-ability (to blame and punish);
8. Engaging all stakeholders in the post-incident review;
9. Placing obligations and accountability on leaders to provide support for all of those in need and to provide professionals with an adequate response to their distress.

These hallmark characteristics are written as planned actions and identify an *intended* implementation of a restorative just culture.

After implementation of a restorative approach, one expects to see the following to have been *realised*: adequate orientation to victims (including both first and second victims); encouragement for practitioners to rec-ognise their contribution to the (potential) harm caused and to be treated as potential second victims; involvement of all relevant stakeholders in rule-development and in processes of restoring trust; enabling dialogue, participation and collaborative decision-making; addressing deeper, systemic issues that gave rise to the incident in the first place; and granting respect to all parties (Dekker & Breakey, 2016, p. 192). As Zehr (2014) and Thorsborne & Blood (2013, p. 37) point out, there are degrees of restorative justice practices.

In the current study, we aim to identify whether, and in what measure, the characteristics of a restorative just culture are in evidence at Mersey Care to ensure that the interventions are indeed of a restorative nature (rather than a concoction of various other approaches). We aim to identify both the *intended* implementation and the *realised* implementation of a restorative just culture.

Expected Qualitative Benefits

Restorative just culture is aimed at moral engagement, emotional healing, reintegration of the practitioner and addressing the causes of harm (Dekker n.d.). Moral engagement means that the people involved in an event are treated as individuals, not as a 'case', and that open conversations are made possible. It ensures that the direct victims, the practitioners that were involved in the event, supervisors and other stakeholders participate in absolving the consequences of an event. Emotional healing allows negative emotions to subside and is the basis for repairing trust and relationships. Reintegrating the practitioner ensures that expensive lessons that have been learned are retained for the organisation, and that trust and transparency are maintained. The causes of harm are more apparent in a restorative just culture because it invites stories and voices and focuses on fixing things instead of apportioning blame.

From the previous study (Kaur, De Boer, Oates, Rafferty & Dekker, 2019), it seemed that many these qualitative benefits had indeed been realised at Mersey Care. Benefits, identified through staff interviews, included: an increase in good faith and sense-making; increased trust within the different levels of the organisation (and also in the system); staff feeling more enabled and aware that a system is in place to enable them to perform their best; awareness of an improved culture within the organisation that helps diffuse stressful situations and restore calm, more compassionate leadership; improved psychological safety; understanding of the relationship between teams' psychological safety and patient safety; fewer 'knee-jerk' reactions to unexpected events; priority for safety, and physical and psychological well-being; reduction in stress; staff more engaged, open and able to speak up; increased motivation and job satisfaction; changing perspective around accountability and human error; tendency to find a local resolution; and more learning.

In the current longitudinal study, we investigate the realisation of these benefits and determine whether and how these have progressively become evident as the restorative just culture has permeated across the trust. The implementation of a restorative just culture has been effectuated at Mersey Care since late 2015, but because of the trust's acquisitions over time not all divisions have been subjected to the interventions simultaneously. We are therefore expecting a gradual increase across the core of Mersey Care, and a delayed uptake for the divisions and services that the trust has acquired recently.

Expected Economic Benefits

In the previous study (Kaur, De Boer, Oates, Rafferty & Dekker, 2019, p. 8), it was concluded that the implementation of restorative justice in Mersey Care shows 'a meaningful saving' of approximately 1% of the total costs and 2% of the labour costs after corrections for inflation and acquisitions. These savings are attributed to higher staff productivity, reduced illness leave, less 'suspension with pay' and a reduction in legal and termination costs. In making the estimate, the authors have credited half of the savings they identified to the implementation of the restorative just culture, and the other half to non-related factors. The authors concede that these estimates are based on a relatively short window after the introduction of restorative practice.

Other studies have confirmed the relationship between a restorative just culture and economic benefits. For instance, Tenhiälä, Linna, Bonsdorff, Pentti, Vahtera, Kivimäki & Elovainio (2013) found that older employees were less susceptible to long illness leave when they perceived a higher level of procedural justice in their work (as is the case in a restorative just culture).

In the current study, we aim to determine whether the original savings have been sustained and whether savings progress across divisions over time as they are subjected to the restorative just culture.

Methodology

The current study aims to report on the qualitative and economic benefits that have been realised at Mersey Care after implementation of a restorative just culture. In this longitudinal study covering the years from 2014 to 2020, we first determine whether, and to what extent, the characteristics of a restorative just culture are in evidence at Mersey Care. We then ascertain the existence of non-economic (qualitative) benefits and then the economic gains associated with the implementation of a restorative just culture.

Implementation of Restorative Just Culture

For the measure of implementation of restorative just culture, we use two measures: the *intended* implementation and the *realised* implementation.

As a measure of the *intended* implementation of a restorative just culture, we utilise the hallmark characteristics from Turner, Stapelberg, Sveticic and Dekker (2020) listed in the introduction. We identify the amount of alignment between the organisation's plans and actions and these hallmark characteristics. Data sources include the previous study (Kaur, De Boer, Oates, Rafferty & Dekker, 2019), Mersey Care propriety data, internal policy documents, action logs and the National Health Service (NHS) publicly available documents.

We will also identify the progression of the *realised* implementation of restorative just culture through analysis of the Trust-wide annual staff survey and the referrals of staff seeking professional support. The staff survey is conducted annually across the NHS and includes overall indicators of staff engagement, summaries of the questionnaire findings and key findings (NHS Survey Coordination Centre, 2014–2019). The survey includes a number of questions about how the organisation treats staff who are involved in an error, near miss or incident; whether the organisation takes action to ensure that adverse events do not happen again; whether feedback is given about changes made in response to adverse events; whether staff members feel secure to raise concerns about unsafe clinical practice; whether staff members are confident that the organisation would address any concerns; and whether the organisation acts on concerns raised by patients or service users. It is suggested that these questions sufficiently mirror the characteristics of restorative just culture (Dekker & Breakey, 2016, p. 192) to be considered proxies for the *realisation* of a restorative just culture.

Another indication of the implementation of a restorative just culture is 'recognising that [staff] too may have needs for support, and ensures these needs are recognised' – Hallmark 5 of the list derived from Turner, Stapelberg, Sveticic and Dekker (2020). To assess whether this has been achieved, we are able to analyse internal Mersey Care data on referrals for staff support, correcting this for the growth in staff numbers. We are also able to categorise the reason for referrals, relating them to aspects of a restorative just culture (such as formal procedures, job situation, employment issues, work conditions and work relations).

Qualitative Benefits

A direct measure of the effect of a restorative just culture is the reduction in investigations and suspensions, available from Mersey Care internal data. An expected secondary benefit of the introduction of a restorative just culture is an increase in staff motivation and job satisfaction, visible through the annual staff survey conducted by the NHS (NHS Survey Coordination Centre, 2014 – 2019). The following questions from the staff survey are proposed to align with motivation and job satisfaction (preceded by the question number from the 2019 survey):

- Q2a – I look forward to going to work
- Q2b – I am enthusiastic about my job
- Q2c – Time passes quickly when I am working
- Q4a – There are frequent opportunities for me to show initiative in my role
- Q4b – I am able to make suggestions to improve the work of my team/ department
- Q4d – I am able to make improvements happen in my area of work
- Q21a – Care of patients/service users is my organisation's top priority
- Q21c – I would recommend my organisation as a place to work
- Q21d – If a friend or relative needed treatment, I would be happy with the standard of care provided by this organisation

Questions 21a and 21d are relevant to job satisfaction, assuming that individuals value working for an organisation that delivers a high-quality service or product. The 2019 survey led to 3079 responses at Mersey Care (44% response rate). The NHS staff survey allows for comparison with a benchmark group. In the case of Mersey Care, this is a group of 32 combined Mental Health/Learning Disability and Community Trusts, with 68,385 responses, a 48% response rate (NHS Survey Coordination Centre, 2019, p. 5).

The survey also allows us to determine work-related stress and the perceived pressure to come to work despite not feeling well:

■ Q11c – During the last 12 months have you felt unwell as a result of work-related stress?
■ Q11d – In the last three months have you ever come to work despite not feeling well enough to perform your duties?

We will be able to mirror these answers with the illness absence data from Mersey Care and NHS (NHS, 2020).

With these four metrics (investigations, suspensions, staff motivation and staff health and well-being), we can determine the quantitative benefits of the application of a restorative just culture at Mersey Care.

Economic Benefits

Two sources of information can be utilised to identify the economic effects of the implementation of a restorative just culture. Firstly, we will study the general ledger from 2014/2015 to 2019/2020 to identify changes in out-of-pockets costs for claims.

Secondly, the increased motivation and smoother collaboration that is inherent in a successful restorative just culture should be evident in increased productivity. We will assess the activity of the different divisions of the trust over the period 2016 to 2020 from the annual reports (Mersey Care NHS Foundation Trust, 2015–2020) and relate this to the volume of staff. Activity is represented as the number of service users, mental health inpatient beds and 'outpatients, community contacts & domiciliary visits'.

Results

In this section, we describe the results of a longitudinal study into the benefits of the introduction of a restorative just culture at Mersey Care. We present in turn the results of the *intended* and *realised* implementation of restorative just culture, the qualitative benefits and the economic benefits.

Alignment with restorative just culture hallmarks *(*intended *implementation)*

In the introduction, the hallmark signs of a restorative just culture as described by Turner, Stapelberg, Sveticic and Dekker (2020) have been listed. In the case of Mersey Care, these nine characteristics can be recognised in their implementation of a restorative just culture (Kaur, De Boer, Oates, Rafferty & Dekker, 2019):

- Restorative conversations are held between all stakeholders after an incident (see characteristics 2, 3, 4, 5, 6, 7, 8);
- Myth/rumour busting by making factual information available quickly to other staff (1, 4, 5, 7, 8);
- Freeze of staff suspensions unless contraindicated by evidence of a threat (1, 2, 3, 5, 7, 9);
- Culling judgemental language about staff performance from HR policies and procedures and patient safety post-incident reviews, and assessing whether they actually empower and enable staff (1, 3, 4, 5, 6, 7, 8, 9);
- Appointment (through self-nominations) of restorative just culture leads and ambassadors to drive the organisational agenda and to advocate restorative justice (1, 3, 4, 5, 6, 7, 9);
- Revitalisation of staff support in general and after adverse events (1, 2, 5, 6, 9);
- Sharing good practice stories (1, 2, 3, 4, 5, 6, 7, 8, 9);
- Encouraging the trickle down of restorative just culture into everyday organisational life, including back-office and administrative work (1, 3, 4, 6, 7, 8, 9);
- Promoting restorative just culture awareness through internal communication to affirm that things will be dealt with differently now (1, 3, 4, 5, 6, 7, 9).

Mersey Care's work, which trust originally called a 'Just and Learning Culture', has been described in an eight-page book (Mersey Care NHS Foundation Trust, 2019b) that spells out their restorative approach. It literally mentions the hallmark signs of a restorative just culture as described

(Turner, Stapelberg, Sveticic & Dekker, 2020): promoting the healing of trust, relationships and people (page 3, note page 4); empowering first victims and second victims (step 2 on page 4); asking what was responsible for things going wrong and how this can be addressed (step 2 on page 4, step 4 on page 5); recognising that staff are accountable for being part of the healing, learning and improvement process after an incident (page 3, step 2 on page 4), and that they have needs for support; assigning roles and responsibilities (page 3, step 2 on page 4); advocating forward-looking accountability (page 2, step 4 on page 5); engaging all stakeholders in the post-incident review (step 2 on page 4 and step 4 on page 5) and placing obligations and accountability on leaders (step 2 on page 4 and step 4 on page 5).

The trust has confirmed its adherence to the hallmarks of restorative just culture in a report to the Board of Directors (Oates, Almond, Lowe, & Raven, 2019). The trust has also maintained an action log that evidences the journey from the first acquaintance with the ideas of a restorative approach until the present day and that was made available to the researchers.

Very recently, the trust has complemented its restorative approach with an initiative to improve respect and civility in the workplace. This approach aims to eliminate poor behaviour such as bullying and belittling, and foster respect, civility and a positive culture (Mersey Care NHS Foundation Trust, 2020b) by asking staff members to speak up when necessary. This approach aligns with the restorative goals of moral engagement and emotional healing (Dekker n.d.) but might be considered as peripheral to a restorative just culture. The approach has been implemented too recently (in 2020) to be of influence on the results of the current study.

From the above, it can be concluded that Mersey Care's *intention* to implement a restorative just culture aligns with the characteristics of such an approach.

Realised Implementation

The annual staff survey conducted by the NHS allows us to identify in how far the intended implementation of a restorative just culture has been realised, as experienced by Mersey Care's staff (NHS Survey Coordination Centre (2019): Mersey Care NHS Foundation Trust 2019 NHS Staff Survey Benchmark Report. NHS, London, UK). The responses for the relevant questions are shown in Figure 12.1.

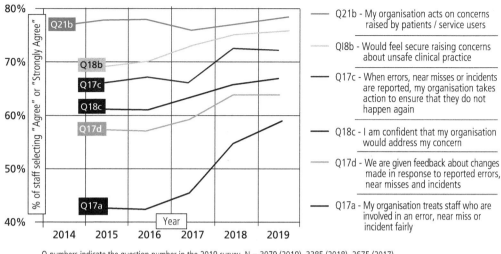

Q-numbers indicate the question number in the 2019 survey. N = 3079 (2019), 3385 (2018), 2675 (2017), 2623 (2016), 2212 (2015) and 1990 (2014). Source: NHS Survey Coordination Centre (2019).

Figure 12.1   Realised implementation of a restorative just culture at Mersey Care over time. Graph shows the staff responses to specific questions over the years 2014–2019. Q-numbers indicate the question number in the 2019 survey. *N* = 3079 (2019), 3385 (2018), 2675 (2017), 2623 (2016), 2212 (2015), and 1990 (2014). Source: NHS Survey Coordination Centre (2019).

In all cases except question 21b, the growth in positive responses between 2015 and 2019 was statistically significant: χ^2 (df = 1, N = 3079, p < 0.01).

It is possible to analyse the data per division of the trust as well. This is illustrated in Figure 12.2 for the last three years. As can be seen, the original Mersey Care divisions (corporate, local, secure and specialist learning disability) show a rapid rise in 2017–2018, after which the increase slows or even declines. The Community division (newly acquired in 2018) shows a similarly large initial increase a year later (2018–2019). We conclude that the staff survey shows a large increase in positive responses directly after implementation of a restorative just culture and a slower further increase after that.

For these questions, Mersey Care responses have been compared to a benchmark group consisting of 32 organisations that are combined mental health/learning disability and community trusts (NHS Survey Coordination Centre, 2019, p. 5). The analysis shows that Mersey Care scores significantly higher on all questions except question 17a by 2–6 percent points: χ^2 (df = 1, N = 3079, p ≤ 0.01); see Figure 12.3.

That the positive responses equal (and do not exceed) the benchmark on question 17a seems surprising given that the focus of a restorative just

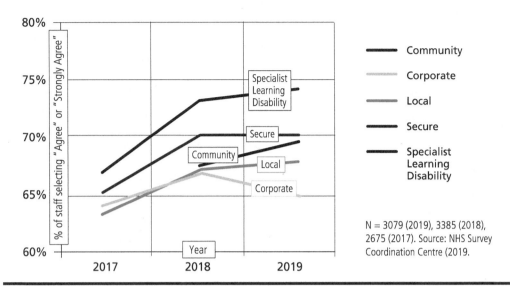

Figure 12.2   Realised implementation of a restorative just culture at Mersey Care per division for 2017–2019. Graph shows the staff responses to the same questions as in Figure 12.1. *N* = 3079 (2019), 3385 (2018), 2675 (2017). Source: NHS Survey Coordination Centre (2019).

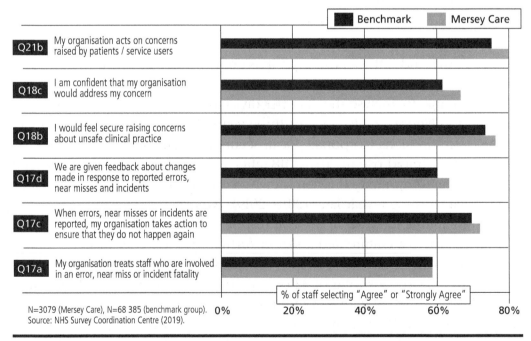

Figure 12.3   Comparison of responses for Mersey Care and for a benchmark group of 32 combined mental health/learning disability and community trusts. *N* = 3079 (Mersey Care), *N* = 68,385 (benchmark group). Source: NHS Survey Coordination Centre (2019).

culture is to 'treat staff who are involved in an error, near miss or inci-dent fairly'. However, this can be explained because previously Mersey Care was actually lagging the benchmark group in response to this question. In 2014, the response for fairness and effectiveness of incident reporting procedures at Mersey Care were rated 3.51 versus 3.52 for the benchmark group on a five-point scale (NHS Survey Coordination Centre, 2014, p. 50). In the 2016 survey (NHS Survey Coordination Centre, 2016, p. 47), fairness and effectiveness of incident reporting procedures at Mersey Care had improved to 3.64 (+0.13) versus 3.71 (+19) for the bench-mark group – temporarily further increasing the gap. In 2019, this gap has now been closed.

Another indication of the implementation of a restorative just culture is that staff are seeking support when needed. We analysed the data on refer-rals for staff support and corrected this for the growth in staff numbers. The results are shown in Figure 12.4.

As can be seen, there is a significant growth in the number of staff refer-rals, signalling that this aspect of restorative just culture is being realised. Interestingly, the percentage of referrals related to aspects of a restorative just culture (formal procedures, job situation, employment issues, work con-ditions and work relations) has decreased from 50% of all referrals to 31%,

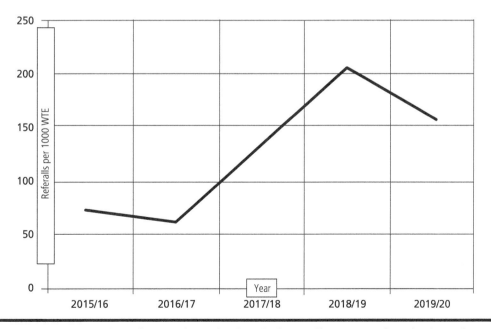

Figure 12.4   Growth in the number of referrals for staff support after the introduc-tion of a restorative just culture in 2016, per 1,000 whole-time equivalents (WTE).

another indication that restorative just culture is being realised at Mersey Care.

We interpret the combination of results presented in this section as evidence that the implementation of restorative just culture has been *realised*, as registered in staff responses to the NHS survey. It is also apparent that the timing of changes in responses is subject to the date of introduction of a restorative just culture in a particular division.

Qualitative Benefits

The expected direct consequence of a restorative just culture is a reduction in investigations and suspensions. The development of these at Mersey Care for the period between 2014 and 2020 is shown in Figure 12.5.

Over the reported period, investigation has decreased by 89% and suspensions have decreased by 91%. The reduction is visible from 2016 to coincide with the introduction of restorative just culture. As is to be expected with the prolongation of the restorative approach at Mersey Care, we have set out earlier in this book that the number of investigations continues to decrease, and the number of suspensions remains low, whilst the workforce has increased by 135%.

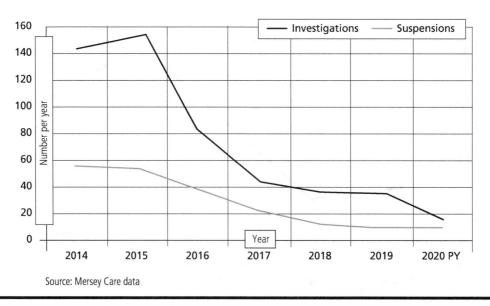

Source: Mersey Care data

Figure 12.5 Number of investigations and suspensions per year from 2014 to 2020 (PY = part year, January–October). Source: Mersey Care data.

The annual staff survey conducted by the NHS allows us to identify whether staff motivation and job satisfaction have improved, as experienced by Mersey Care's staff (NHS Survey Coordination Centre, 2019). The responses for the relevant questions are shown in Figure 12.6. In all cases except question 4d, the growth in positive responses between 2014 and 2019 was statistically significant: χ^2 (df = 1, N = 3079, p < 0.01).

The analysis per division is illustrated in Figure 12.7 for the last three years. As can be seen, the original Mersey Care divisions (local, secure and specialist learning disability) show a rapid rise in 2017–2018, after which the increase slows. The Community division (newly acquired in 2018) shows a similarly large initial increase a year later (2018–2019). The Corporate division shows a slight increase from 2017 to 2019 with a dip between in 2018. We conclude that the staff survey shows a large increase in positive responses directly after implementation of a restorative just culture and a slower further increase after that.

The Mersey Care responses for these questions have again been compared to the benchmark group (NHS Survey Coordination Centre, 2019).

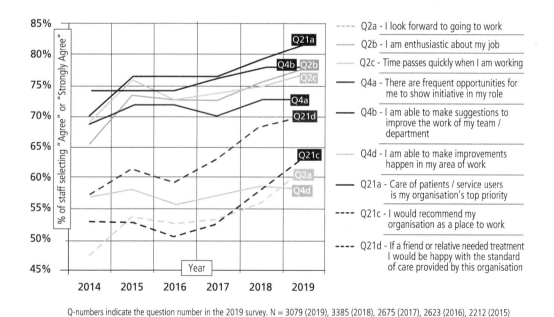

Q-numbers indicate the question number in the 2019 survey. N = 3079 (2019), 3385 (2018), 2675 (2017), 2623 (2016), 2212 (2015) and 1990 (2014). Source: NHS Survey Coordination Centre (2019).

Figure 12.6   Realised qualitative benefits of a restorative just culture at Mersey Care over time. Graph shows the staff responses to specific questions over the years 2014–2019. Q-numbers indicate the question number in the 2019 survey. *N* = 3079 (2019), 3385 (2018), 2675 (2017), 2623 (2016), 2212 (2015) and 1990 (2014). Source: NHS Survey Coordination Centre (2019).

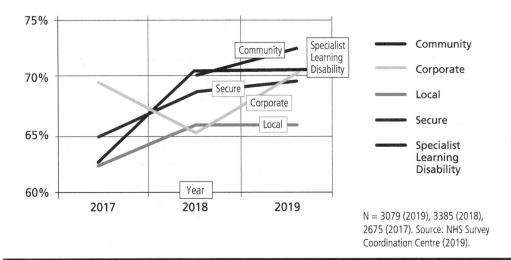

N = 3079 (2019), 3385 (2018), 2675 (2017). Source: NHS Survey Coordination Centre (2019).

Figure 12.7   Realised implementation of a restorative just culture at Mersey Care per division for 2017–2019. Graph shows the staff responses to the same questions as in Figure 12.5. *N* = 3079 (2019), 3385 (2018) and 2675 (2017). Source: NHS Survey Coordination Centre (2019).

The analysis shows that Mersey Care does not significantly differ from the benchmark on all questions except question 21a (in which it scores 5 percent points better) and 21d (2 percent points better): χ^2 (df = 1, N = 3079, p < 0.01). These two questions pertain to the quality of care to service users. It is somewhat surprising that most of the responses to these questions do not significantly differ from the benchmark despite the positive development at Mersey Care over the years. However, this is perhaps because in previous years Mersey Care was lagging in comparison to the benchmark group. For instance, in 2014 staff motivation at work scored 3.74 compared to 3.84 for the benchmark group on a 5-point scale (NHS Survey Coordination Centre, 2014, p. 51). In 2016, staff motivation has increased to 3.86 (up by 0.12) but the benchmark has also increased by 0.06 to 3.90 (NHS Survey Coordination Centre, 2016, p. 48). The implementation of a restorative just culture has enabled Mersey Care to make good this lag.

Work-related stress at Mersey Care has reduced from 41% of staff members in 2014 (N = 1990) to 37% in 2019 (N = 3079), χ^2 (df = 1, N = 3079, p < 0.01). The reported stress level is now below the NHS benchmark of 40% (N = 68,385): χ^2 (df = 1, N = 3079, p < 0.01). The staff members coming to work despite not feeling well enough has also decreased from 66% in 2014 to 57% in 2019, χ^2 (df = 1, N = 3079, p < 0.01). This is equal to the NHS benchmark.

Economic Benefits

The direct benefits of the application of restorative just culture is a reduction in termination and suspension costs. These have dropped from nearly £3 million in 2014–2015 to less than £0.5 million in 2018–2019 but have recently spiked again. Costs pertaining to employee liability claims have dropped from over £1.6 million in 2016–2017 and 2017–2018 to less than £400,000 in the three fiscal years from 2018 to 2019 (based on year of incident). Note that these claims are not paid by the trust directly but are pooled by NHS.

The productivity of Mersey Care staff over the period 2016 to 2020 has generally risen, as can be seen in Table 12.1. Activity is presented as number of service users, mental health inpatient beds or 'Outpatient, Community Contacts & Domiciliary Visits' (abbreviated to 'outpatients'). A significant increase in productivity is visible across all metrics between earliest and latest available years except in the case of former Liverpool Community Health (–7%). The increase in outpatients for former Sefton from 2018/2019 to 2019/2020 seems an outlier, as does the increase in service users between 2017/2018 and 2918/19 for Local division.

Taking a 15% increase in productivity (the average excluding local and former Sefton divisions), this equals a savings of about 3–4% per annum (assuming a 70% labour component of total costs), on top of the out-of-pockets savings described earlier. We conservatively attribute 50% of these savings to the implementation of a restorative just culture to correct for other factors (such as economies of scale, advances in technology and process improvements not linked to a restorative just culture).

Discussion

The current longitudinal study, covering the years from 2014 to 2020, aims to report on the qualitative and economic benefits that have been realised at Mersey Care after its implementation of a restorative just culture. Through the use of the Mersey Care propriety data, internal policy documents, action logs and NHS publicly available documents, we have been able to determine whether, and to what extent, the characteristics of a restorative just culture are in evidence at Mersey Care, what the qualitative benefits and the economic gains of this approach have been.

We have been able to establish that Mersey Care's *intention* to implement a restorative just culture aligns with the characteristics that we have

Table 12.1 Productivity Increase for Various Divisions of Mersey Care over the Period 2016–2020.

		2016/2017	*2017/2018*	*2018/2019*	*2019/2020*	Δ%
Local division	WTE	1485	1503	1581	1645	
	Service users	20,387	22,068	37,169	37,125	
	Ratio	**13.73**	**14.68**	**23.50**	**22.57**	**+64%**
	Outpatients	351,306	343,169	384,232	423,064	
	Ratio	**236**	**228**	**242**	**257**	**+9%**
Secure division	WTE	1809	1619	1668	1618	
	Service users	240	245	309	n/a	
	Ratio	**0.13**	**0.15**	**0.19**	**n/a**	**+40%**
	Beds	760	766	766	765	
	Ratio	**0.42**	**0.47**	**0.46**	**0.47**	**+13%**
Former Sefton	WTE		337	356	339	
	Outpatients		225,782	263,053	392,724	
	Ratio		**669.98**	**738.91**	**1,158.48**	**+73%**
Former Liverpool	WTE			1649	1624	
	Outpatients			1,217,683	1,117,746	
	Ratio			**738.44**	**688.27**	**−7%**
Corporate	WTE	1055	1081	1257	1319	
	WTE trust	4349	4540	6511.51	6545	
	Ratio	**4.12**	**4.20**	**5.18**	**4.96**	**+20%**

Activity is presented as number of service users, mental health inpatient beds or 'Outpatient, Community Contacts & Domiciliary Visits' (abbreviated to 'outpatients'). Productivity increase in percentage (column headed 'Δ%') between earliest and latest available years. Visible is a significant increase in productivity except in the case of former Liverpool Health (acquired in 2018).

Source: Mersey Care annual reports over the respective years.

identified from Turner, Stapelberg, Sveticic & Dekker (2020). We have also found that the implementation of the restorative just culture has been *realised*. The annual staff survey showed a rise in agreement to questions that were considered proxies for the characteristics of restorative just culture described by Dekker and Breakey (2016, p. 192). It is also apparent that the timing of these increases was linked to the introduction of a restorative just culture in a particular division. The number and type of referrals of staff seeking professional support also indicated the *realisation* of a restorative just culture. This implies that the planning and execution of steps for the implementation of the restorative just culture have been effective in creating a restorative just culture and confirms that these are relevant.

As expected, there was a significant reduction in investigations and suspensions after the introduction of a restorative just culture. Other qualitative benefits included improved staff motivation and job satisfaction as identified through the staff surveys, and a reduction in work-related stress and staff members coming to work despite not feeling well. The staff surveys showed a large increase in staff motivation and job satisfaction directly after implementation of a restorative just culture and a slower further increase after that.

The increase in staff illness can (at least in part) be explained by the decrease in staff members coming to work despite not feeling well enough, and in that sense can be interpreted as a qualitative benefit of a restorative just culture (that may however influence the business case negatively).

The Business Case

The economic benefit of the introduction of a restorative just culture has been conservatively estimated at 1.5–2% per annum, primarily due to an increase in productivity. A significant reduction of more than £1 million in employee liability is also in evidence that is however covered by an NHS pool. The results match and even surpass those of the earlier study (Kaur, De Boer, Oates, Rafferty, & Dekker, 2019) that identified a 1% per annum economic benefit. This study has been able to address one of the limitations of the previous by taking a multi-year longitudinal view and identifying the sustainment of improvements over that period. The results mirror the findings of Tenhiälä, Linna, Bonsdorff, Pentti, Vahtera, Kivimäki and Elovainio (2013) that (older) employees experiencing a high level of procedural justice are less likely to miss work due to illnesses.

Recent acquisitions such as former Liverpool Community Health show a lag of about a year to realise the qualitative benefits associated with the introduction of a restorative just culture and a little longer to generate productivity improvements. This is a relatively rapid improvement compared to culture changes generally, signalling the efficacy of the leadership team at Mersey Care.

With savings of 1.5–2% per annum, the business case for the introduction of a restorative just culture seems obvious. The required up-front costs or investments are minimal, as described elsewhere in this volume. It is therefore expected that the results of the current study help overcome the reluctance to implement a restorative just culture, be it a lack of time or the reservations that Cook & Nemeth (2010) identified, such as the wish of the organisation's leaders to distance themselves from the event and to absolve themselves of guilt. The business case for a restorative just culture will overcome all of these.

Limitations

Contrary to the previous study (Kaur, De Boer, Oates, Rafferty, & Dekker, 2019), the analysis has been limited to what is available as hard data – the staff surveys and the productivity data might have been enriched with supplemental narratives from the workplace. The previous study estimated the benefits through the analysis of the general ledger, whereas this study utilised an activity-based approach. Although this represents a direct and therefore more reliable basis for the analysis, the activity data in the annual reports (Mersey Care NHS Foundation Trust, 2015–2020) are inconsistently grouped across divisions and seem erratic across years. This has confounded the productivity analysis for the present study, and more generally makes comparisons for consecutive years and across the NHS difficult. It is recommended that Mersey Care and the NHS at large consider the value of activity-based reporting and converge to a stable reporting base. The data on out-of-pocket costs may be confounded by a lag in effects and other situational factors that could not be identified within the scope of the current study.

This study represents a single case study at Mersey Care. At the time of the introduction of the restorative just culture, the organisation was characterised by a relatively large number of investigations and disciplinary actions.

Other organisations may form a more favourable position, or already have partially adopted a restorative approach, possibly reducing the expected economic impact.

Conclusion

The objective of the current study is to report on the qualitative and economic benefits that have been realised at Mersey Care after implementation of a restorative just culture from late 2015. As in a previous study executed in 2018, we have first ascertained the existence of non-economic (qualitative) benefits of a restorative just culture, as these are considered the cause for any economic gains that are identified.

Mersey Care's *intention* to implement a restorative just culture aligns with the characteristics that were identified, and we have also found that the implementation of the restorative just culture has been *realised*. As expected, there was a significant reduction in investigations and suspensions after the introduction of a restorative just culture. Other qualitative benefits included improved staff motivation and job satisfaction as identified through the staff surveys, and a reduction in work-related stress and staff members coming to work despite not feeling well.

The economic benefit of the introduction of a restorative just culture was conservatively estimated at 1.5–2% per annum, primarily due to an increase in productivity. These results match those of the 2018 study that identified a 1% per annum economic benefit. The results of the study demonstrate clear economic benefits after adopting a restorative just culture. Therefore, apart from a possible intent to 'do the right thing', economic benefits should be an additional argument for (more) restorative practice. The savings should hopefully convince organisations to adopt a restorative just culture and overcome any reluctance to do away with more traditional (retributive) just culture approaches.

Acknowledgements

The authors would like to thank Mersey Care NHS Foundation Trust for supplying the data that have made this study possible.

References

Bitar, F. K., Chadwick-Jones, D., Nazaruk, M., & Boodhai, C. (2018): From individual behaviour to system weaknesses: The re-design of the just culture process in an international energy company. A case study. *Journal of Loss Prevention in the Process Industries*, 55, 267–282.

Cook, R. I., & Nemeth, C. P. (2010): "Those found responsible have been sacked": Some observations on the usefulness of error. *Cognition, Technology & Work*, 12(2), 87–93.

De Boer, R. J. (2021): *Safety Leadership: A Different, Doable and Directed Approach to Operational Improvements*. CRC Press, Boca Raton, FL.

Dekker (n.d.): Restorative Just Culture Checklist. Available at https://www.safetydif-ferently.com/wp-content/uploads/2018/12/RestorativeJustCultureChecklist-1.pdf, accessed 28 Febraury 2022.

Dekker, S. W., & Breakey, H. (2016): Just culture: 'Improving safety by achieving substantive, procedural and restorative justice. *Safety Science*, 85, 187–193.

Dekker, S. (2017): *Just Culture: Restoring Trust and Accountability in Your Organisation*, 3rd edition. CRC Press. Boca Raton, FL.

Kaur, M., De Boer, R. J., Oates, A., Rafferty, J., & Dekker, S. (2019): Restorative just culture: A study of the practical and economic effects of implementing restorative justice in an NHS trust. In MATEC Web of Conferences (Vol. 273, p. 01007). EDP Sciences.

Mersey Care NHS Foundation Trust (2015): *Annual Report 2014/15*. Prescot, UK.

Mersey Care NHS Foundation Trust (2016): *Annual Report 2015/16*. Prescot, UK.

Mersey Care NHS Foundation Trust (2017): *Annual Report 2016/17*. Prescot, UK.

Mersey Care NHS Foundation Trust (2018): *Annual Report 2017/18*. Prescot, UK.

Mersey Care NHS Foundation Trust (2019a): *Annual Report 2018/19*. Prescot, UK.

Mersey Care NHS Foundation Trust (2019b): *Supporting Just and Learning Culture – A Four Step Process for Managing Our People Processes in a Supportive Way*. Mersey Care NHS Foundation Trust, Prescot, UK.

Mersey Care NHS Foundation Trust (2020a): *Annual Report 2019/20*. Prescot, UK.

Mersey Care NHS Foundation Trust (2020b): *Respect & Civility Work Stream – Just and Learning Culture*. Prescot, UK.

NHS (2020): NHS Sickness Absence Rates August 2020, Provisional Statistics. Available at https://digital.nhs.uk/data-and-information/publications/statistical/nhs-sickness-absence-rates/august-2020, accessed December 30th, 2020.

NHS Resolution (2019): *Being Fair: Supporting a Just and Learning Culture for Staff and Patients Following Incidents in the NHS*. NHS Resolution Report, London, UK. available at https://resolution.nhs.uk/wp-content/uploads/2019/07/NHS-Resolution-Being-Fair-Report.pdf, accessed December 13th 2020.

NHS Survey Coordination Centre (2014): *National NHS Staff Survey 2014*. Available at www.nhsstaffsurveys.com, accessed December 14th, 2020

NHS Survey Coordination Centre (2015): *National NHS Staff Survey 2015*. Available at www.nhsstaffsurveys.com, accessed December 14th, 2020

NHS Survey Coordination Centre (2016): *National NHS Staff Survey 2016.* Available at www.nhsstaffsurveys.com, accessed December 14th, 2020

NHS Survey Coordination Centre (2017): *National NHS Staff Survey 2017.* Available at www.nhsstaffsurveys.com, accessed December 14th, 2020

NHS Survey Coordination Centre (2018): *National NHS Staff Survey 2018.* Available at www.nhsstaffsurveys.com, accessed December 14th, 2020

NHS Survey Coordination Centre (2019): *National NHS Staff Survey 2019.* Available at www.nhsstaffsurveys.com, accessed December 14th, 2020

Oates, A., Almond, C., Lowe, L., & Raven, I. (2019): *Learning Lessons to Improve Our People Practice.* Mersey Care NHS Foundation Trust, Prescot, UK.

Ross, M. (2019): *Interview: Amanda Oates, Mersey Care NHS Foundation Trust.* MIP Health, London. https://www.miphealth.org.uk/home/news-campaigns/Features/interview-amanda-oates-mersey-care.aspx, accessed December 12th 2020.

Tenhiälä, A., Linna, A., Bonsdorff, M. V., Pentti, J., Vahtera, J., Kivimäki, M., & Elovainio, M. (2013): Organisational justice, sickness absence and employee age. *Journal of Managerial Psychology,* 28(7–8), 805–825.

Thorsborne, M., & Blood, P. (2013): *Implementing Restorative Practices in Schools: A Practical Guide to Transforming School Communities.* Jessica Kingsley Publishers, London, UK.

Turner, K., Stapelberg, N. J., Sveticic, J., & Dekker, S. W. (2020): Inconvenient truths in suicide prevention: Why a restorative just culture should be implemented alongside a zero suicide framework. *Australian & New Zealand Journal of Psychiatry,* 54(6), 571–581.

Zehr, H. (2014): *The Little Book of Restorative Justice* (Rev. and Upd. ed.). Good Books, New York, NY.

Chapter 13

Civility Saves Lives

Joe Farmer, Penny Hurst and Chris Turner

Contents

DOI: 10.4324/9781003162582-13

Civility Saves Lives is a grass roots campaign that aims to raise awareness of the impact of incivility (rudeness) on team performance.

As Mersey Care were starting on their journey so were we. Civility Saves Lives (CSL) started over a coffee when Joe and Chris were pushing around ideas about work, life and potential projects when Joe recounted an episode that he had been involved in.

These are his words.

I had been working in the department for two months as a Foundation Year 2 (FY2) doctor. I was usually paired with one specific senior registrar for our shifts out of hours and they had supported me through a multitude of emergency situations. One day we were allocated to a daytime surgical list together, along with a consultant. The procedure was a major one and we were both required, me as a support, while the registrar and consultant conducted the procedure. The registrar requested to lead and the consultant agreed. As the registrar began to prepare the patient, which required placement of internal instruments through small incisions in the skin, the consultant observed. I sat at the end of the operating table waiting to assist. The registrar attempted to insert the first instrument, but quickly came across some difficulty. To my surprise, the consultant snapped at the registrar; 'What are you doing? Place the port, it's simple'. Within an instant, I felt the operating theatre tension increase, and I could see the registrar had become flushed and flustered. They apologised, and made another attempt to site the port, but again had difficulty. The consultant responded with 'Why are you having such difficulty with this?!' in an accusatory tone, 'this should be easy, you're delaying us'. The registrar apologised again to the consultant, but I could see they were almost trembling now. On the third failed attempt, the consultant lost patience completely 'move out of the way, I don't have time for this, I'm leading, you assist, if you can manage that?' For the remainder of the procedure, the registrar was nervous, lacked confidence and appeared visibly impacted by this interaction. I didn't know where to look, and there was a palpable tension throughout the whole team. People were looking away, the theatre assistant was on edge, and I couldn't wait for it to be over.

The story was simultaneously horrifying, anxiety producing and, sadly, recognisable.

In his governance role, Chris had noticed an intermittent pattern for a number of years. Incidents would be identified and, if deemed serious enough, they would be investigated. There would be a forensic search for protocol breaches, eventually resulting in the finger of accusation being pointed at some poor soul; whilst buried within the story would be a comment, often glossed over, alluding to poor interactions between healthcare professionals that occurred along the way. These negative interactions felt important but, in the absence of evidence that they had a material impact on the ability of individuals and teams to perform well, they were not generally felt to be of significance. When Joe told the story, Chris had an epiphany (OK, well, more of a low energy light bulb moment that slowly dawned on him) as he realised that the academic evidence that this was both important and impactful and had begun to amass.

Chris had recently been introduced to the work of Christine Porath by Trevor Dale, a human factors expert. Professor Porath works at Georgetown University's McDonough School of Business and she writes and researches extensively in the field of incivility. Her work shows how behaviour can affect individual and team performance, and this felt to Joe and Chris like the missing link between how we are treated and the quality of our work. They started to ask the question; what if these negative interactions were not insignificant, what if they had the potential to result in harm for patients and staff?

The Impact of Incivility in the Workplace

Most of us dislike rudeness in the workplace and almost all of us have experienced it with studies showing it has increased in frequency over recent years (Porath and Pearson). Incivility can leave us feeling disrespected and sometimes humiliated but, beyond our feelings, does it matter? What if incivility did not impact performance or if, instead of decreasing performance, incivility actually improved performance? If rudeness resulted in better results, there are many in healthcare who would not see addressing incivility as an issue.

Over the last few years, however, what started as a trickle has led to a torrent of evidence that behaviour impacts performance in the workplace. In the vast majority of cases, negative behaviours such as rudeness have corresponding negative outcomes on performance. In healthcare, this can cost lives.

How Does Incivility Work to Reduce Performance?

Modern healthcare, like much of business, is a team sport. We deliver our results in complicated and sometimes complex environments with workplaces that can be unpredictable, often changing from moment to moment. This means that generating solutions requires us to gather information to understand the current situation and to then process this information to create solutions that fit the moment.

Many of these creative solutions are formed in our 'working memory' (Figure 13.1) where we juggle the available evidence and come up with what seems to be the best solution at a given time. Incivility has been shown both to steal from our working memory and to change the nature of solutions we come up with from positive solutions to more negative, punitive solutions (Porath and Erez, 2007). This means in uncivil environments, team members are likely to generate fewer ideas and those they do generate will be more negatively orientated.

The capacity of our working memory is dependent on our level of stress (Figure 13.2). Too little stress and we don't fire up, too much and we are overloaded and unable to think. This is classically illustrated by the performance/arousal (Yerkes-Dodson) curve, shown in Figure 13.3

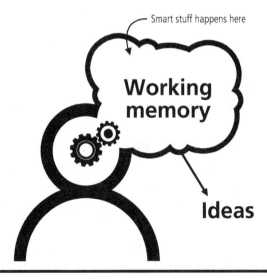

Figure 13.1   Working memory.

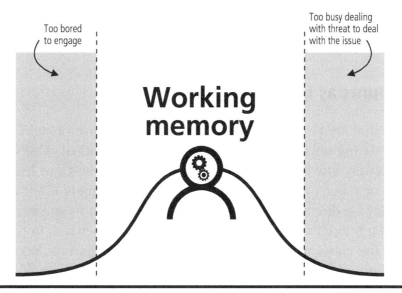

Figure 13.2   Level of stress.

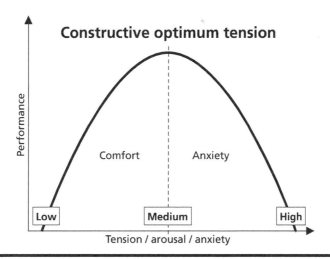

Figure 13.3   Yerkes-Dodson curve.

Stress in the workplace can be caused by multiple factors, for example, being given impossible tasks or not being given the correct tools for the job. For many people though, the most likely cause of stress at work is having negative interpersonal relationships. Recent evidence states that incivility between co-workers can exacerbate both physical and mental health problems. At an executive level, Ray Williams' 2015 study estimated that 13% of the total time is be taken up on resolving issues between individuals. This illustrates the tip of the iceberg as, in large organisations at least, very few of the interpersonal problems in workplaces make it as far as the executive level.

What Counts as Incivility?

Behaviours that are perceived as discourteous, dismissive or rude are regarded as being uncivil, as interpreted by each individual. Although often seen as relatively low-level, incivility has direct effects and can lead to significantly worse behaviours such as bullying or harassment if left unchecked. Incivility may be directed at individuals or may be of a more pervasive nature, being normalised as how someone generally behaves in the workplace, with the classic response of 'Oh, that's just how Jack is, don't worry about it'. The problem, as we'll show in the chapter, is that we do seem to worry about it and it continues to have an impact.

Some examples of incivility (a very non-exhaustive list):

Ignoring, undermining, interrupting, belittling, dismissive gestures (such as eye rolling, tutting, heavy sighing in a meeting), personal put-downs (ad-hominems) and talking negatively about others behind their back (see Keltner, 2017). In general, it takes the form of behaviours that leave people feeling negative about the interaction but without being certain of the intent of the other person.

How Does Incivility Affect the Various Groups Who Are Exposed to It?

Effect on the Individual

Being on the receiving end of incivility has a measurable impact on performance. In a study by Porath and Erez in 2007, they found that there was a 61% decrease in creative test performance after exposure to incivility. This is probably due to our working memory being hijacked by a combination of us trying to understand what just happened and fight/flight emotion, resulting in overstimulation and the loss of effective working memory. We then end up ruminating for variable lengths of time, prolonging this period of working memory hijack resulting in poorer ongoing performance.

This is one of the reasons that when we are treated poorly we can't think of the great retort at the time; it only comes to us sometime later, once our working memory is back online (Figure 13.4).

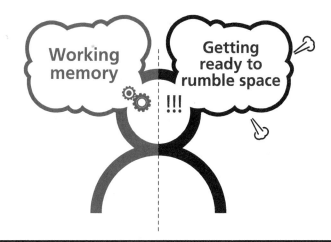

Figure 13.4 Working memory back online.

Effect on Co-worker Bystanders

Many of us have been witness to workplace incivility/hostility and can probably remember how it felt: often a combination of anxiety and morbid curiosity. It is not immediately obvious but just witnessing incivility measurably
affects performance. Despite knowing it is wrong we cannot help but keep
paying attention, possibly because our primitive centres in our brains detect
the threat and need to keep tabs on it. Observers of workplace incivility
have been found to have, on average, a 20% reduction in their cognitive
ability (Porath and Erez, 2009). This can add up to a huge cumulative cognitive decline when many people work near each other. Unfortunately, the
impact on bystanders extends beyond the immediate moment and we carry
the cognitive and emotional burden into future interactions – if, for example,
someone asks us for help after we have witnessed incivility, then we are a
full 50% less likely to help that person than if we had not witnessed the incivility (ibid.). Negative behaviours affect more than just the parties who are
immediately involved.

A 2020 work by Gadi Gilam shows that the impact of witnessing incivility
is not equal across all personality types. Those people who are at the more
empathic end of the spectrum are more negatively affected by incivility,
having a greater reduction in their cognitive abilities versus those at the less
empathic end of the spectrum. This means that the very people we are trying to encourage into healthcare, those that care, are those most negatively
impacted by cultures that permit incivility.

Just being around incivility is bad for many of us.

Effect on Patients/Relatives/Clients

Studies on the impact of seeing rudeness in organisations are more common in business than in healthcare. One area of business that has similarities with healthcare is banking, because in banking trust is central to our relationship, and this is equally true of healthcare. Rudeness between employees has been found to result in consumers being impacted in three ways; they generalise this behaviour towards the whole organisation; they lose trust in the organisation (from 80% net promotors to 20% after witnessing a single negative staff–staff interaction), and they believe this behaviour can be expected from others in the organisation. Interestingly, these findings did not appear to change whether or not the observer felt the reprimand was warranted. We simply don't like to see people being treated poorly, possibly because we know we might be next (see for example Porath et al, 2020)

Effect on the Team

In team situations, 'information sharing' is a vital component for understanding a complex and evolving situation, be that a complicated office issue, a difficult diagnosis or a cardiac arrest. Incivility has a major impact on team performance by reducing the amount of information that is shared.

Under stress, our working memories are already squeezed by the enormity of what is going on around us, so we start with less thinking space (see Figure 13.5). This means we risk becoming overloaded and task

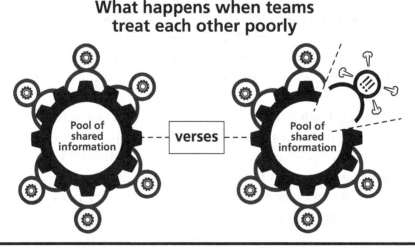

Figure 13.5   What happens when teams treat each other poorly.

focussed, leading to us missing things. Incivility compounds this over-arousal by directly reducing the amount of information the team shares, effectively turning off the flow of data just when it is needed most possibly because the team does not feel safe (Riskin et al., 2015). When we have less information to base our decisions on the consequence is that we cannot take advantage of the knowledge in the room. Decisions are then frequently worse and have been shown in landmark studies (ibid.) to cause poorer outcomes for critically ill patients, with 40–60% of the variance in information sharing being explained through incivility in teams. Good teams learn to rely upon the eyes and ears of the whole group, making space to share information, especially when under pressure. Treating each other with civility helps create this environment.

Leadership Incivility

Most people would agree that leadership is important, having potentially both positive and negative effects on the ability of a team to complete tasks. We can name the good leaders we have worked for and unfortunately also the bad. Leaders come in many different styles. But does incivility from the leader influence performance? And who counts as a leader?

We know that people look to leaders for guidance about what is permitted in an environment, for example, spending more time in meetings watching the leader's conduct and being role modelled by them rather than anyone else. The style of the leader then becomes normal for the team. In general, leaders set the tone and others follow.

Unfortunately, evidence around the change in our behaviour as we become more senior is, frankly, often discouraging. What appears to happen is that as we ascend the hierarchy, we have fewer constraints on how we conduct ourselves. We can fall into the trap of treating leadership as our right to behave as we like rather than the responsibility of getting the most out of those around us.

Many of us will have had an experience of co-workers who appear to have a personality change once they became the boss, displaying dominant behaviours that were not previously visible and acting as though their thoughts had intrinsically more importance than those of others. This change in behaviour is most likely to occur during the transition into leadership positions (perhaps we later come to realise the value of others), and it can be highly disruptive for those involved. Elevation of status and the accompanying authority appear, for some at least, to take off the self-regulatory brakes. This can translate into what becomes rude, disrespectful and dismissive acts that are hard to challenge when we are trying to work out our new relationship with the person concerned. On elevation to positions of authority, we are three times more likely to interrupt people, three times more likely to raise our voices at them and three times more likely to say insulting things about others. This can be the starting point of an incremental creep from microaggressions to full-blown bullying and harassment. We slowly boil the frog and hostile work environments become normalised. Obviously this does not happen to all leaders, but it is something all leaders should be aware of so that we might keep a check on it.

When Walsh et al. (2018) studied this, they found positive leader behaviours normalised respect and positive behaviours in their workplace. This normalisation of respect resulted in lower workplace incivility. The value of respect by leaders is something that may seem obvious written down; however, many of us will have experienced leadership behaviours that feel like anything. Consciously respecting co-workers appears to bring out the best in them.

You might be reading this and thinking 'I'm glad I'm not a leader'; however, it turns out that if we have people who are lower than us on the hierarchy, then we tend to be seen as leaders by those people (see Figure 13.6). These 'direct reports' look to their immediate boss for the norms, the expected and accepted behaviours. When negative behaviours are modelled and go unchallenged, they become normalised.

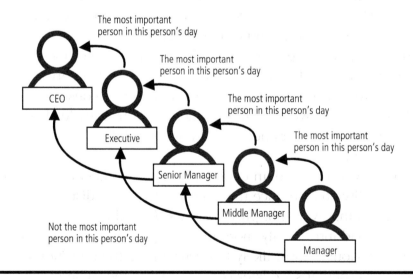

Figure 13.6 Leaders' hierarchy.

In fact, the relationship with our immediate superior is one of the most influential components of our working day. The single most important factor determining the engagement of an employee at work is how engaged their immediate boss is, and engagement is the number one predictor of organisational success (according to Randall Beck and Jim Harter's report of a 2015 Gallup study). When our boss is engaged, we are likely to be engaged, when they are disengaged it is far harder for us to be engaged. On the one hand, this is bad news because we are having our day determined to a significant extent by someone else's; on the other hand, this is a tremendous opportunity as it means that we have the chance to energise and support those whom we supervise so that they have a better work experience. Because well-being and engagement are intimately linked, this results in improved well-being (see SHRM's toolkits).

The impact of positive behaviours in the workplace is far less heavily researched than the impact of incivility but a couple of recent papers give cause for genuine optimism. In the first paper, Jones and Plunkett showed that introducing a positive feedback system when doctors wrote a perfect prescription resulted in a 50% increase in perfect prescriptions over four months – people responded to the positive feedback by doing more of the same. In a further paper, Bertrand et al. (2021) examined technical performance in a high stress-simulated scenario. In their simulation, anaesthetic teams were confronted with a patient that they could not intubate or ventilate – an extreme emergency requiring them to make an incision in the patient's neck in order to ensure survival. The researchers found that performance was significantly improved when the team had been briefed in a positive rather than neutral manner.

So What Does It All Mean?

The evidence that behaviours matter and that civility underpins respectful teams and organisations is compelling. How we feel treated as individuals and as groups has a direct and measurable impact on our performance. When civility is the norm, then staff respond better in a crisis, they share information more willingly and they help both the individual and the team to perform at their best; the result of this is that we have better outcomes, for patients and for staff.

But what were we going to do about it (Figure 13.7).

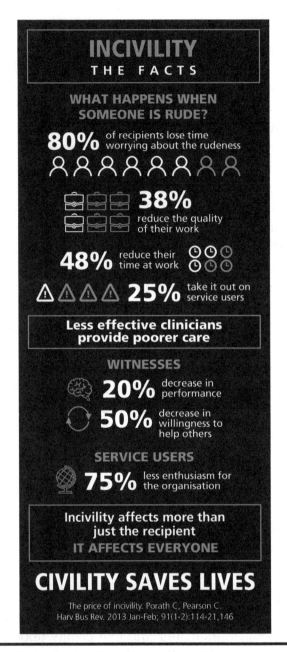

Figure 13.7 Civility Saves Lives – the price of incivility (Porath and Pearson, 2013).

Starting Civility Saves Lives

Having concluded that this was a worthwhile message, we knew we couldn't just leave this lie. Penny (another junior doctor) heard about this idea from Joe and was immediately keen to help spread the word. She had experienced various instances of incivility in her training and felt the times of civility stood out as being infrequent rather than normal.

> I can clearly remember the first time I had to bleep the on call Medical Registrar for advice. I was a newly qualified first year doctor in general surgery and my patient had a high blood sugar level, but I had never managed this for myself. Looking back now, I can see how the Medical Registrar could have been annoyed at being bothered by an easy question like this, but they were polite and supportive, helping me work out how much insulin to give. This encouraged me to feel comfortable contacting seniors for advice when my patients needed it, therefore improving their care. As I've become a Registrar myself, I'm now the one called for advice, so I try to remember how nice that doctor was to me.

We all felt a responsibility to share this information but weren't sure how. An immediate issue was around what method we should use to get people thinking about rudeness in healthcare. Initially our ideas involved audits/quality improvement/formal research, a standard but pretty dry approach. We quickly realised that this would not work if people didn't feel behaviour mattered; we could shout as loud as we liked about the rates of incivility, but if staff didn't think incivility had an impact on them and their patients then they would simply ignore us. Something more fundamental was required, something that tapped into the values held by staff in healthcare. We decided to start to raise awareness of the effect of rudeness on outcomes, not through the research/audit/QI route, but by talking about it, using our experiences and the evidence that others had already generated. Perhaps if we could talk honestly about how we had felt in these situations, then others would relate to this and they would then let us talk through the evidence that feeling disrespected at work resulted in negative consequences for individuals and teams.

We knew that this approach would benefit from some kind of snappy title, because people don't have time to spend working out what the purpose of something is if it is not immediately obvious. We met a few times, knocking about ideas, having listed, and discarded, 'Civility Saves Lives' early in the process. There was a definite temptation to run with one of the ' Don't be a …' titles, perhaps 'Don't be a dick', or 'Don't be an arse' or really 'Don't be a (insert rude anatomical area of your choice)', each of which felt highly impactful. Then we thought about the Learning from Excellence movement and how their prosocial, aspirational message had resonated with us and many others. People don't go to work to treat others poorly, they go to work to do a difficult job to the best of their abilities, so we decided to use 'Civility Saves Lives' (and if it hadn't worked we'd probably now be writing about the amazing success of 'Don't be a dingus'). Rather than pointing the finger, we tried to appeal to the values of staff.

Getting the Message Across

There was something of a tightrope to be walked, we wanted to get the message over but without sounding preachy or accusatorial. We recognised that over the years, incivility has become normalised in many areas of healthcare, with such luminaries as Gary Kaplan, 'Poor behaviours are omnipresent in Healthcare' and Lucian Leape, 'Poor behaviours are pervasive in Healthcare' acknowledging this. Some staff may even have felt that disregard for the emotions of co-workers was integral to good care, accepted under the guise of 'putting the patient first'. As a result, we knew that this could be a challenging message to many good, diligent, committed healthcare workers; delivering it with evangelical zeal might only serve to leave them feeling criticised for acts they felt were in the best interest of patients. To try to avoid any accusations of finger pointing we made it clear that we have all screwed this stuff up, usually illustrating this with stories about ourselves.

We settled on a combination of giving talks and creating a social media presence and a website. We used Twitter as it is used heavily in healthcare and called our feed @civilitysaves. Having a multi-platform approach was not an option for us as we did not have the spare time to administer a variety of different accounts and Twitter proved to be a good tool for us as a combination of positive messages and infrequent but graphic-heavy tweets meant we ended up with credibility and high levels of engagement.

We have found that infographics help get ideas across in an easily digestible way, with what they lack in nuance being more than made up for by their ability to convey key ideas quickly. We chose to use Canva to generate graphics, having been introduced to this by Ross Fisher (2013), a paediatric surgeon in Sheffield who is an expert of presentations. Using this platform has allowed for a reasonably uniform and recognisable brand identity, and Penny's infographic 'Incivility: The Facts' has been shared by professionals around the world (see Figure 13.7)

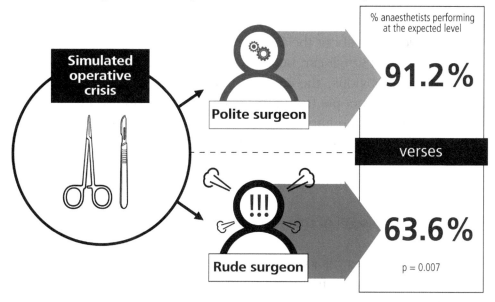

Rude surgeons impair anaesthetist performance

Simulated operative crisis

Polite surgeon

% anaesthetists performing at the expected level

91.2%

verses

Rude surgeon

63.6%

p = 0.007

However staff reported anaesthetist performance was not significantly different (p = 0.112). This is interesting because it shows we are rubbish at self assessment.

Exposure to incivility hinders clinical performance in a simulated operative crisis. Katz D et al. BMJ Qual Saf 2019.01.g

Figure 13.8   Exposure to uncivility hinders clinical performance in a simulated operative crisis (Katz et al., 2019).

The mainstay of raising awareness though was speaking at events. Soon we were all receiving regular invitations to talk. On one occasion, Chris was talking when his PowerPoint presentation failed, and he was left speaking without the safety net these provide. This was seen by one of the team from TEDxNHS and this led to an invitation to talk at TEDxExeter (Turner, 2019). Around the same time, there were people beginning to speak under the Civility Saves Lives banner in many different places, often people whom we had not met or spoken with. We started to join people up via WhatsApp and gradually we formed a small community of like-minded individuals.

Writing this down makes it sound far more strategic than it actually was. We took what we knew, decided how we wanted to position the message and tried to be consistent in how this was presented whilst allowing for any individual variation that people wanted to introduce. We also took the decision to not try to control this if other people wanted to get on board. Our self-generated work is creative commons and, possibly most importantly, we committed that anyone who wanted to use the name or logo could do so in any non-commercial way they saw fit. For us, this seems to have worked and has allowed us to work alongside organisations like Mersey Care.

Once people know about the impact of behaviour on performance (see for example Figure 13.8), it can become easy to forget that this may not always have been obvious, 'the curse of knowledge'. When we talk, our main aim is to bring people from a place of pre-contemplation to a place where they mull over the impact of behaviours in healthcare. If people leave thinking that 'behaviour matters', then this is a success.

People talk about this in various ways – an example of the arc of Chris' narrative looks something like this:

1. Tell an anonymised but true story about when behaviour impacted performance.
2. Speak briefly about his journey to the realisation that how we treat each other has a material impact on our ability to work well together.
3. Describe complexity – because we would generally agree that we work in a complex environment, articulating what that actually means can be difficult. The key points are that we get into positions of power through personal mastery but for us to function well in a team, particularly if we are leading the group, we need mastery of how to get the most out of our team. This leads to how we might think differently, the need for diversity and a little psychology around how we underestimate other people's roles.
4. Discuss the evidence for what makes teams work well in healthcare and beyond. This draws upon the work of Michael West and personal experience of working in particularly challenging environments such as the ED and Mid Staffs. This then leads to the work done by Riskin and Erez (2015), who showed that team performance is measurably diminished when people are treated poorly.
5. Finally, he talks about the evidence base around creativity and our working memory. This is because working in healthcare is a relentlessly creative process. We are constantly bending and flexing in order to get the best outcomes whilst functioning in a complex adaptive system and to be consciously creative we need working memory.
6. The talk is wrapped up with a message of hope and about doing things in a different way (Figure 13.9).

CIVILITY SAVES LIVES

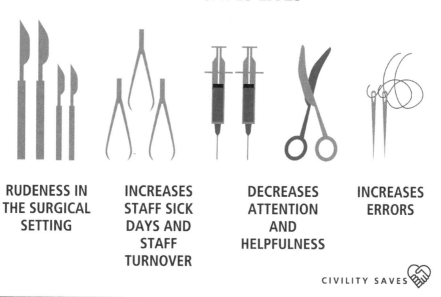

| RUDENESS IN THE SURGICAL SETTING | INCREASES STAFF SICK DAYS AND STAFF TURNOVER | DECREASES ATTENTION AND HELPFULNESS | INCREASES ERRORS |

CIVILITY SAVES

Figure 13.9   Doing things differently.

Here is a list of the core messages that we hope to get across:

Rudeness impacts the performance of individuals and teams.

Rudeness steals from our working memory and makes us cognitively less able.

Rudeness affects those around us, even if they are not directly involved.

We don't necessarily start out as rude, but some positions allow us the permission to be ruder. This is particularly true when we move into authority positions.

Despite what we think, most people who are being rude do not recognise this is happening. Usually they are incredibly stressed or this way of behaving has become normalised over time.

We believe that we can mitigate for the rudeness of others but this is not upheld by the evidence. We are not good at stress inoculation when the stress comes from individuals rather than situations.

Rudeness from an employee makes those using the service less likely to trust the service. We want to get back at people who are rude. When the person being rude is seen as representing an organisation, >80% of people are happy to get back at the organisation rather than the individual.

Different Evidence for Different Groups – Horses for Courses

Early on, we learned that just because something was important to us, this did not make it important to other people. Making the point over and over, but with more vigour, ran the risk of sounding like the archetypical Englishman abroad, using the same language both louder and slower in order to be understood by someone who simply does not understand our words.

If we were going to be heard by different groups, we needed arguments that resonated with their internal or corporate values. Our experience has been that clinical staff respond to arguments based on clinical excellence. This is fortunate because this was mostly what we were doing.

When we present to organisational boards, the arguments require augmentation and sometimes wholesale change, for example, both financial and reputational concerns appear to be important at an executive level. An example of the financial perspective would be the excellent work of CREW with the Veterans' Affairs hospitals in the US (2016). In 2011, they found that the hospitals with the most civil cultures spent $2.2 million less on equal opportunities of lawsuits per year than those with the least civil cultures, and that this was compounded by the cost of sickness leave in the least civil organisations, where they were spending $26.2 million more per year on filling sickness absence, a consequence also linked to incivility.

Unsurprisingly, we found that even within medicine, people had different drivers, with those who have a governance perspective wanting to know about the safety implications and those with educational perspectives wanting to hear about the impact of behaviour on teaching and retaining information. Sometimes, this meant that we had to bring together the information in a digestible form, such as when Josie Cheetham and Chris Turner (2020) wrote a summary article for the *Future Medicine Journal*, published by the Royal College of Physicians.

Approaches for different groups of staff:

Staff group	Values	Evidence
Direct clinical staff	Clinical excellence, education, safety	Riskin and Erez Cheetham paper RCP Future Dr journal Gerry Hickson (Vanderbilt)
Managers	Discretionary effort, efficiency	OscarKilo.org work on discretionary effort
Executives	Finance, reputation	CREW work from VA

We speak to many groups, but we were particularly keen to make sure the message was delivered to those at the start of their professional lives, hopefully allowing the development of a generation of staff who are raised on the idea that civility has intrinsic professional value. In order to minimise the hierarchy and therefore to seem less patronising, Joe and Penny gave talks to medical students and foundation year doctors about Civility Saves Lives. These were keenly received by the trainees and trainers alike and have led to further talks across the UK; some organisations have incorporated it into their annual induction programmes.

Connecting with Other Groups

We also found that we shared values with many other groups and that together with our voices became louder. Adrian Plunkett is a paediatric consultant who formed the 'Learning from Excellence' movement some years previously and whom we were lucky enough to get to know. From Adrian we learned of the value of organic spread, of not trying to control the message and instead letting people interpret this in their own way. The values of CSL seem to resonate strongly enough that others take this and head off in a variety of directions. It can feel a little like being held responsible for the tide, but the alternative is trying to relentlessly manage the message, so we made an active decision to trust in the positive intentions of those who wish to promote the concepts.

Gradually we found ourselves being invited to join other groups, in particular the Anti-Bullying Alliance that is run by two Royal Colleges, the National Freedom to Speak Up Guardians, the Royal College of Surgeons of Edinburgh and the Royal College of Obstetricians and Gynaecologists. This led to more chances to talk, including at the Houses of Parliament and around the country.

Being part of these larger groups provided both the opportunity to learn from others (particularly Adrian and Emma Plunkett) and to spread the message.

Beyond Civility Saves Lives

Initially, we believed that once we got the message out there that would be enough. People would listen, hopefully be sold on the idea and then choose to change. Our job would be done. It became clear though that there were some who completely bought into the idea, who even espoused it to others, but who were somehow leaving a trail of devastation behind them. These people were often senior in organisations. Whilst it is possible that they were using this work for Machiavellian means, we thought it was more likely that they were not aware of the impact they were having on those around them. After all, many of us were displaying the leadership behaviours we had been exposed to and that were role modelled to us. They were probably being misunderstood. This opened the door to further work aimed not at raising awareness of the impact of incivility, but of finding ways to let people know when they had been perceived as being uncivil.

A little on perception and communication:

The Importance of Perception

One important aspect of incivility is that whether it is intended or not the impact is the same, because it is all about perception. When someone causes offence, it may just be how they are, they may not mean anything by it, but it still has a negative impact on the performance of those around them.

This negative impact is present even when, as recipients, we think we have compensated for the negative behaviour. This was beautifully illustrated in a study by Dan Katz.

Dan studied the impact of rudeness on the ability of senior healthcare workers to perform when under pressure, comparing those with a rude co-worker to those with a polite co-worker. He found that staff knew when their co-worker had been uncivil, but felt they compensated for this, so that there was no impact on the simulated patient's care. But when the performance of the staff involved was assessed by experts who didn't know if the co-worker had been rude, they found the impact to be highly significant. Just less than 64% of the subjects worked at the expected level of expertise when the co-worker was rude, whereas just over 91% worked at the expected level when the co-worker was polite.

This has further implications – if someone perceives rudeness, then this has an effect on their performance, whether or not the offense was intended.

Incivility can be difficult to pin down as so much of it is in the interpretation – for example, two people may engage in an interaction that neither of them finds offensive but the same words, delivered in the same way may be highly offensive to others. This requires sensitivity on both sides, as words and behaviours may not be intended in the way they are perceived. Our intentions can easily be misunderstood.

Misunderstandings

For Chris, an example of this came when he asked a junior colleague a poorly worded question.

> It was morning and the emergency department had been through a typically difficult night. As I arrived, the department looked like it had been under assault. At the time many nights were like this and, intending to understand a little more about when things had become impossible to control, I asked the registrar, 'When did the wheels fall off?' To me this was a simple question about time, I knew the wheels regularly fell off overnight and that the team would have still managed to provide care to our patients, I just wanted to get a handle on when it happened. Unfortunately, my junior colleague heard not a question but two statements 1) you don't run the department well and 2) you're not a good doctor. I would never have known this was an issue except for the fact that one of the senior sisters, asked me what I had said to upset the registrar. Once I discovered that this was what had happened, it took considerable time and effort to get our working relationship back on track.

So what happened? There was no intent on Chris' part; however, there was a significant amount of bad feeling generated by it and he would never have known if a colleague had not told him.

Fortunately, this has been researched by Kruger and Epley, see Figure 13.10. They have shown that, whether it is written or verbal communication, we tend to believe others will understand about 80% of what we say, but when we are the recipients, we think we understand about 90%. This means that for a significant proportion of the time we not only do we fail to understand what others mean, we also find it hard to accept that we have misunderstood: a potentially toxic combination.

This situation becomes even more imbalanced when we consider different forms of communication. We tend to believe that we understand the same percentage whether the information is written or verbal. When tested in experimental conditions, we understand about 78% of communication via voice, but when we communicate via email our understanding drops to a potentially catastrophic 56%. Amazingly, we still believe we have understood 90%. The reasons we misinterpret written

Figure 13.10 What we believe (Kruger et al., 2005).

communication so impressively are because it is stripped of much that we rely upon to make the correct sense of a message. When we talk, we have words, tone, movement, the sender's reputation and mood, and the mood of the receiver, all of which contribute to our understanding of what is happening. When we send a written message, we are left with the words, the reputation of the sender and the mood of the receiver, and this is simply not enough for us to understand nuance. Add in the certainty we have about the correctness of our interpretation, then we have a situation that can be nothing short of a communication disaster (Figure 13.11).

If this was the case, then we needed ways to raise this issue with the supposed perpetrators; perhaps they were being misinterpreted? There has been much work done around this area and many different models are available. One of the main differences between the 'speaking up' models is that some are about the victim addressing the (supposed) perpetrator, whilst others use an intermediary.

There are many attractive features to being able to address the perpetrator directly, particularly that it feels strong and learning to do this speaks to our desire to have personal mastery. Different ways of doing this are promoted and this can undoubtedly be an effective approach; however, some aspects of this approach are concerning. This pushes the responsibility back onto the shoulders of someone who is often already feeling vulnerable and asks them to speak directly with a person who they feel has not got their best interests at heart. Our ability to confront someone who we believe has treated us poorly is compromised by the emotion we feel in the situation, with our working memory being hijacked by our fight/

Determinants of communication

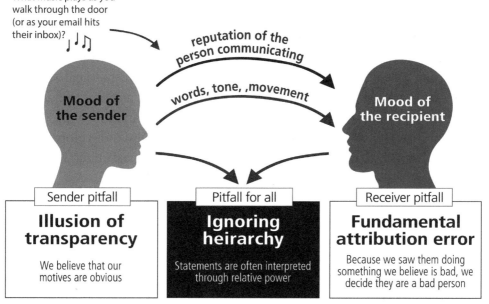

Figure 13.11   Determinants of communication...or at least some of them.

flight response (see Porath et al, 2015). The result is that we are not usually our 'best selves' when confronting these behaviours. Even very senior people often need to rehearse the conversation in advance, with many steeling themselves for the interaction. Another issue is that the speaking up agenda is often driven by people in positions of power, partly because they have the platform and partly because that is the world they live in. The intention is good, but they have forgotten what it is like to be a person who is a long way down the authority gradient who is trying to raise an issue. The reality is that, for people with authority, making themselves heard is a quite different process compared to someone at the bottom of the hierarchy. When we speak up the hierarchy gradient, the potential negative effects on us are much greater, the incentive to raise our voices diminished by the magnitude of the negative potential outcomes. After all, it is rare for someone to thank another profusely when they have brought negative information about the person whom they are approaching. Add in that the person being approached has often got power to hurt/harm the supposed victim, then we have an anxiety producing situation that is strong enough to deter all but the most hardy of people who feel they have been disrespected.

Because of the potential deterrents mentioned above, we feel that second messenger systems, where there is an intermediary between the perpetrator and victim, have their place. In fact, the evidence for them in healthcare settings is strong, with the work of Gerry Hickson and the team at Vanderbilt able to show a >80% positive behavioural response from medical staff when they are approached in a respectful way that does not assume the act was deliberately designed to cause hurt/disrespect. In conjunction with Hadas Levy at the Royal College of Physicians Ireland (RCPI), we developed a system that supports teams deciding to use a second messenger approach, shown below:

1. Establish that behaviour matters. This is the core message of Civility Saves Lives.
2. Establish that people are trying to 'do the right thing' (Chris uses ethics for this but it can be done a number of ways), that they are not fundamentally bad.
3. Show how easily we can be misunderstood.
4. Show how the current system of gathering evidence, triangulation and 'proving' bad behaviour drives a whole bunch of negative responses from both organisations and the individuals they are addressing (the so-called 'failure zone of HR').
5. Find out if the team would like to know earlier if they had been party to an incident where others felt disrespected. Most teams and team members want to know.
6. Discuss how they will identify the second messengers – we usually get teams of peers to have blind ballots and then select out those that are seen by their colleagues as having the required skill set.
7. We let those individuals who were voted for know about the esteem their colleagues hold them in. We then go on to offer them the chance to talk about the process (we call it 'Calling it out with compassion') with no obligations. It is rare for people to turn down the chance to talk about this further.
8. Over coffee, we discuss the aim of the process and the structure for the conversation. The aim of the conversation is twofold. Firstly, the aim is to care for the supposed perpetrator – after all we know that people who hurt others are often in emotional pain themselves. The second purpose of the conversation is to land the idea that, after

an interaction, an individual (or individuals) was left feeling disrespected. It is not to apportion blame, it is not to say how it really happened, it is to land the idea so that the person receiving it can make the choice about how they wish to respond. We discuss the conversation itself, describing three components – checking in 'Are you OK?.....no, really, are you OK?'; listening to their perspective 'What happened in XX yesterday?' and finally (supposing the incident has not been surfaced already), landing the idea of how others felt 'so, I'm here today because after you had an interaction with Joe yesterday he was quite upset and I know that you would want to know'. There isn't a follow up question of 'So what are you going to do about it' because that does not seem necessary – the purpose of the conversation is to care and to make clear how others felt after an interaction (because how we feel has a direct impact on our performance).

9. We talk about when to do it, where to do it.
10. Agree where this sits in a continuum of interventions (usually after two interventions in a year the next step is a more formal authority intervention).

This system has been taken up in hospitals across the UK – though at this stage it is impossible to state how effective it is in our context.

Summary

As Mersey Care has taken on a new way of thinking and moulded this to suit them over time, so have we. The Civility Saves Lives story has, like that of Mersey Care, been one of recognising the impact we have on each other and moving from a place of blame and recrimination to one where we want to help people to 'be their best selves' in the workplace so that we might get the best results for patients. This has required us to have faith in the people we interact with and to accept that our interpretations of event may be flawed, as may all of our behaviours at times. We hope that soon all health care professionals will feel empowered to embody, practice and spread the key messages.

Thank you very much for choosing to take the time to read this
Penny, Joe and Chris
Civility Saves Lives

References

Bertrand, B., Evain, J.-N., Poit, J. et al (2021). Positive communication behaviour during handover and team-based clinical performance in critical situations: a simulation randomised controlled trial. *Quality and Patient Safety*, 126(4): 854–861, 1 April 2021.

Beck, R. and Harter, J. (2015). Managers account for 70% of variance in employee engagement. http://news.gallup.com/businessjournal/182792/managers-account-variance-employee-engagement.aspx

Cheetham, L.J. and Turner, C. (2020). Incivility and the clinical learner. *Future Healthcare Journal*, 7(2): 109–111. doi:10.7861/fhj.2020-0008

Dacher Keltner, D. (2017). *The Power Paradox*. New York: Penguin Books.

Fisher, R. (2013). TEDx. www.tedxstuttgart.com/events/2013-2/ross-fisher/

Gilam, G., Horing, B., Sivan, R., Weinman, N., and Mackey, S.C. (2020). The decline in task performance after witnessing rudeness is moderated by emotional empathy-A pilot study. *Frontiers in Psychology*, 11: 1584. Published 2020 Jul 7. doi:10.3389/fpsyg.2020.01584

Hickson, G.B, Webb, L.E., Dmochowski, R.R., Moore, I.N., Pichert, J.W., Catron, T.F., Troyer, M., Martinez, W., and Cooper, W.O. (2016). Using coworker observations to promote accountability for disrespectful and unsafe behaviors by physicians and advanced practice professionals. *The Joint Commission Journal on Quality and Patient Safety* 2016 Apr, 42(4): 149–164. doi:10.1016/s1553-7250(16)42019-2. PMID: 27025575.

Jones, A.S., Isaac, R.E., Price, K.L., and Plunkett, A.C.(2019). Impact of positive feedback on antimicrobial stewardship in a Pediatric Intensive Care Unit: A quality improvement project. *Pediatric Quality & Safety*, 4(5): e206. Aug 30 2019. doi:10.1097/pq9.0000000000000206

Katz, D., Blasius, K., Isaak, R., et al (2019). Exposure to incivility hinders clinical performance in a simulated operative crisis. *BMJ Quality & Safety*, 28: 750–757.

Kruger, J., Epley, N., Parker, J., and Ng, Z.W. (2005). Egocentrism over e-mail: can we communicate as well as we think? *Journal of Personality and Social Psychology* 2005 Dec, 89(6): 925–936. doi:10.1037/0022-3514.89.6.925. PMID: 16393025.

Porath, C. and Erez, A. (2007). Does rudeness really matter? The effects of rudeness on task performance and helpfulness. *Academy of Management Journal*, 50(5), 1181–1197. doi:10.2307/20159919

Porath, C. and Erez, A. (2009). Overlooked but not untouched: How rudeness reduces onlookers' performance on routine and creative tasks. Organizational Behavior and Human Decision Processes, 109, 29–44. doi:10.1016/j.obhdp.2009.01.003

Porath, C. and Pearson, C. (2013). The price of Incivility. *Harvard Business Review*. https://hbr.org/2013/01/the-price-of-incivility

Porath, C., Foulk, T., and Erez, A. (2015). How incivility hijacks performance. It robs cognitive resources, increases dysfunctional behavior, and infects team dynamics and functioning. *Organizational Dynamics*, 44(4), 258–265. 0090-2616 doi:10.1016/j.orgdyn.2015.09.002

Porath, C., MacInnis, D., and Folkes, V. (2020). Witnessing incivility among employees: Effects on consumer anger and negative inferences about companies. *Journal of Consumer Research*, 37(2), August 2010, 292–303. doi:10.1086/651565

Riskin, A., Erez, A., et al. (2015). The Impact of rudeness on medical team performance: A randomized trial. *American Academy of Pediatrics,* 136(3), (August 1985), cited on www.researchgate.net/publication/280967683_The_Impact_of _Rudeness_on_Medical_Team_Performance_A_Randomized_Trial

Riskin, A., Erez, A.,Foulk, T.A., Kugelman, A., Gover, A., Shoris, I., Riskin, K.S., Bamberger, P.A. (2015). The impact of rudeness on medical team performance: A randomized trial. *Pediatrics* September 2015, 136(3): 487–495.

Turner, C. (2019). TEDx. www.ted.com/talks/chris_turner_when_rudeness_in _teams_turns_deadly?language=en

US Department of Veterans Affairs (2016). www.va.gov/NCOD/docs/CREW_Civility _Brochure_electronic.pdf

Walsh, B.M., Junghyun, L., Jensen, J.L., McGonagle, A.K., and Samnami, A. (2018). Positive leader behaviors and workplace incivility: The mediating role of perceived norms for respect. *Journal of Business and Psychology*, 33, 495–508.

Williams, R. (2015). Workplace rudeness is contagious – Study. www.linkedin.com/ pulse/workplace-rudeness-contagious-study-ray-williams

Chapter 14

Training Your Staff for Restorative Practices and a Just and Learning Culture

Nico A. Kaptein, Kristina Brown and Robert J. de Boer

Contents

DOI: 10.4324/9781003162582-14

Introduction

Within this book, we have described the change process towards a restorative just culture as a journey. A journey requires a significant level of planning, investment, commitment and engagement from all levels of the organisation. Like any journey of organisational change, there are barriers and enablers that you will endure. However, a determination to plan and resource through these challenges will result in benefits and tangible results, some of which can be seen and felt fairly soon – and by all stakeholders. In this chapter, we position where that journey should start, if you like – a pre-requisite of this journey, which is in the training and development of your workforce to successfully implement organisational culture change.

Science does not (yet) help us with reviews or evaluations of restorative just culture 'implementations' – or rather with evaluations of successful change processes towards a restorative just culture. However, numerous scientists and practitioners have tried to understand organisational change. If anything, they have learned that to change is not easy, depending on the 'depth' of the change (see for instance Van Olffen, 2014). Deep and lasting change can be extremely difficult and requires hard work, perseverance and passion. And culture change *is* deep change.

It is not possible to just 'train' a new culture, defined in this sense as one that exists independently of an organisation's workforce. A culture emerges from within an organisation and is driven by and relies upon the real people who form and work within that organisation. It is from this understanding of culture and change that we have gained experience and learning of the importance of incorporating the role of development and training into any programme for change, highlighting what *can* be done and how training staff members can support culture change (Davies, Nutley and Mannion, 2000).

In this chapter, we discuss the ways in which training and development can support the change process towards a restorative just culture. In this specific context, the empirical evidence so far of the role of training may be limited, but we are able to share results based on what we do know and on participant's feedback.

We will also explore and argue for the need of training and development of the workforce as an essential part of the initial phase of culture change and the opportunity for failure if this is overlooked. Although we draw on empirical examples of training and development in restorative practices and just and learning cultures from the healthcare sector, our aim is that the teachings and learnings of this chapter can be adapted to all industries and sectors regardless of context.

A Personal Experience of Training and Development for Restorative Practices

A couple of years ago, when I was in the process of setting up my own research, consulting and training company, I had a conversation with Professor Sydney Dekker, Griffith University who – together with Dr Robert de Boer, Northumbria University, was supporting Mersey Care NHS Foundation Trust on their journey towards a 'Just and Learning Culture' (Kaur, De Boer, Oates and Rafferty, 2019). In their case, the culture they were implementing was a restorative just culture but it's good to remind ourselves that just cultures can be retributive, restorative or a mix of both. In this chapter, we imply a meaning of restorative just culture when using the term 'just culture' unless otherwise stated. At the time, there was the *Just Culture* book, there was Sidney himself and there were Mersey Care's experiences from the first couple of years on their journey (Dekker, 2012). There was an emerging and informative literature on restorative just cultures (Thorsborne and Blood, 2013;Vaandering, 2014; Zehr, 2015; Dekker and Breakey, 2016; Dekker, 2018). This literature however was limited as to any practical tools and guides as to how to implement a just culture and did not contain many relevant examples. To our knowledge, any material, tools, guides or reference to training and developed simple did not exist. At this time, it became evident that implementing a restorative just culture means first and foremost to take all staff members and stakeholders on board. Not just to inform them of what is going to change, but to design and implement the change together. To empower these staff members and stakeholders to participate, Mersey Care herself needed a training programme. Soon after, many other NHS Trusts became interested to learn from Mersey Care.

We decided to tailor the training and use it as an answer to this need. In this way, other organisations can benefit from the learning of Mersey Care NHS FT as well as from what we know from scientific literature and from what we learned in other industries such as the military, road authorities and airlines, and in other countries, such as The Netherlands and Australia (Soeters, Winslow and Weibull, 2006; Dekker, 2009; Kahtri, Brown and Hicks, 2009; Anund, Fors, Kecklund and Leeuwen, 2015; Dekker, 2018). 'Training' has in reality been a highly interactive experience, since we as trainers have in return learned a lot from all participants. We have used these learnings to improve and enrich the trainings. None of this could have happened without the drive and energy of all in the core team. I will never forget late night hotel sessions to discuss last-minute changes to the next day's programme, in-car Karaoke sessions without proper warning - and the contagious passion Amanda Oates (Mersey Care's Executive Director of Workforce) expressed again in each opening session with a new group. The result has been incredible. More than in any other training, I have facilitated throughout the years, the personal and emotional impact on participants and on myself and my fellow trainers has been enormous. Time and again participants expressed the profound impact restorative practice had and how it changes the way they appreciated their relationships with colleagues, staff members – and patients.

The Argument for Training and Development for Change

Training is a necessity in the workplace (Elnaga and Imran, 2013). A definition of training given by Abiodun (1999), is shown as the 'systematic development of the knowledge, skills and attitudes required by employees to perform adequately on a given task or job. It can take place in a number of ways, on the job or off the job, in the organisation or outside organization'. Effective training programmes equip employees and organisations to develop the skills, abilities and knowledge required to implement any change which can then positively impact the motivation and commitment of an employee to implement that change (Meyer and Allen, 1991). Therefore, the success of any organisational efforts to change can be linked to the planning and investment of associated training and training programmes to effect that change. A review of the organisational literature reveals that unsuccessful organisational change efforts are directly attributed to insufficient education and training, whereas rigorous and well-designed training that encourages a systems approach enable the development of those employee skills needed to cope with the uncertain conditions that any change implementation will bring.

As the need for change in blame and harmful cultures becomes universally/nationally accepted, a spotlight has shone on the role that efficient and effective training and development plays in this and some would argue is even dependent on this (Olaniyan and Ojo, 2008). Restorative just culture (RJC) is one such culture change that organisations are turning to as a way of creating a range of quality improvements that are brought about when restorative as opposed to retributive approaches are taken in the management of employee relations, such as employee well-being, psychological safety, high-performing teams and significant reductions in human resource and organisational development and design support (Kaur, De Boer, Oates, Rafferty, Dekker, 2019).

Human resources are the most important asset of any organisation, and in all of our organisations there will be a breadth of talent, knowledge and skills upon which the effectiveness and success of our organisation depends (Yahya and Goh, 2002). However, where there is a new drive for change requiring a significant change in practices, policies and processes, a new and further development of workforce knowledge, skills and attitudes is now required, relevant to the new organisational needs. Therefore, the need for the training and development of any workforce in restorative practices when the organisational goal is to implement a restorative culture is critical if this change is to be implemented successfully.

Intuitively, any change process would benefit from:

- *Awareness*: being aware of the possibility to do things differently.
- *Understanding impact and business case*: understanding the potential impact of implementing a restorative just culture, as input for decision-making.
- *Knowledge*: understanding the (scientific) principles behind a restorative just culture (and related concepts such as psychological safety).
- *Tools*: identifying examples of specific elements of change/tools/'micro-experiments' and their impact.
- *Lessons*: taking lessons learned by those who have started their journey earlier.

The principles of a restorative just culture do not prescribe how *your* culture should be. It makes no sense to teach what your vision and values should be or what the design of your organisation should look like. Instead, it makes a lot more sense to provide you with relevant awareness, knowledge, insight, tools and lessons learned elsewhere as input for your decision-making and change process.

Also, all organisations have at least some values, structures and processes that already support a restorative just culture: no one starts from scratch. It is up to you to decide what of what is provided makes sense in your context to actually use and apply.

All training and development should have learning outcomes that support the restorative goals the organisation is aiming to achieve, or the change process. Dee Fink (2003) provides a useful guide as to six domains that the learning outcomes of any training and development should be mapped to:

1. *Foundational knowledge* is about understanding and remembering information and ideas. This is the traditional training content that is represented by the guidance material and input from experts, and made available through reading material, videos and lectures. By using a variety of means and ensuring that reading materials and presentations have an attractive layout, we facilitate the urge to absorb information.

2. *Application* is the skills, thinking and management of projects to apply the foundational knowledge to generate change in processes. Application is trained through the small and large practical exercises that are included in the programme. We give ample opportunity to practice and ensure specific feedback is given.

3. *Integration* is connecting ideas, people and realms of life, and is achieved through the acquaintance with experts (face to face or online), networking events, and the small-group work (in which different ideas need to be consolidated into an answer to an assignment). Our experienced and knowledgeable trainers are able to help trainees connect the dots.

4. *The human dimension* is represented by learning about oneself and others. Small-group work and plenary discussions contribute to this, as do presentations by experts if they touch upon the emotional aspects of their work. The assignments include moments of self-reflection. The diversity of cultures in some training settings will also contribute to learning about oneself and others.

5. *Caring* is about developing new feelings, interests and values, and can be a result of the human dimension but can also be triggered by the new knowledge that is conveyed. The social networking activities contribute significantly and are particularly relevant to the creation of a Just and Learning Culture.

6. *Learning* how to learn is necessary to become a better student, to be self-directed and to be inquisitive. It is cultivated through the in-class and homework assignments and motivational feedback by the trainer. Learning how to learn is essential for the participants to allow them to apply their newly learned knowledge and skills in their workplace successfully.

In the next section, we will discuss the ways in which the learning outcomes of our own training and development programme and approaches are defined across these six domains, and the ways in which this has enabled organisations to implement culture change successfully.

Training and Development Programmes for Restorative Practices and just and Learning Cultures

Our training and developing programmes takes a human resource and organisational development, design, effectiveness and learning approach to culture change, an approach which can be adapted to the structure and make-up of any organisation.

We see the learning outcomes of our own training and development programmes mapping to the six domains of Dee Fink (2003) as shown below:

1. *Foundational knowledge* – enable participants to understand the theories and concepts that underpin the practices relating to a Restorative Just Culture and that contributes to safe levels of patient care (foundational knowledge).
2. *Application* – support participants in critically analysing the current approach to employee relation matters that have arisen from bullying, harassment, grievances, disciplinaries and/or an adverse event or serious incident (application, integration, human dimension, caring).
3. *Integration* – support participants in developing and supporting high-performing teams that are psychological safe and resilient to deliver sage and continuous care whilst working in a context of work imagined versus work as done (application, human dimension, caring).
4. *The human dimension* – develop participants learning in RJC to design a framework/plan to implement restorative just culture within your own organisation and link this to strategic-level organisational goals (application, integration, caring, learning to learn).
5. *Caring* – facilitate participants confidence and learning in applying Mersey Care's four-step process to manage employees' relations which is the framework designed and used within Mersey Care NHS Foundation Trust (foundational knowledge, application, human dimension, learning to learn).
6. *Learning* – identify individual and organisational learning needs that are needed to support the implementation of a restorative just culture within your own organisation (application, integration, human dimension, caring).

These learning outcomes are achieved through the application of a variety of tools, such as live speaker sessions, presentations, group facilitated sessions, role play, small-group and plenary discussions. An important element of the training is role play, watching both pre-recorded role play videos and active role playing by the participants themselves, observed by the trainers.

In reality, the preparation and training of staff members is built up gradually. First, a group of frontrunners is trained to prepare them for the role in the start-up phase of the change process, where the organisation's vision and ambitions are discussed, where it is decided whom to involve and what preconditions need to be met before the process can start. Also, a certain level of awareness, understanding and insight is supportive of developing one's own business case. In this phase, training will typically involve all of the above.

Later on in the process, when the journey has started, training becomes more targeted. Separate trainings are designed based on what people exactly need in their roles and with their individual backgrounds. Now trainings, attended by much larger numbers of staff members, are generally shorter and more targeted and specifically address a limited set of learning outcomes.

Person Focused Training – Who Need to Be Trained?

We have come to realise that those who drive the change process for their roles need to be prepared – and trained first.

The above applies to the training of leaders and key staff members that drive the change process first. These key drivers do not need to be the leaders and/or senior management of an organisation. Preferably, the key drivers of the change are a group of people who are motivated to invest in the culture change and represent different perspectives, disciplines and groups within the organisation and perhaps even from outside of the organisation (Cameron and Green, 2019). Later, if and when you have re-designed or adapted you values, strategy, structures, processes and tools, more staff members need to be trained to apply to do their jobs the new way and work with the new tools.

Typically, senior leadership, HR and OD are among the people that drive culture change. Obviously, many of the established and proven methods within each of these disciplines are just as useful and valid in the context of a restorative just culture as they have been before. A fair understanding of the principles behind a restorative just culture may be sufficient to enable leader and practitioners to do their job and lead the change process, especially if specific tools are made available as well. Obviously, this process is accelerated; one has the advantage of benefiting from experiences elsewhere.

Much that is described in this chapter on training is the result of our collaboration with Mersey Care and Northumbria University, inspired by Sidney Dekker's *Just Culture* (Dekker, 2012, 2019).

Organisations are not necessarily able to find another organisation that may serve as an example and that is highly similar, with similar strategy, goals, systems, processes, stakeholders and tools. Within healthcare and specifically with the NHS this is different. Much of the context, values, goals, structures, processes, stakeholders, issues and dilemmas are similar for any NHS Trust.

Therefore, much of Mersey Care's learnings, choices, tools and results make just as much sense elsewhere within the NHS. When Mersey Care started their journey towards what they originally called a Just and Learning Culture, no other NHS Trust had done so. Although elements of a restorative Just Culture have been implemented in other countries, with different healthcare systems and traditions, and organisations in other sectors, such as oil and gas companies and airlines, there was no example of any organisation that is sufficiently similar to serve as an example. This is different now: any NHS Trust that chooses to implement (elements of) a restorative just culture may benefit from Mersey Care's experience.

Obviously, in spite of the similarities, many things are different across these Trusts. Because of these differences and local context and circumstances, the goals, choices and change and implementation approaches will be different. Each organisation needs to make their own decisions on what strive for, what specifically to do and how and when and with whom to do it.

CASE STUDY: THE NORTHUMBRIA UNIVERSITY AND MERSEY CARE 4 DAY PROGRAMME: TRANSFORMING ORGANISATIONAL CULTURE – PRINCIPLES AND PRACTICES OF RESTORATIVE JUST CULTURE

Over the last couple of years, Mersey Care has increasingly been asked to share their story and experiences with colleagues across the NHS. And they did share: they inspired colleagues, shared lessons and insights and transparently shared what they would have wanted to have done differently – with hindsight. When it became increasingly difficult to find the time and resources to honour all these requests, the need arose to structure this process of sharing. Hence, the four-day programme (https://www.northumbria.ac.uk/study-at-northumbria/continuing-professional-development-short-courses-specialist-training/restorative-just-culture/) that Northumbria University and Mersey Care have developed together has been delivered to representatives of NHS Trusts across the UK.

In June 2019, Northumbria University and Mersey Care NHS FT developed an accredited four-day training and development programme in restorative just culture and practices. The programme is relevant for professionals and practitioners who are involved in the management and welfare of employees, patients and/or clients. Although the focus of the programme is on how to respond to employee relations matters, such as bullying/harassment/grievances/disciplinary and/or an adverse event or incident, such as patient safety-related incidents, the programme also concerns restorative practice in daily work. The key purpose of the programme is to train and develop participants in restorative practices and approaches to implement a restorative just culture. There is a further and optional element of accreditation to the programme and upon successful submission of an academic assignment, participants will be awarded 30 credits at HE Level 7 (master's level) and from 2022 an additional CIPD qualification.

The Impact of COVID-19 on Training and Development and the Emergence of an Online Programme

The programme was originally designed for face-to-face delivery and a number of programmes had been successfully delivered around the UK at training venues provided by the host organisation. However, when the COVID-19 pandemic impacted on the UK, a number of trainings that were planned to take place in the first half of 2020 were postponed until further notice. Initially, we stopped all programmes until Government and organisational guidelines would safely allow us to reconvene.

However, when we began to realise that this could take some time, we realised we needed to think creatively and to borrow a phrase coined by

Amanda Oates: we took the approach of 'Business Better than Usual' rather than 'Business as Usual'. This has inspired the development of an online version of the course – into which we poured every ounce of energy we had (or at least it certainly felt like that). At this point, we are keen to convey that the online programme is not an e-learning programme and should not be considered as one. Although there is a time and a place for e-learning based on our knowledge of certain industries, e-learning has earned a certain amount of stigma as being online and remote modules without any facilitator or live participation. In recognition of the interaction that is the core of the training, this programme delivery was designed around the core elements of live speaker sessions, group facilitated sessions with a limited self-directed learning, which are supported by live Q&A sessions, ensuring that we have kept as much interaction as realistically possible.

We have learned that the structure and materials of a face-to-face programme cannot merely be picked up and dropped online. There is so much to consider when putting a programme online, so much risk, so much that can go right and so much that can go wrong. As a result of this, the programme developed in a more structured way where we work towards the same learning outcomes. More or less unexpectedly, the sessions have become more balanced than we anticipated, since all participants have an equal opportunity to put their questions in and the facilitators can easily organise all of these questions to be answered.

Framework Programme Development

In the early co-creation stages of developing this programme, we settled on the framework by Kirkpatrick and Kirkpatrick (2006) as the factors that should be carefully considered when planning and implementing an effective training and development programme:

1. Determining needs – determining needs in this sense related to the needs of the participants and after consultation with many organisations that expressed a desire for this training and based on the experience of Mersey Care and Northumbria University in this specific area and the underlying theory and empirical evidence with regard to (restorative) just cultures.
2. Setting objectives – objectives were set by determining what the learning outcomes of the programme needed to be if we were to enable

participants to have the knowledge, skills and behaviours necessary to implement a restorative just culture in their own organisations. This resulted in the learning units shown below.

3. Determining subject content – this was shaped by the learning outcomes which influenced the level and specification of unit content.
4. Selecting participants – this was based on self-selection of any person, not limited by profession, employment status or industry.
5. Determining the best schedule – this was designed to encourage accessibility for all by: avoiding busiest touch points of start and end of weekdays, not before 9:30 hours or after 15:30 hours to support childcare times and later develop into an online programme accessible from any location, hardware and Wi-Fi connection depending.
6. Selecting appropriate facilitators – for the face-to-face sessions as well as the online sessions.
7. Selecting appropriate instructors – this is critical to the success of any programme and we were fortunate to have a core teams of practitioners, consultants and academics with the qualifications, knowledge, evidence base and with the relevant teaching and learning skills to meet participants learning needs and with the necessary facilitation skills.
8. Selecting and preparing audiovisual aids – Blackboard Ultra was used as the learning portal for all of the programme materials. This software is a responsive interface which enables participants to interact with the materials at any time and via computer, tablet or smartphone. The training and development materials comprised of interactive web pages supplemented with audio and video to support a range of learning styles. This was also linked to the wider Northumbria University online facilities such as interactive links to the library reading lists and student resources such as academic skills for critical reading and writing.
9. Coordinating the programme – programme organisation, both generically and specifically the technical facilitation of online programmes, takes a different role from that of teacher and facilitator. Trustworthy and proactive coordination are key success factors for any training programme of a certain complexity, such as this one. In addition, using online platforms requires everyone to be familiar with the platform of choice to have the correct hardware, as participants need to be moved in and out of groups. Slides need to be shared, participants need to be brought back to the (online) main room several times throughout the day, there are electronic registers to sign for attendance and probably more than we have mentioned here. In addition to the delivery of the

programme content, we cannot underestimate the need for a skilled technical facilitator. For this element, we recruited a skilled and experienced online coordinator from Mersey Care, without whom we would be lost.

10. Evaluating the programme – although there are many reasons as to why training and development should be evaluated, we focused on determining the effectiveness of the programme and the ways in which it could be improved. For this point, we considered eight factors which outlined further on in this section.

Professionals and practitioners are given the opportunity to explore and critically analyse the concepts of restorative approach and how these can be applied within their own organisation and the wider context. Training and development outcomes are developed to enable the management of issues in a restorative way that minimises the negative impacts of current cultures to maximise the learning and develop and organisational culture where people feel safe and the one they can trust. The learning outcomes also incorporate the theory behind the approach of restorative just cultures and the tools and practical guides as to implement this practically in an organisation, and therefore reap the associated benefits such as better relations with your employees, improved staff survey results, less labour conflicts and more motivated colleagues.

The training and development learning outcomes of the programme are developed in ways that enable participants to:

■ Explore and critically analyse the concepts of restorative just culture approaches with application to organisations of any appropriate context.
■ Manage issues in a restorative way that minimises the negative impacts, maximises the learning and develops an organisational culture where people feel safe and one they can trust.
■ Develop knowledge of the theory behind the approach of restorative just cultures and practical tools and guides to implement this practically in organisations, therefore reaping the associated benefits: better relations with your employees, improved staff survey results, less labour conflicts and more motivated colleagues (Northumbria, 2020).

Underpinning all of these learning outcomes is one of the key guiding philosophies of a restorative just culture, which is an approach to managing and learning that is system focused with a focus on what went right rather than person focused, asking who is to blame and what went wrong. Following this approach, we do so by asking:

- Who is hurt, what do they need and whose obligation is it to meet those needs?
- Do our teams feel psychologically safe to speak out, take interpersonal risks and make decisions to provide necessary care without fear of retribution or marginalisation?
- Do we understand work done versus work imagined and how this facilitates Safety II approaches such as the need to understand system dynamics and the way people adjust or make trade-offs to be able to continue to provide safe and good quality care when equipment or documentation is unavailable? (Zehr, 2002; Dekker, 2018).

Achievement of the learning outcomes is through the delivery of a range of topics that represent the core elements of any organisational culture change, underpinned with human resource, organisational design, development and effectiveness frameworks which makes it particularly relevant to current organisational contexts, such as listed below.

Programme Units:

Unit 1 – Introduction to Industry/Sector Context

Unit 2 – Just Cultures: Understanding Restorative and Retributive Just Cultures

Unit 3 – Incident Management: What Does Empirical Evidence Tell Us About How to Effectively Respond to and Learn From Incidents?

Unit 4 – The Mersey Care Four-Step Process for Dealing with Incidents, Events and Employee Relations;

Unit 5 – Partnership Working/Staff Side/Freedom to Speak Up Guardians

Unit 6 – Organisational Design, Development and Effectiveness, Including Change Management and Facilitating Psychological Safety with the Organisation.

Unit 7 – Patient Safety I and II: Learn from What Goes Right, Not Only from What Goes Wrong and Facilitate Organisational Learning in a Psychologically Safe Manner for All Involved.

Unit 8 – People Processes, Including Mersey Care's 'Civility and Respect Framework'.

Unit 9 – Implementation and Evaluation: Tools and Methods to Monitor Progress and Impact.

Unit 10 – Next Steps: A Workshop to Facilitate Participants to Make a Plan for What to Do Next, as First Steps Towards an Analysis of Just Culture in Your Own Organisation and an Implementation and Evaluation Plan as to How You Can Affect This After the Programme.

Programme Delivery – Training as Fact Sharing and Facilitation and Not as Prescriptive Teaching

This programme by no means aims to prescribe to other organisations the ways in which they should make their decisions. We do not tell organisation and their participants what norms, rules and standards to implement – and even not what their decisions should be in specific cases. Rather, our intention is to support the development of the knowledge, skills and behaviours that enable other to implement a restorative just culture in ways which facilitate their own decision-making and planning.

Although we call the programme 'training', it involves a lot of 'sharing'. We share experiences and tools. Many of these are Mersey Care's. Also experiences and examples from other sectors and countries are shared and discussed. The programme is a highly interactive experience that benefits from discussions with participants.

That we introduce the concept of a restorative just culture does not mean that Trusts until now have been 'retributive'. On the contrary, any organisation we have worked with was able to identify both retributive and restorative practices within their organisation. Obviously, all organisations have something in place to look after and care for patients and staff members after an adverse event – which in its nature is a restorative act.

Also, all organisations have processes in place to learn from incidents. In many cases, the organisation's patient safety strategy already includes measures and process that protect the individuals involved from unintended harm. Similarly, some of the Trusts have been able to reduce the amount of suspensions and investigations in recent years.

However, so far none of the Trusts we worked with already had an integrated approach for HR, OD and patient safety. And none of the Trusts had a systematic way to prevent to focus on 'the who rather than the what' after an issue or incident. Also, all of the Trusts have retributive language hidden in many of their forms and procedures.

With this aim, we maintain and align the learning outcomes of our training and development in restorative practices and just and learning cultures with the definition of training by Abiodun (1999) referred to earlier in this chapter as the 'systematic development of the knowledge, skills and attitudes required by employees to perform adequately on a given task or job. It can take place in a number of ways, on the job or off the job, in the organisation or outside organization'.

Active Participation: The Impact of Recognition of Hurt as a Consequence of a Review of Past Cases

As part of the learning on the programme we invite and encourage where appropriate those participating to identify past situations where an employee's relation matter has been handled in a manner now felt to be retributive or in a way that they would have wished had been handled differently. Often this amounts to recognising and wanting an outcome that could have caused less harm to those involved and one where the learning prevented the situation from (hopefully) happening to anyone else again. Typically, this involves retributive responses to adverse events, unwillingly hurting staff members by not hearing their account of what happened and/or (with hindsight) unnecessarily suspending and investigating them. When applying the Mersey Care 4 Step Process (the practical tool in which participants are trained in on this programme) to such a case, more often than not participants realise they would make different and more restorative choices which result in less harmful outcomes for those involved. As a consequence, participants may feel guilty of having hurt staff members with the decision they made in the past.

This part of the learning process is an essential one and can be a hard learning curve for those involved in the reflection. However, we are mindful in supporting these reflections, helping participants to be mindful that those decisions were in line with the policies at the time and where judged fair and just. Of course, none of the people we met intended to hurt anyone. Peers will have made similar decisions. It is important to recognise this and organise support for those who are confronted with their past decisions. We came to realise this over time and now proactively discuss support and care.

Ensuring Psychological Safety in the Programme: Chatham House Rules

Psychological safety is a key principle of creating a restorative just culture and plays a key role in the training and development of participants that engage with this programme. In this sense, we align to the definition of psychological safety given by Edmondson (1999, 2004) as 'the taken for granted beliefs that others will respond in a positive and non-blaming way when a team member exposes their thoughts by asking a question, reporting a mistake or proposing a new idea' and we strive to create a programme climate that is 'characterized by trust, respect, concern for members, and confidence in members' abilities' (Edmondson, 1996, 1999). In this way, when participants share experiences and examples – personal or with respect to their organisation as part of their group work with the programme, we take great care to facilitate the safety of the sessions. We aim to ensure the psychologic safety of the sessions. We find it important that no information or evaluations about events, processes or persons from the participants' organisations are exposed.

During the training sessions, Chatham House rules apply. We encourage participants to anonymise examples and only share within the session what they are comfortable to share. If they need to share specific information in the context of an exercise, we make sure this information is not shared or used outside of the session, other than by these participants themselves.

Programme Evaluation

Evaluation is an important part of any programme outcome and we are mindful of the need to be reflective and honest with ourselves, just as we encourage our participants to be when they are on the programme.

We have highlighted in the framework by Kirkpatrick and Kirkpatrick (2006) that in evaluating the effectiveness of this training and development programme and the ways that it could be improved, we focused on the following eight factors:

1. To what extent does the subject content meet the needs of those attending?
2. Is the leader the one best qualified to teach?
3. Does the leader use the most effective methods for maintaining interest and teaching the desired attitudes, knowledge and skills?
4. Are the facilities satisfactory?
5. Is the schedule appropriate for the participants?
6. Are the learning materials effective in achieving the training and development learning outcomes?

7. Was the coordination of the programme satisfactory?
8. What else can be done to improve the programme?

There were two main data capture points that we relied on to address these factors: the review of our own practice from a facilitator perspective and the perspective of the participants who had received the training and development. We are mindful of the need to be reflective and honest with ourselves, just as we encourage our participants to be when they are on the programme.

Evaluating our own practice came after each programme delivery where we were careful to record what worked well and what didn't work so well and used the above framework as our discussion basis. As a result of this, we made minor amends to some of the session timings and provided access to all materials even earlier than the standard two weeks to account for working and shift patters and the COVID-19 context which had significantly impacted participants' daily workload regardless of practitioner or professional role.

To capture the participants' voice, we wanted to use a tool that would allow participants to provide honest feedback in a safe, anonymous and confidential space with an option to allow consent for communication purposes. That would include purposes such as this one being used here. For this, we used an online programme evaluation form with pre-populated sections designed to capturing information regarding the eight factors outlined above with a response scale ranging of: insufficient, poor, satisfactory good and excellent. A free-text section was also provided to allow participants any other feedback they felt relevant and important to their perception and experience of the programme. For all of the pre-populated questions on which participants could choose responses raging from insufficient to excellent, our lowest score was good, and our highest score was excellent. From these responses, excellent received the high percentage of responses. Analysis of the free form data showed that the participants' perceptions of their experience of the training and development were in the main very positive and we used these data to support our decisions regarding the programme. Where analysis of participants' data showed that their experience could have been improved, it is often matched with our own reflection and we incorporated this feedback into our revisions. Extracts of these data are published below – with participants' consent.

Feedback Indicating Positive Affirmations of Training and Development Programme:

'All of the speakers were engaging and really bought the material to life – Thank you'

'All facilitators were knowledgeable about the subject.'

'Theoretical aspects – very good. In practice how it can be applied – very good'

'Honest reflection and experience – really enlightening and easy to understand'

Feedback Indicating Further Revision of Training and Development (showing action taken):

'Some delivery of the programme was a little dry and took too long to explain'

Action Taken – this aligned with our own reflections and we revised the timings of two of the sessions. Later evaluations highlighted no further comments of this nature.

'Although having understood this broadly and the challenges, would have been useful to get the "little" things that help create the bigger "Just Culture", for example tools and techniques used on an everyday level, i.e., any documents, checklist, etc. and would have been good to know how it was like for our floor/ middle/ line managers. The kind of conversations and interactions etc.'

Action Taken – we added HR and OD policies and checklists to help participants understand the everyday nature of implementing restorative tools and techniques.

'The only negative is completely out of your control! It is so difficult being on a prolonged team meeting especially for a subject such as this. It would be so lovely to face to face meet the group. Thank you for making is so good though.'

Action Taken – we scheduled further breaks and injected good humour wherever possible.

'More practical examples of implementing RJLC would be helpful.'

Action taken – we added further case studies with answers to support learning from a range of different contexts with varying restorative outcomes.

Conclusion

We strongly recommend that anyone who chooses to embark on a journey towards a restorative just culture should carefully consider what staff training and development may be needed to improve the chance of success. Depending on the specific circumstances and analysis, this may be a programme similar to the one we described in this chapter or something different. To benefit from the experience and learnings from elsewhere does make a difference.

For us being allowed to work with Mersey Care and all of the Trusts that have participated on their journeys has been an honour and a pleasure – and foremost an experience that has taught and brought us much in return that we are happy to share.

References

Abiodun, E. J. A. (1999). *Human Resources management, an overview.* Concept Publication, Shomolu, Lagos. P. 110–121.

Anund, A., Fors, C., Kecklund, G., Leeuwen, W. V., & Åkerstedt, T. (2015). *Countermeasures for fatigue in transportation: A review of existing methods for drivers on road, rail, sea and in aviation.* Statens väg-och transportforskningsinstitut https://transportstyrelsen.se/globalassets/global/om_oss/forskning-och-innovation/r852a.pdf

Cameron, E., & Green, M. (2019). *Making sense of change management: A complete guide to the models, tools and techniques of organizational change.* Kogan Page Publishers, London.

Davies, H. T., Nutley, S. M., & Mannion, R. (2000). Organisational culture and quality of health care *BMJ Quality & Safety*, 9(2), 111–119.

Dee Fink, L. (2003). *Creating significant learning experiences: An integrated approach to designing college courses.* John Wiley & Sons, San Francisco, CA.

Dekker, S. W. (2009). Just culture: Who gets to draw the line? *Cognition, Technology & Work*, 11(3), 177–185.

Dekker, S. (2012). *Just culture: Balancing safety and accountability.* Ashgate Publishing, Ltd.

Dekker, S. (2018). *Just culture: restoring trust and accountability in your organization.* Crc Press.

Dekker, S. (2019). *Foundations of Safety Science: A Century of Understanding Accidents and Disasters.* Routledge.

Dekker, S. W., & Breakey, H. (2016). 'Just culture': Improving safety by achieving substantive, procedural and restorative justice. *Safety Science*, 85, 187–193.

Edmondson, A. C. (1996). Learning from mistakes is easier said than done: Group and organizational influences on the detection and correction of human error. *Journal of Applied Behavioral Science*, 32, 5–32.

Edmondson, A. (1999). Psychological safety and learning behavior in work teams. *Administrative Science Quarterly*, 44(2), 350–383.

Edmondson, A. C. (2004). Learning from mistakes is easier said than done: Group and organizational influences on the detection and correction of human error. *The Journal of Applied Behavioral Science*, 40(1), 66–90.

Elnaga, A., & Imran, A. (2013). The effect of training on employee performance. *European journal of Business and Management*, 5(4), 137–147.

Kaur, M., De Boer, R. J., Oates, A., Rafferty, J., & Dekker, S. (2019). Restorative just culture: a study of the practical and economic effects of implementing restorative justice in an NHS trust. In *MATEC Web of Conferences* (Vol. 273, p. 01007). EDP Sciences.

Khatri, N., Brown, G. D., & Hicks, L. L. (2009). From a blame culture to a just culture in health care. *Health Care Management Review*, 34(4), 312–322.

Kirkpatrick, D. L. and Kirkpatrick, J. D. (2006). *Evaluating Training Programs: The Four Levels*. Berrett-Koehler, San Francisco, CA.

Meyer, J., & Allen, N. (1991). A three-component conceptualization of organizational commitment. *Human Resource Management Review*, 1(1), 61–89.

Northumbria University (2020). Restorative Just Culture website https://www.northumbria.ac.uk/study-at-northumbria/continuing-professional-development-short-courses-specialist-training/restorative-just-culture/ accessed 28 February 2022.

Olaniyan, D. A., & Ojo, L. B. (2008). Staff training and development: A vital tool for organizational effectiveness. *European Journal of Scientific Research*, 24(3), 326–331.

Soeters, J. L., Winslow, D. J., & Weibull, A. (2006). Military culture. In Giuseppe Caforio and Marina Nuciari (eds) *Handbook of the sociology of the Military* (pp. 237–254). Springer, Boston, MA.

Thorsborne, M., & Blood, P. (2013). *Implementing restorative practices in schools: A practical guide to transforming school communities*. Jessica Kingsley Publishers, London.

Van Olffen (2014). Change caught in the act. Towards a stronger connection between change knowledge and change management (in Dutch: 'Verandering op heterdaad. Naar een sterker verband tussen veranderkennis en -kunde). Inaugural speech May 9 2014. TIAS School for Business and Society, Tilburg University.

Vaandering, D. (2014). Implementing restorative justice practice in schools: What pedagogy reveals. *Journal of Peace Education*, 11(1), 64–80.

Yahya, S., & Goh, W. K. (2002). Managing human resources toward achieving knowledge management. *Journal of Knowledge Management*, 6 (5).

Zehr, H. (2002). *The little book of restorative justice*. Simon and Schuster.

Zehr, H. (2015). *The little book of restorative justice: Revised and updated*. Good Books, Intercourse, PA.

Chapter 15

The Restorative Just Culture Manifesto: A Call for Action

Amanda Oates and Mersey Care's OE Team

Contents

In this 'manifesto', we want to propose a united purpose and vision through ten interconnected commitments that improve the experience and safety of all our people.

These are what we offer in good faith and we trust are suggestions of value. They serve as a guide to those organisations and colleagues who want to work together within a framework that transcends current organisational boundaries and ways of working, to create a consistently compassionate, inclusive, diverse and values-driven culture, underpinned by restorative principles and practices. We believe they should be set as actions for your organisation.

We recognise that regardless of sector or industry, organisations are essentially an interacting and adaptive system of actions, processes, behaviours and attitudes, where things do not always go as planned or expected. In complex environments such as healthcare, the risks associated with things

DOI: 10.4324/9781003162582-15

not going as planned or expected become heightened. How we respond to incidents or events is critical to what this means for our people, the impacts to their career and lives and their ability to provide safe and continuous care.

Creating a restorative just culture is a commitment to your workforce, patients, organisation and the wider system, in which you pledge to take every opportunity to listen, act, learn, improve, support and create an environment that enables your people to be the very best they can be and to do the very best they can do.

What Does It Mean for Your Organisation and for Us?

All too often in healthcare and other sectors we are inundated with the latest campaign, or toolkit, or guidance to read and/or implement. That's not to say that they don't add value and purpose in their own way. So how do you prioritise one over the other? How do you stop you or your teams feeling overwhelmed with the 'ask'?

How do we address all the different asks? How do we make the connections and relationships between them all? In other words, what will help you have a line of sight to your ultimate organisational goals and help you connect all the pieces of the jigsaw together – a restorative just culture approach can embody it all and the commitments of this manifesto offer the practical foundational steps that can help bring about this implementation.

To be clear, a restorative just culture as one mechanism does not mean you are opposed to another. Implementing the design principles of the restorative just culture manifesto is not at the expense of 'inclusivity', neither is it leadership at the expense of psychological safety. However, saying we have a restorative just culture does not make your staff feel safe. This comes from how you take practical actions to building that culture that charts new territory based on the science of human behaviour and the emerging concepts of Safety I and Safety II (Figure 15.1).

Ten Proposed Actions for You

The commitments of this manifesto are drawn from two areas. They come from the critical evidence-based learning of Mersey Care's journey

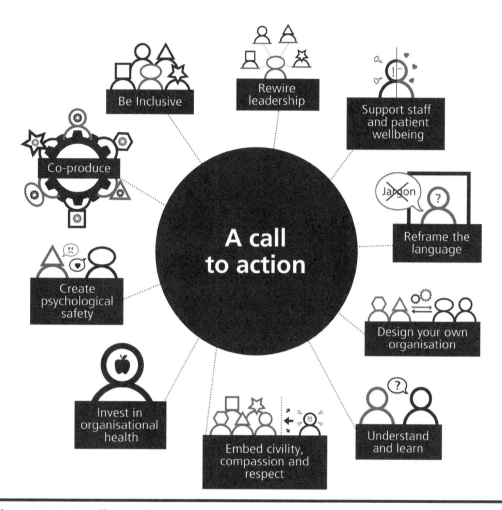

Figure 15.1 A call to action.

of implementing a restorative just culture. They are also informed by the insights and learning of scholars and practitioners including academic contributors to this volume and colleagues with powerful examples of lived experiences. All these people have dedicated their time so that others may benefit from restorative practices. We are grateful to them.

1. **Be inclusive**

Including the voices of all stakeholders enables you to understand your organisational context and circumstances in multiple dimensions. Listening to the views and perspectives of your workforce, patients and communities can help you comprehend the populations that you serve and their needs. The combination of a diagnostic approach, understanding evidence and data, and a dialogic approach, conversations and feedback, is incredibly powerful to understand the evidence and the context for our people holistically. Inclusion of all voices encourages valuing diversity, cooperative working, innovation and improved health outcomes when organisations and communities work together.

2. **Coproduce**

By patients and stakeholders meaningfully collaborating and contributing to the provision of healthcare services, and building on dialogue and insight from inclusive conversations, you can identify action that could lead to meaningful improvement and optimal health outcomes. Working with your workforce, patients and communities, and taking action and solutions based on their analysis and understanding of issues can lead to positive outcomes. Hearing the experiences of patients and coproducing improvements can improve patient care and experience, enhance value and give urgency to improvement as the benefit and impact to the patient is clearer. It enables prioritisation of change that will be valued by patients and stakeholders and legitimises improvements and investment in them. Coproduction of health services can be used as a means to rethink how healthcare is delivered at all levels, from ward to board.

3. **Design your organisation**

It is critical to create an organisational design that ensures people can speak up and be listened to without fear of blame or consequences and ultimately support your people to do their best job even when things don't go as planned. People should feel confident and safe to raise concerns or highlight vulnerabilities in systems, practices, protocols, values, behaviours, conduct, capability and environments. There must not be that fear of blame or of being ignored or isolated as a consequence. Your design must enable reporting to assist learning, support safety and experience and it must make it easier for people to do the right thing and harder to do the wrong thing. It must also enable system thinking so you need to distinguish between direct causation and contributory factors and ignore systematic issues which effect or cause safety concern and issues. Safety should be considered as part of the organisational design and within the context of overall system design, recognising complex and adaptive systems for what they are, and understand the difference between work done versus work imagined at organisational and systematic levels.

4. **Create psychological safety**

This leads into having an organisation where people can speak up and be listened to. Team members who are psychologically safe are able to contribute their views, ideas and opinions in a civil and respectful way without fear of being embarrassed or ridiculed. They feel able to contribute their views and ideas in the most difficult of circumstances and challenge decisions or ideas, or ways of working. We recall the example of the car industry where pulling the cord immediately halts production, or in a clinical setting calling out immediate risk when it appears, regardless of the levels of seniority. This can help to identify risk and leads to learning and innovation.

5. **Embed civility, compassion and respect**

Place civility, compassion and respect at the organisation's heart, which are visible in your organisation's polices, processes, practices and leadership. Every member of an organisation and team should feel safe and be without fear of discrimination of any kind. However, fear can often start when incivility and disrespect are tolerated or not recognised or challenged. We should not have to ask people to be polite, but if we can challenge behaviours before it becomes bullying or intimation, we have the opportunity to support people who have been hurt and upset before it becomes more serious. Furthermore, we are not promoting those behaviours within our organisational life.

6. **Understand and learn**

Become a forward learning organisation by measuring and evaluating the impact of your actions and interventions to recalibrate future actions. Your people must seek to understand events or incidents in the context in which they occurred. They must account for the perspective of the colleague who enacted their role. In other words, always ask questions to learn through appreciation and professional discussion. This way, team members can ask questions to understand not blame. They can avoid the application of hindsight bias, saying 'I would have done this', or 'I'd have taken this action' with the benefit of knowledge of the outcome. Colleagues in such teams will feel able to freely admit, discuss and understand everyday things that went better than expected, or did not go as expected. They will also feel safe to seek support or advice when and if needed.

7. **Reframe the language**

Semantics that support restorative just culture are crucial. Restorative just culture influences our language and cognitively reframes the words of accountability, failure and forgiveness. Language is difficult to separate from culture and the relationship between the two is very complex. The language chosen can fundamentally change the response to it; both to the content and to the speaker. Language is unique to cultural norms, social systems and cognitive processes. Some words or expressions simply don't translate, so may need local explanation and adaption for the words to be understood how intended. Your language can support psychological safety or challenge it; by cognitive reframing of language, it can improve communication and information sharing, safety, honesty, openness, support and trust. Moving away from overuse (or indeed any use) of 'wrong', 'mistake' or 'failure' is a significant step. What to replace them with will require careful consideration by parties at many levels in your organisation. As with jargon and acronyms, which can also silence those who aren't included in the inner circle, word choice matters. All your audience needs to be included and clear what is meant, free of euphemism, ambiguity or unintended judgement.

8. **Support staff and patient well-being**

   Personal resilience is the way we cope with challenging and difficult situations in order to overcome them and how we personally recover from stress. Supporting staff and patient well-being contributes to improved resilience and working preventatively to encourage good health supports compassion, productivity and best outcomes in sustainable ways. Healthcare workers are typically hugely resilient, committed and skilled, although it's fair to note that this resilience has been tested in extremis in recent years globally. Proper support functions are essential and well-being offers must be fit for the world as it is now. Leaders' role modelling is powerful: taking care of themselves, asking after the well-being of others and watching out for the behaviour of colleagues, offering support and signposting to help available. There remains a place for self-help choices: by understanding the reality of their own personal circumstances and the things they may need to act on, people may be better prepared to start taking positive actions, no matter how small, to give them a sense of moving forward with their lives.

9. **Rewire leadership**

   Leadership needs to be collective, inclusive and compassionate. It is vital that leaders and managers model and promote compassion in an enduring way including self-compassion. Compassionate leadership is a potent way that people can deal with what feels frightening and over-whelming, supported by an appreciation of core human needs at work. The role of the leader is crucial to guide and support, keep the holistic view and plan for emergencies. Necessary actions include: acknowledge complexity and unprecedented circumstances, model fallibility, no one has all the answers to navigate changing circumstances and ask the question 'how can I help you?', to understand the challenge and pressure staff are feeling. People need to feel autonomy and control, with that psychological space to perform at their best. It is important to give voice and influence over decisions which affect care and environment and create a sense of connection, belonging and support. This plays a significant role in helping people cope with being frightened or overwhelmed.

10. **Invest in organisational health**

Organisational performance involves reviewing performance against objectives and goals: looking at real results compared with intended outputs and typically reviews key performance indicators. Organisational health is concerned with the health, well-being and 'flourishing' of the workforce and typically reviews staff metrics. Historically the focus of many organisations has been only on their organisational performance. Evidence today suggests that the best way to run an organisation is to balance short-term organisation performance and long-term organisation health. Investing in keeping people well and engaged influences the organisation's ability to function effectively, cope with change appropriately and grow and innovate, all of which can facilitate higher performance. Performance is driven by behaviour and behaviour is driven by context. Cultivating a long-term positive context and relationship between people and an organisation can contribute to sustainability, growth and success.

Make an overt pledge to restorative just culture – have a statement of organisational or individual commitment, a pro forma for individuals or organisations to complete. Together we can link to a community of practice.

Together, we've come this far. With all the experience and knowledge we have gained in the process of building a restorative just and learning culture, there is no excuse to once again slide back into blame, retribution and risk secrecy.

The future of your organisational cultures is in your hands—we figured out what to do, and you now know what to do. A just, restorative culture isn't easy to build. But it can be done, rigorously, reliably. And the rewards—for your colleagues, your clients, your community, yourself—are more than worth the effort.

Index